D1527960

OVID SURVEYED

. . . le plus gentil et le plus ingénieux
de tous les poètes grecs et latins.

GASPAR BACHET, SIEUR DE MÉZIRIAC (1626)

BY THE SAME AUTHOR

HORACE AND HIS LYRIC POETRY

LETTERS OF CICERO (Bles and Grey Arrow Books)

OVID RECALLED

OVID SURVEYED

AN ABRIDGEMENT FOR THE GENERAL READER OF

'OVID RECALLED'

BY

L. P. WILKINSON

Fellow of King's College
and Lecturer in Classics in the
University of Cambridge

CAMBRIDGE
AT THE UNIVERSITY PRESS
1962

PUBLISHED BY
THE SYNDICS OF THE CAMBRIDGE UNIVERSITY PRESS

Bentley House, 200 Euston Road, London, N.W.1
American Branch: 32 East 57th Street, New York 22, N.Y.
West African Office: P.O. Box 33, Ibadan, Nigeria

Printed in Great Britain at the University Press, Cambridge
(Brooke Crutchley, University Printer)

TO

Barbara Proctor

CONTENTS

INTRODUCTION

COMPARATIVELY little has been written recently about Ovid, especially before his bimillenary year of 1958, considering the volume of his work and its historic as well as intrinsic interest. The present book is an abridgement of my longer work of 1955. It is designed for Latinless readers, and I have therefore omitted not only the extensive Latin quotations, but anything that presupposed a knowledge of that language or of specialist classics. But since I hope it may still be of some use to classical students, there is an index, under pages, of the pieces translated, so that they can look up the original. The whole apparatus of documentation, including acknowledgements, has had to be removed; but any reader who wants to check anything should have little difficulty in finding the place in *Ovid Recalled*. I have taken the opportunity of making alterations suggested by reviewers or correspondents, or by some of the essays included in Professor N. I. Herescu's admirably edited bimillenary volume *Ovidiana*.

The translations are nearly all in heroic couplets, not because I have any illusions about the possibility of reproducing in English verse the streamlined neatness of Ovid's Latin, even when the full sense can be fitted into the shorter medium in the more verbose language and fortune proffers appropriate rhymes, but simply from a hope that rhyme and metre of any kind may prove more palatable to the non-classical reader than plain prose would be. I have stuck to this traditional medium because it is the closest counterpart we have to the Ovidian elegiac (indeed a direct descendant, as I shall indicate), compact, subject to clear restrictions, and familiar to all educated readers. Anything modern, such as *vers libre* or sprung rhythm, would be wholly foreign to the spirit of the original. And I have not scrupled to use various poetic licences and words that belong to the convention of heroic couplets.

Ovid's writings are voluminous and too repetitive. As in the case of Wordsworth or Tennyson, only a selection can do him justice. There is much in him that we can enjoy today, but the casual reader might well be discouraged in the search. For this reason I have translated at length most of the passages that seem to me to deserve it, so that the book is somewhat in the nature of an anthology with running commentary.

I conclude with two chapters and an epilogue on the posthumous fortunes of the poet. The study of these from original sources could be the work of more than a lifetime, and I have pieced together my account from a limited number of secondary authorities who have dealt with various aspects. It seemed better to do even this than to leave the reader with a wholly false impression of Ovid's status by ending at his death. No ancient author, not even Cicero, has had so great a posthumous importance in proportion to his intrinsic merits. Ovid has been part of the cultural history of Western Europe; and the study of the classics is shorn of a great deal of its interest and justification if we overlook what it has meant to others down the ages, and how they have turned it to peculiar uses of their own, as Dante did in the case of Virgil, to the enrichment of the heritage passed on to us.

But if you ask anyone whether he likes Ovid, the chances are that he will reply that he did not care for what he read of him at school, and has read nothing since. Further inquiry may elicit the fact that he was introduced to him by way of selections from the *Heroides* or *Fasti* or *Tristia*, works which have this in common, that they are not 'unsuitable' for schoolboys. But what are the preferences of a mature reader? Macaulay may serve as a witness, since he read Ovid all through at least once during his residence at Calcutta, and his biographer has obligingly assembled his opinions for us. Well, 'He was evidently surfeited by the *Heroides*, but pleased by the *Amores*. Of the *Ars* he said, "Ovid's best".' 'The *Fasti* were almost too much for him', the *Tristia* he found 'a very melancholy set of poems'. With the *Metamorphoses*, though they contained 'some very fine things', he was disappointed at first reading, though he liked them better on reperusal. So the works that are commonly set before schoolboys are precisely those which a literary man of the world found least palatable. I should myself be inclined to begin my order of preference *Metamorphoses*, *Amores*, *Ars*, but the point remains: there is a case for offering the individual reader a reintroduction to Ovid.

And in a wider sense also there is, I venture to think, a case for offering our generation a reintroduction. For nearly two centuries

Ovid has been out of fashion. Suggested reasons for this, which are cumulative, I will postpone to where they belong chronologically—in the Epilogue; here we are only concerned with the fact, and with posing the question whether the attitude of recent generations has not been, in a temporal sense, rather provincial. For six centuries, roughly from 1075 to 1675, Ovid's position as one of the greatest poets, comparable with that of Virgil, was scarcely challenged. Thus in the fourteenth century at one end of Europe Maximus Planudes was rendering the *Metamorphoses* and *Heroides* into Greek prose for Byzantine readers, a unique distinction in an age when all the cultural traffic was going the other way, while at the other his name was one to conjure with in the poetry of Dafydd ab Gwilym, who, though he may only have known him at second hand, invokes as his source of inspiration a fictitious 'Book of Ovid'.

It is perhaps significant that Ovid has always appealed most to the young. The *Metamorphoses*, read at the age of seven or eight, before he knew French, was the first work of literature to delight Montaigne. Petrarch, Boccaccio, Shakespeare and Milton are among those who seem to have enjoyed him especially in their youth. More surprising is the testimony of Wordsworth: 'Before I read Virgil I was so strongly attached to Ovid, whose *Metamorphoses* I read at school, that I was quite in a passion when I found him in books of criticism placed below Virgil.' At Eton Swinburne, about 1850, wrote Ovidian poems on Byblis, Clytië, and Apollo and Daphne; and there, a few years later, Robert Bridges' eyes were first opened to poetry by reading some elegies of Ovid. The most striking evidence, however, of his power to affect the young is Goethe's recollection in *Dichtung und Wahrheit* of how he had struggled to vindicate him against Herder's strictures:

> Try as I might to take my favourite under my protection, saying that for a youthful imagination there could be nothing more delightful than to linger with gods and demigods in those gay and glorious surroundings and be a witness of their actions and their passions, . . . all that was not allowed to count: there was no genuine, first-hand truth to be found in these poems: here was neither Greece nor Italy, neither a primitive nor a civilized world, but mere imitation throughout of what already existed, such as one could expect only of an over-cultivated man. And when I finally tried to establish that whatever an outstanding individual produces is also 'Nature', and that among all peoples,

old and new, it is always only the poet who has succeeded in being a poet, these facts were allowed to count for absolutely nothing in my favour, and I had to endure much, indeed I was nearly put off my Ovid by it.

Again and again it is clear that the qualities in Ovid which appealed to these young poets were his fertility in invention, his power of conjuring up vivid pictures, his unphilosophic gusto, his preoccupation with love, and his knowledge of the human heart. They were also enchanted by the wild, free, romantic world he had imagined as background for his *Metamorphoses*, careless whether it was *Natur* or not. I would not suggest for a moment that we should put him back on his pedestal beside Virgil; indeed, I have tried to remain conscious throughout of the danger of overpraising through eagerness to redress the balance. It was absurd of Landor, reacting against his contemporaries, to say that Ovid's contest of Ajax and Ulysses is 'the most wonderful thing in the whole range of Latin poetry', and that it 'has more continued and unabated excellence than anything in Dante'. But has not the time come for the exile to have his case impartially reviewed, to plead at any rate to be brought nearer home? Is it not possible that a poet who could say so much to Shakespeare, Milton and Goethe may still be able to say more than we have realized even to us?

L.P.W.

CAMBRIDGE
May 1960

CHAPTER I

EARLY YEARS

FEW of the poets of Rome were natives of the city. They came from all over Italy—in later times, from all over the Empire. Inevitably, however, they gravitated to the capital, there to find the life and audience that suited them; only the shy, sensitive Virgil could keep away for long. But even when their name was made they did not forget the humbler town of their origin, Mantua or Verona or Venusia, proud to have added fresh laurels to it, and not ashamed to say so. And the towns in turn were proud of their sons.

Less than a hundred miles east of Rome, on the railway to Pescara, the Apennines enclose a small, undulating plain watered by many streams and graced with poplars:

> Here Sulmo lies amid Pelignian hills,
> Small, but for ever fresh with watering rills.
> Though sun draw near and soil begin to crack
> Under the Dogstar's merciless attack,
> Pelignian fields with trickling streams abound,
> And luscious herbage clothes the softened ground.
> Corn-crops are grown, and vines surpassing these,
> With here and there a patch of olive-trees,
> And where the brook glides softly through the reeds
> Thick tufts of grass cover the watermeads.*

One is not surprised to find a Corso Ovidio among the streets of the modern Sulmona, and a renaissance statue credited with representing Ovid in the courtyard of the Palazzo del Convitto; for who (save some prisoners in the last war) would ever have heard of Sulmona, *bel paese* though it is, or gone out of his way to visit it, if the poet had not been born there?

> So shall the stranger, gazing on the walls
> That watch o'er Sulmo's plots and waterfalls,
> Cry, 'Thou that such a poet didst beget,
> Small though thou be, yet will I call thee great.'

* The unfailing water and greenness were what remained in Ovid's memory. He recalls them quite irrelevantly at *Fasti* IV, 686, for instance.

From time to time in the course of his works Ovid tells us this or that about his life. At *Amores* I, 3, 10, for instance, he mentions that both his parents find it necessary to economize, or to make him economize (it is not clear which); and he begins an account of a festival at Falerii by saying that he only chanced to witness it because his wife comes from there. In the nostalgia of exile he becomes still more reminiscent, and in *Tristia* IV, 10 he gives us an unusually detailed piece of autobiography.

Publius Ovidius Naso was born on March 20, 43 B.C., exactly a year after his brother. The name Ovidius, common on inscriptions in that Pelignian neighbourhood but not found elsewhere, would attest his origin from that race even if he had not himself claimed to be its glory. The sturdy Pelignians had been ringleaders in the Social War, when their town of Corfinium was selected as capital by the Confederates and renamed Italica. Ovid rejoiced in the free spirit in his race,

> Whom love of freedom drove to righteous arms
> When Allied bands filled Rome with dire alarms.

All this was long happily over. The Pelignians were proud of the Roman status they had fought to gain; and some recent forebear distinguished for his nose had earned for Ovid's family the Latin *cognomen* of Naso.

Ovid's father, without being rich, was reasonably well off and of good standing locally. He sent his two sons to Rome, probably about 31 B.C., the year of the Battle of Actium, and put them under distinguished teachers. With the *grammaticus* they would study Latin, and no doubt also Greek, grammar and literature in a rather cut-and-dried way. They would then proceed to the *rhetor*, under whom they would learn to declaim on set themes—rather unreal ones now, since the establishment of Augustus as sole ruler had made discussion of contemporary politics pointless or dangerous. The elder Seneca tells us that Ovid was a good declaimer; but 'already at that time his style seemed nothing else than free verse'. To what extent the casuistical atmosphere of the rhetorical school debates had a bad effect on his character we cannot know; but we may suspect that he would never in any case have been a Virgil, or even a Horace. What he was, and what he has given us, is perhaps the best that could ever have been hoped of him. At all events it could never do anyone harm to be taught to arrange his thoughts on a given subject, while an ability to make epigrams, unless it becomes an obsession, does at least enliven social intercourse and literary style.

But from his earliest days, so he tells us, he felt the urge to write poetry, incurring from his father the censure that fathers reserve for sons who lift their eyes from lower ambitions. Whether because of his own promise or through some other connexion, he was drawn into the ambit of a noble patron of literature, Messalla, almost as soon (it appears) as he reached Rome, when he was scarcely more than twelve years old. Messalla was then at the height of his prestige, having recently commanded the centre of Octavian's fleet, as consul, at the Battle of Actium. Ovid certainly did not lack contemporary stimulus, for during the first year or two after his arrival at Rome several events of great importance occurred in the world of poetry: Horace collected and published in book form the remainder of his satires and iambic pieces which he thought worth preserving and began to recite in the circle of his friends the earliest of the *Odes*; Virgil published his *Georgics*, and embarked on the *Aeneid*; and Propertius brought out the first book of his elegies. During the next few years Propertius published two more books of elegies, and Tibullus his two books; Horace published *Odes* I–III and *Epistles* I; and the *Aeneid* was nearly completed. Few decades of literature can compare with the years 30–20 B.C. The fact that a poem had not yet been finally published did not mean that work in progress was unknown to other poets.

In a famous passage Ovid recalls in exile his associations with the poets of that time. Four he knew well, including Propertius. Virgil, who rarely came to Rome, he had only seen, and whether the phrase he uses means literally that he heard Horace recite or metaphorically that his ear was charmed by the *Odes*, we cannot determine. He laments that the early death of Tibullus in 19 B.C. prevented their friendship from ripening. At some period—his early twenties would be the natural time—he went to study at Athens, and he also completed the Grand Tour, spending the greater part of a year in Sicily and visiting the famous cities of Asia Minor in company with another poet, Pompeius Macer. With what excitement must he have contemplated the scenes of the many legends he was later to recount so vividly! Like

Catullus, he visited the site of Troy, and like him also had the great grief of losing his beloved brother, who died at the age of twenty.

Meanwhile he acquired a wide knowledge of both Greek and Roman poetry. So long as books were in papyrus rolls, it was laborious to look up a passage, the left hand rewinding as the right unwound. Even after the place was found, the entire process had to be repeated backwards. Consequently people relied on their memories, and though they might not always remember or quote accurately, the amount they kept in their head seems to have been remarkable. Ovid's literary allusions range so widely within short poems or passages that we may infer that he was drawing on a well-stocked memory. Messalla, he tells us, encouraged his early poetic efforts. Already his 'Corinna' was the talk of the town by the time he gave his first public recitation, presumably of early pieces destined to form part of the *Amores*. At some time Augustus admitted him to the order of the Knights. He was even destined originally for a senatorial career, a distinction which had rarely been opened in Republican times to the local aristocracy of Italian townships, and as an earnest of this assumed the broad-striped tunic. Indeed, he held some judicial offices (creditably, he claimed). But he soon abandoned any ambition for a public career (which in any case was losing substance under the principate), preferring to live at ease and write, dividing his time between Rome and his garden villa on the pine-clad slopes between the Clodian and Flaminian Ways. Henceforward he adopted in real life, possibly under the influence of his friend Propertius, what had become the traditional attitude of the elegist: a polite respect for the successful man of action combined with a firm refusal to have anything to do with action himself. Even the polite respect tended to shade into agreement to differ, and from that into open contempt. Not attached to Maecenas, he never really became, what Virgil, Horace and Propertius became in turn sooner or later, an Augustan.

When he was scarcely grown up he had been given a wife (presumably by his father), but she was 'neither worthy nor useful' and the union did not last for long. His second wife 'had nothing against her'. She was probably the mother of the poet's only child, a daughter; but again the union was destined, for whatever reason, to be short-lived. And here we may leave his life for a while and turn to his poetry.

CHAPTER II

LATIN EROTIC ELEGY

To give a full account of Latin erotic elegy would be beyond the scope of this book; but something must be said about its traditions, and then about the nature of the love affairs it purports to reflect.

It used to be assumed that that 'subjective' love-elegy in which a poet told of his own experience was an invention of the Greeks. The loss of the great bulk of Greek elegy, an important genre especially in Hellenistic times, made it difficult to check the assumption, which in itself was natural enough; but in the last half-century it has been generally abandoned. Two of Catullus' poems, 68 and 76, give him as good a claim as any known poet to be called the inventor of subjective love-elegy. Some fifteen years after him, about the time of the Battle of Philippi, Cornelius Gallus wrote four books of erotic elegies to 'Lycoris' (the celebrated stage artistc Cytheris). Of these only one line survives; but by a curious chance we possess a handbook of stories in prose about legendary lovers dedicated to him by the Greek poet Parthenius for use in his epic and elegiac verse. The interest of the elegiac poets in such love-stories is most marked. At the end of his short epic on the *Marriage of Peleus and Thetis* Catullus laments that 'the world is too much with us', human nature is degenerate and gods and heroes no longer walk the earth. To him, and to the sensitive poets who followed him, the imaginary world of Greek mythology became a refuge from the corruption and banality of modern life. In his Allius elegy (68) he compared with his divine Lesbia the heroine Laodameia, and so inaugurated one of the chief features of Roman elegy, the parallel from Greek legend. Turn to Propertius and begin the opening elegy: the first eight lines state the theme, his constant devotion to Cynthia, the next eight give the parallel, the story of Milanion's devotion to Atalanta.

Throughout his work Propertius constantly used this device, and Ovid, without being so much obsessed with it, followed suit. To us it is apt to seem a tiresome substitute for thinking of something to say:

we may find it hard to recapture the romantic aura, to feel the thrill that a Roman elegist may have felt in comparing his present situation with that of fabled heroes half-divine. Yet even in our own poetry it occurs, sometimes most effectively, as in Dryden's elegy to the memory of Mr Oldham:

> To the same goal did both our studies drive;
> The last set out, the soonest did arrive.
> Thus Nisus fell upon the slippery place,
> Whilst his young friend perform'd, and won the race.

Here the reminiscence of the *Aeneid* prepares the reader's mind for the intensely moving allusions to Roman poetry in the concluding lines:

> Once more, hail, and farewell; farewell, thou young,
> But ah too short, Marcellus of our tongue!
> Thy brows with ivy, and with laurels bound;
> But fate and gloomy night encompass thee around.

Catullus in his Lesbia poems had generally written straight from the heart, but all the other Roman elegists made frequent use of traditional motives. Source-hunting has occupied a great deal of scholars' time, and it is important to be clear about the extent of its usefulness. The fact that a poet can be shown to have taken much from others, consciously or unconsciously, need have little bearing on his originality. Classical poets had no idea of copyright. They prided themselves not on originality of thought, but on originality of treatment and on perfection of form. Brandt remarked of Ovid: 'There is no motive of any importance in the *Amores* to which one cannot point out a literary predecessor.' The knowledge that some detail is traditional can sometimes save us from falsely taking it as autobiographical evidence; and Ovid will sometimes echo his predecessors with obvious intent to recall the associations of their poems, or in a spirit of contrast or burlesque. But when all is said, most of his poems can and should be read simply for themselves, regardless of their debt to tradition.

The ancients did not set the object of their love on a pedestal: the 'ever-feminine' did not draw them upwards. The attitude of medieval chivalry, still not without its effect today, would have been incomprehensible to them, let alone the attitude of Dante to Beatrice. The idealism of Plato's Academy remained unique, aside from the main stream of literature, and probably also of life. In Homer, indeed, love is much as we know it today. But when we emerge from the Dorian invasions and the Dark Age we find a curious change. Whatever feelings husbands and wives may then have had for one another, love as expressed in poetry has become homosexual. But in the Athens of Pericles, while a wife's place, as he himself reminded her in Thucydides, was in the home, outside the home, to provide men with stimulating companionship, there were cultivated courtesans like the beautiful Laïs or the clever Aspasia. The fourth century was throughout Greece the golden age of these courtesans, whom the ever-popular New Comedy introduced as characters into literature; but in the third, when the literary centre of gravity shifted to the eastern Mediterranean, the love of boys emerged again, in the Ionic-Alexandrian epigram and lyric, and in the idylls of Theocritus. It was these last two phases that set the tone for the Greco-Roman world. Courtesans could not be expected to remain constant, and boys could not be expected to bloom for long. And yet there may often have been in these affairs something which it would be fairer to call love than merely lust.

At Rome things were somewhat different. Paederasty, though it remained a fit subject for literature, was considered by many to be no fit mode of behaviour. It is noteworthy that, whereas Propertius and Tibullus, not to mention Virgil and Horace, dealt on occasion with the love of boys, Ovid not only omitted it altogether, but went out of his way once to deprecate it, for the sympathetic reason that the parties do not derive equal enjoyment. Moreover, wives at Rome did not lead a cloistered existence: they played much the same part in society as they do today, and it followed that they might become the subject of love poetry. Catullus' Lesbia was a consul's wife. Nevertheless, the cultivated, or at least accomplished, courtesans, usually Greek freedwomen, were not displaced, though a Cicero might feel obliged (not very seriously) to explain how he came to be at table with the aforesaid Cytheris. To this class belonged also the Cynthia-Hostia of Propertius, the Delia-Plania and the Nemesis of Tibullus, and the various mistresses, whether real or fictitious, of Horace. As such too is Ovid's Corinna envisaged.

In their treatment of old material the three Roman elegists were diverse. Propertius gave his elegy a romantic, Tibullus an idyllic, Ovid a realistic and humorous colouring. Through the veil of conventional matter the differences in their temperament make themselves apparent. Propertius was an aesthete—passionate, neurotic, imaginative, intense, sometimes morbid and abject, sometimes triumphant, occasionally noble and even tragic. Tibullus was a milder spirit—refined, fastidious, hypochondriac, sentimental, not without wit and humour, in his less plaintive moods as fitting a friend for Horace as Propertius was not. But Ovid is no more passionate, romantic or sentimental than Chaucer. However much he may affect to be the victim of the erotic situations he depicts, we feel, and are surely meant to feel, that he is really, like the Horace of the *Odes*, a detached observer of the tragi-comedy of sex, a witty connoisseur, no doubt experienced himself, but steeped in the literature of his subject. As such he came before the world in his first poems, the *Amores*, which are more often intended to entertain us by their art and wit than to move us as a record of personal experience.

CHAPTER III

THE ELEGIAC COUPLET

IN order to explain how Ovid's favourite metre, the elegiac couplet consisting of a hexameter and a pentameter, came to be what it is, a short but somewhat technical exposition is necessary. Catullus and Cicero, in their hexameters, had adopted as a rule what had always been a tendency in Latin, though not Greek: the line must end with a disyllable or trisyllable (or two monosyllables). The effect of this was to make word-accent coincide with verse-beat in the last two feet. Many scholars, notably those whose native tongues have no stress-accent, will maintain that this effect was a chance by-product. But it is notoriously a principle of versification that, whatever variations are allowed or encouraged earlier in the line, the basic rhythm should be brought out clearly at the end; and like most English-speaking scholars I prefer to believe that this was the intention behind an otherwise hampering rule.

Pentameters proved more recalcitrant, because by the laws of Latin word-accentuation perfect coincidence of accent and verse-beat at the end was impossible (except by ending with a monosyllable, which every verse-form avoided). However, ending with a disyllable secured an overall preponderance of two coincidences to one clash in the second half of the line. Catullus let ill alone; but by about 25 B.C. both Propertius and Tibullus had come to feel that this severe restriction was aesthetically worth while, and Ovid followed suit. The result was to revolutionize the previously free-flowing elegiac verse-form. The new rules tended to make the lines more self-contained. And more important, the emphasizing of the metre in the second half of each pentameter marked the couplets off from one another. The verse thus acquired a more regular flow and ebb. The parallel development in English poetry is well described by Lytton Strachey in his Leslie Stephen Lecture on Pope (1925):

It was not until the collapse of blank verse, about 1630, that the essential characteristics which lay concealed in the couplet began to be exploited. It was Waller who first fully apprehended the implications of regularity; and it is to this fact that his immense reputation during the succeeding hundred years was due. Waller disengaged the heroic couplet from the beautiful vagueness of Elizabethanism. He perceived what logically followed from a rhyme. He saw that regularity implied balance, and that balance implied antithesis; he saw that balance also implied simplicity, that simplicity implied clarity, and that clarity implied exactitude. The result was a poetic medium contrary in every particular to blank verse—a form which, instead of being varied, unsymmetrical, fluid, complex, profound and indefinite, was regular, balanced, antithetical, simple, clear and exact.

How well these last words describe the elegy of Tibullus and Ovid! The regularization of the second half of the pentameter had much the same effect as rhyme: the couplet became an artistic unit. Catullus had used no tricks of style, not even anaphora. Tibullus was the Waller of the Latin elegy; he paved the way for Ovid, its Pope. Elegiacs now become affected by the new rhetoric, with its short sentences of parallel, antithetical members. Pentameter restates hexameter; the roughness of elision is almost gone; assonance and alliteration tune the verse. The couplet has become a plaything, fascinating in itself, liable to become an end in itself; stock themes tend to supply the place of thought and feeling.

Ovid absorbed the stock-in-trade of his predecessors; but his wit, always in control, gave individuality to his style. Strachey maintained that Pope's heroic couplet was itself his 'criticism of life'; and to some extent the same may be said of Ovid's elegiac couplet, at any rate in his erotic elegies. Its intricate subtleties and surprises reflect the paradoxes and complications of love's psychology. Let us take as an example *Amores* III, 11*b*.

A tug-of-war distracts my wavering breast,
Love versus hate: methinks love comes off best.
If hate I cannot, grudging I will love:
Ox bears the yoke he hates but cannot move.
I flee from sin—I look, and flee no more:
Your ways I shun—your body I adore;
Nor with you nor without you can I live,
And scarcely know for what my prayers should strive.
Would you less lovely or less vicious were!
Fair form belies so foul a character.
When I should hate, your looks implore my love;
Alas that looks should then the stronger prove!

O spare me, by our bed's confederate ties,
By all the gods that tolerate your lies,
By your fair face, to me a power divine,
And by your own eyes which have ravished mine,
Whate'er you be, I'm yours! But would you have
Me love you, choose, a volunteer or slave?
Nay rather, with the wind I'll trim my course,
And will to love whom else I'd love perforce.

The fascination of elegiacs is hard to define. There are times when we seem to hear them 'like Ocean on a western beach': every successive billow gathers in the first four feet of the hexameter, curls over in the dactylic fifth and breaks on the final spondee, to ebb again with the backwash of the pentameter. On another occasion we may conceive of them as horses, trotting, cantering, galloping or weaving intricate patterns. Turn to another poem and we may find still lighter verses, tripping like dancers who now advance boldly, now gracefully retire again; or we may see with the mind's eye of Schiller, as reproduced by Tennyson:

In the hexameter rises the fountain's silvery column,
In the pentameter aye falling in melody back.

As a sequence of rise and fall it was felt by Ovid himself: 'Let my work *rise* in six feet and *sink back* in five.' Perhaps no other verse-form generates of its own mere motion so haunting a melody. For a while it can be sheer delight. The fatal thing is for it to go on too long; for then it becomes as cloying as the later stages of the dance 'Sir Roger de Coverley' when there are too many couples on the floor.

In Propertius, although the couplets are normally self-contained, the sense of the hexameter is often incomplete without the pentameter, which is therefore weighty and important. But in Tibullus, and still more in Ovid, the unit tends to be the line, and as far as sense goes the pentameter may be only an echo or variant of the hexameter. There can be virtue however in this, for it produces the effect known as parallelism. Why this should be pleasing is a mystery of aesthetic psychology, but its appearance in many literatures is sufficient evidence that men feel it to be so:

When Israel came out of Egypt,
And the house of Jacob from among the strange people,
Judah was his sanctuary,
And Israel his dominion.

The sea saw that, and fled;
Jordan was driven back;
The mountains skipped like rams,
And the little hills like young sheep.

There is something soothing and satisfying in the leisurely antiphony. The English heroic couplet likewise lends itself to parallelism:

Learning and Rome alike in empire grew,
And arts still followed where her eagles flew;
From the same foes, at last, both felt their doom,
And the same age saw learning fall, and Rome.

On the other hand, the compact form of the pentameter makes it a better vehicle for epigram and wit even than the hexameter, which sometimes seems to exist only to compère its brilliant young partner.

But the subject-matter of elegy, often trite enough, required heavy spicing to make it palatable. The spice was provided in a multitude of ways. There are the recognized rhetorical figures of speech, which impart life and energy—*anaphora*, *apostrophe* and the rest. But there are other devices not so easy to name which contribute no less. One of these we may call syntactical pattern. Its effect can be illustrated again by analogies from the heroic couplet of Pope, but the much greater flexibility of Latin word-order gave a great advantage to the Roman poet. First there are patterns of symmetry, as in 'that verse which they call Golden, of two substantives and two adjectives with a verb betwixt to keep the peace' (Dryden). The corresponding type in heroic couplets (less effective because English obliges the adjective to come next to its noun) is very common; for example,

The lonely woodcocks haunt the wat'ry glade.

The symmetry may extend throughout a couplet as in

Though learn'd, well-bred; and though well-bred, sincere:
Modestly bold, and humanly severe.

It may also be 'chiastic' (ABBA). These six lines from Pope's *Messiah* contain three examples:

Lo, earth receives him from the bending skies!
Sink down, ye mountains, and ye valleys, rise;
With heads declin'd ye cedars, homage pay;
Be smooth, ye rocks; ye rapid floods, give way!
The Saviour comes, by ancient bards foretold:
Hear him, ye deaf, and, all ye blind, behold!

The separation of adjective and noun, and the principle of balance which tended to make the one occur before the caesura and the other at the end of the line, produced, in the inflected Latin language, something very like rhyme. It seems likely that this was an accidental by-product; but it must have had its effect. And it is only one form of the assonance which, together with alliteration, imparted melody to elegiacs as to other forms of Latin poetry. The perfect blending of vowels and consonants is, however, a faculty of the true poet which ultimately defies analysis. It is surely not so much the metaphor, trite enough in all conscience, as something in the sounds, that makes us thrill when the curtain goes up and Gloucester begins to speak:

> Now is the winter of our discontent
> Made glorious summer by this sun of York.

None of these stylistic devices may seem of much importance in itself; but taken together they represent a genuine art.

CHAPTER IV

THE 'AMORES'

It is not surprising, from what we can gather about his natural bent, that Ovid should have decided to devote himself to elegy rather than to some other form of poetry. When he was in his teens the *Cynthia* of Propertius was being 'read all over the Forum', while within Messalla's circle there was the example of Tibullus and others. Propertius, who would have found congenial spirits in nineteenth-century Paris, once wrote in a mood of unconscientious objection to military glory,

> Let me, whom Fortune willed a profligate,
> Breathe my last breath in unregenerate state.

One side of Propertius seems to have been really like that, a blend of *nostalgie de la boue* and defiant moral nihilism. Ovid, I believe, saw the literary possibilities of a pose on these lines, and deliberately adopted it. Might it not repel readers? A few perhaps. But Ovid knew human nature well. We often have erotic feelings which we suppress as discreditable; all the better when someone else confesses without shame to giving the same feelings free rein. The confession may earn sympathy or contempt, according to the rigidity of the reader's moral censorship; but in either case the underlying impulse receives vicarious satisfaction. The character of Don Juan was invented as a dreadful warning; in due course he became a popular hero. Some Sunday papers expose vice under pretext of cleaning it up, others simply expose it; in either case sales prove equally good.

There is, in fact, no need for anyone to be shocked. Human nature has an apparently infinite capacity for not applying what it reads to how it lives. The world of Roman love-elegy can be taken as a 'conventional' world, like that of Restoration comedy, and there is a good deal of sense in Lamb's remarks in his essay *On the Artificial Comedy of the Last Century*, for all Macaulay's strictures:

I confess for myself that (with no great delinquencies to answer for) I am glad for a season to take an airing beyond the diocese of strict conscience—not to live always in the precincts of the law-courts—but now and then, for a dream-while or so, to imagine a world with no meddling restrictions....I come back to my cage and my restraint the fresher and more healthy for it. I wear my shackles more contentedly for having respired the breath of an imaginary freedom. I do not know how it is with others, but I feel the better always for the perusal of one of Congreve's—nay, why should I not add even of Wycherley's—comedies. I am the gayer at least for it; and I could never connect those sports of a witty fancy in any shape with any result to be drawn from them to imitation in real life.

Indeed, the enjoyment to be derived from this vicarious wickedness is enhanced by the pleasing shocks of blasphemy. The more blandly impudent and unconscionable the rascal is, the more we laugh in spite of (indeed, because of) the affront to any censor we may have within. It must be emphasized, however, that the mere fact of having a mistress would not have shocked a Roman. In all countries where marriages have been made for reasons of convenience and often at the instigation of parents the husband at least has been pardoned a certain amount of amusement with the *demi-monde*, still more so the young bachelor.

Naturally Ovid pretended that his poetic world was real, and himself its hero; but he pathetically abandoned his *bravura* when trouble forced him to do so: 'Believe me, my conduct is different from my verse; my life is pure though my Muse be wanton. A large part of my work is fiction and imagination: it allows itself liberties its author denies himself. My book is no evidence of character, but an innocent diversion: you will find in it much to beguile the ear.' It is beside the point to seek for autobiography in his erotic elegies. Even in Propertius genuine experience was thickly overlaid with traditional motives. There is nothing to convince us that Ovid's Corinna really existed. His statement to her that he knows someone who is spreading it round that *she* is really Corinna, whereas none but herself will be sung by him, need only be a characteristic piece of Ovidian fun—assuring an imaginary character of his unswerving loyalty. It is hard to believe that even the least reticent genuine lover would have had the face to publish *Amores* II, 8, the outrageous blackmail of Cypassis, or III, 7, the complaint of his own temporary impotence. And Apuleius, who can tell us confidently the real name of Lesbia, Cynthia, Delia and others, does not even mention Corinna, though he is obviously recalling every identification of a poetic pseudonym he can. The clue to the *Amores* is a passage in the proem to Book II (7–10):

> And may some youth whose wounder is the same
> Perceive the signs and recognize the flame,
> And, musing long, demand, 'What tell-tale spy
> Has told this poet all my history?'

Ovid is bent on representing every phase and situation of love, every twist and paradox of love's psychology. No doubt he was not without amorous experience, but reading and talk could have given him most of the motives that occur. To try to fit a Corinna episode into the framework of his authentic biography with its three marriages is labour lost.*

It is all represented as a great game, played seriously at times, but regarded by the player between-whiles with amused and indulgent astonishment. The introductory epigram, written for the second edition of the *Amores*, is suitably light-hearted and disarming:

> The five small books of Naso once we were:
> Now we are three, for so he did prefer.
> Granted we still may not appeal to you,
> You'll be relieved to find us minus two.

Next follows a literary squib. When first the Alexandrian poet Callimachus set the tablets on his knee, Apollo spoke to him: 'Poet, you must always offer me the fattest possible victim, but song that is slender.' So he tells us in the famous prologue to the *Aetia* against the poets of grand epic, of all passages in Greek poetry the one most quoted by the Romans. Since then no reputable poet ever began right; he invariably embarked on some epic theme, only to be interrupted by a pinch on the ear from Apollo and an admonition to do what he had really wanted to do all along. Not to be outdone, Ovid claimed to have begun an epic about martial deeds, when Cupid with a laugh stole a foot from the second line and turned hexameters into elegiacs. The poet protested with a string of arguments from Olympus *ad hominem*, but to no purpose: Cupid chose a shaft:

> Firm with his knee he flexed the sinuous bow,
> And crying, 'Poet, here's your theme!', let go.

* As is done, for example, by Owen, *Tristia* I, Introd., p. xvi. Sir Edmund Gosse was similarly astray in supposing on the evidence of Donne's youthful elegies, themselves imitations of Ovid, that about 1596 he was having an intrigue with some married woman (J. B. Leishman, *The Monarch of Wit* (1951), p. 56).

So love is to be the theme, and elegiac, of course, the metre must remain.

A slight piece, perhaps, but already there are touches of a distinctive, rococo wit: and, sure enough, in the piece that follows we have the whole paraphernalia of Hellenistic baroque—the Triumph of Love, the golden boy, in a car drawn by doves. There he stands, driving elegantly, his head bound with myrtle, his wings and hair sparkling with jewels; at his golden chariot wheels follows a long train of captive youths and girls, among them Ovid with his wounds yet fresh, and such obvious enemies as Sanity and Modesty, while Charms, Error and Madness act as escort. Venus looks down with approval from heaven, and scatters roses from her altar offerings. Thus tricked out he passes through the throng, dealing many a wound with flame or shaft. The conventional elegiac metaphor of love as a form of soldiering is here carried to its impudent extreme. The first poem is an introduction to the *Amores* as a whole, an intimation that in them love will be treated not seriously, but in a half-humorous, detached, Hellenistic spirit; the second well illustrates this programme: whereas Propertius introduced his Third Book with a poem in which he himself, crowned with laurel, is driving in proud triumph with his Muse, Ovid makes Cupid the Triumphator, and himself one of the captives in his train. We are being introduced to a new mood of Latin elegy; we are to be entertained, not moved.

Cupids can be charming if kept in their proper sphere, but a few go a long way; and the intrusions of such symbolism into realistic descriptions of love can be tiresome. Ovid generally, though not always, avoids this pitfall. The fact that Cupid, owing to the unfortunate incident described by Demodocus in *Odyssey* VIII, could be called Mars' stepson was a godsend for the manufacture of conceits, while the other fact that, as Aeneas' half-brother, he was related to the Emperor, gave good scope for baroque, and perhaps faintly mischievous, flattery.

But for the most part the *Amores* are realistic enough. The rules of the game are that 'All's fair', and the character of the lover is represented on this assumption. He is a real lover, of Mediterranean temperament. Though he never speaks of anything so irrelevant as marriage, he can contemplate a liaison sufficiently long for the end not to need thinking of, sometimes even for life; but at other times he can love two women at once, or even be distracted between twenty different types. He is potent enough for anything—and yet on another occasion he fails inexplicably. He is comparatively poor, and it kills his love if his mistress asks for money; not even beasts, but only prostitutes, do that. The union he wants is one on equal terms, based on the assumption that both parties get equal pleasure from the act. If money passes, the transaction is completed, and there survives none of the mutual gratitude which cements love affairs. As a lover he hates war and soldiers (how can Corinna bear the feel of hands stained with blood?); indeed, he hates all men of affairs, who ruined the Golden Age of Saturn with their ploughing, sailing and gold-digging that lead to war. Their only use is to supply Roman girls with false hair from captured Germans. But let them have their reward—if only they do not use it to tempt away the girls of poor, innocent poets. Not that he has no gift to bring; a poet's gift, rightly valued, surpasses all money—the hope of an immortal name.

He is jealous, of course, sometimes insanely jealous. In a fit of passion he is capable of pulling his mistress' hair and slapping her face, only to suffer violent remorse. He fears that his praise of her has attracted rivals. Yet jealousy and variability are sauces his love requires, and he inveighs against her complacent official lover for spoiling the sport by providing a sitting bird. At another time, infuriated by her open infidelities, he meditates revolt; but though he hates her character, he still loves her face: 'Thus I can neither live with you nor without you.' He knows he must be her slave eternally, and only prays she will make it easy and not degrading for him. He does not want to be free from love; life would be empty without it. If necessary, he will share his mistress with rivals, if only she will take pains to deceive him: 'She sins not who can feign she has not sinned;' she will find him a most willing dupe. To sum up, his greatest desire is to have her love; failing that, to find her ever worthy of his love; at worst, to be allowed to love.

And what of the girl? Her status is left vague, but she may be taken to be an amateur of the kind that receives a generous allowance for expenses. She is not a common prostitute, but more like the educated and accomplished courtesans of Athens. Her relatives are only mentioned once, when the bawd suggests they too should cadge from her lovers, and so increase the family resources. Sometimes we hear of her 'vir'. In I, 4 he seems to be something very like a husband, who can shut her in at night and claim her favours *de jure*. The term can denote any reigning lover, and at times Ovid seems himself to claim this position. A janitor keeps the door of her house; she is also guarded by a eunuch, who cannot be expected to sympathize with the suitor, and she walks abroad with a dusky chaperone. At such times a furtive tablet may be slipped to her in the new Portico of the Danaids, or at Isis' temple, with a space left in the wax for her reply. But there are times when her husband is careless: a bawd can give her corrupting advice, while Ovid eavesdrops from a cupboard; she can visit him alone at noon, and go alone to the theatre or circus.

She is, of course, beautiful. She has highly skilled maids to do her hair. This is remarkably fine, with a natural wave, but on one occasion it all comes out through injudicious use of hair-dye, whereupon Ovid teases her with the prospect of a German wig (well knowing that it will in fact grow again). Once she has recourse to abortion on her own and makes herself dangerously ill, the poet's reaction being a mixture of indignation and solicitude, untempered by any sympathy for her motives or sense of personal responsibility. Her own feelings are seldom revealed. She is capable of jealousy, not without cause. She is keen on racehorses and their drivers, rather than literary or artistic like Propertius' Cynthia. Ovid does not expect anyone so lovely to be chaste, but only discreet. However, even discretion does not seem to be one of her strong points. And the gods laugh at her perjuries.

These portraits should not be taken seriously as such; they are simply convenient devices for assembling motives. The man indeed has a shadow of reality, because, though variability of mood is his chief characteristic, he is not without singleness of purpose; and after all, the pretence at least is that he represents Ovid of Sulmo. But the woman is a composite figure, or a number of incompatible figures. In twelve elegies she is named Corinna; these pieces may be survivors of the first edition. In the rest she may or may not be envisaged as the same person. All that matters is that the variety of moods and situations be such that every lover who reads may recognize much of his own experience. So we are free to take each poem on its merits and enjoy it without ulterior speculation.

Let us begin with a straightforward account of a successful act of love (*Am.* I, 5). It is surprising how rarely poets have felt urged to communicate so intense and universal an experience; since many can scarcely be credited with reticence, one can only suppose that, when content and gratified, they lose the itch for verbal self-expression. 'Lips only sing when they cannot kiss.' Propertius, however, did write two such poems (II, 14 and 15), and his success in communicating his felicity may well have encouraged Ovid.

It was full noontide on a sultry day;
Taking siesta on my bed I lay;
One shutter closed, the other open stood,
Making a half-light much as in a wood,
Like the dim gloaming at the set of sun,
Or when night's gone but day's not yet begun:—
A light beloved of timorous girls and shy
That seek to veil their maiden modesty.

Sudden, Corinna comes: ungirt her dress:
On either side her neck a braided tress.
E'en so, methinks, into her chamber moved
Semiramis, or Laïs much-beloved.
I snatched the dress, so fine, it half revealed;
Though e'en with this she strove to be concealed;
Yet strove she not as one intent to win:
Easily, self-betrayed, she soon gave in.

So there she stood all naked to my gaze.
In all her body not one fault there was.
What shoulders and what arms I saw, I held,
What dainty nipples, asking to be felt,
Beneath the shapely breast what belly smooth,
Hips large and beautiful, the thighs of youth!

Why single out? No part but stood the test.
Her naked to my naked form I pressed.
All know the sequel. We relaxed in swoon.
O, oft may Fortune grant me such a noon!

The erotic elegist is so single-minded, he imposes on himself such limitations, that he cannot be read for long without tedium. But Ovid does find ways of keeping us amused, and his glimpses of Roman life are particularly delightful. His account of laying siege to a girl at a race-meeting (III, 2) is surely one of the most witty and spirited poems in all

Latin. It is a dramatic monologue, except for the stage direction given in the penultimate line. The sudden transitions from the intense to the banal are worthy of Byron.* Long though the poem is, it deserves quotation in full.

'For thoroughbreds I do not care a pin;
Only I hope that he you back may win!
I came to talk to you, with you to sit,
Lest I should love and you not know of it.
You watch the horses, I watch you; and thus
Let's feast our eyes each on what pleases us.
Thrice happy he, the driver you support!
So that's the lucky one who holds your thought?
Let me be he, right from the very start
I'll urge my horses on with fearless heart,
Now give the rein, now searing lashes deal,
Now graze the turn-post with my near-side wheel;
But, sighting you, in full career I'll stop
And from my heedless hands the rein let drop.
How nearly Pelops fell in Pisa's chase
Through gazing on Hippodameia's face!
Yet sure his lady brought him victory:
So may we each to ours beholden be!

Why edge away? The line must keep us close†
(These rules are not entirely otiose!).
You on the lady's right, sir, please keep clear:
She does not care to feel your side so near.
And you behind, sir, please control your legs:
Don't stick your knees into her back, she begs.
But look, your skirt is trailing here below:
Lift it—or rather, let me lift it so.
O jealous dress to hide such comeliness!
To make you look the more—O jealous dress!
Such were the legs Milanion longed to raise
When Atalanta bared them for the chase;
So artists paint the limbs of Artemis
That of brave beasts the braver huntress is.

* Byron had more than a touch of Ovid. For Corinna struggling unconvincingly in I, 5 cf. Julia in *Don Juan*:

A little while she strove and much repented,
And whispering 'I will ne'er consent'—consented.

† In the Roman circus the individual seats were marked off by a line.

With these still hid I burned, but seeing these
Is adding flame to flames, or sea to seas;
From these can I those further joys infer
Which lurk beneath that robe of gossamer.

But would you, while we wait, care to be fanned?
My programme, I will wave it with my hand.
Or is this heat not in the air around
But in my burning heart, to woman bound?
Look, there's a speck of dust upon your dress:
Off, dust! How dare you soil such loveliness?

But hush! Attend! the great procession draws
Near us, the pomp of gold: prepare applause!
In front, with wings outstretched, is Victory;*
Hail, goddess! Grant my love victorious be.
Cheer Neptune, you that brave the billows rough;
No seas for me: my land is room enough.
You soldiers, clap for Mars: I hate alarms;
Peace is my love, and love in peace's arms.
Phoebus, aid augurs; Phoebe, hunters aid;
Pallas, to thee the craftsman's court be paid;
Farmers, for Ceres rise and Bacchus dear;
Boxers, cheer Pollux; horsemen, Castor cheer.
For thee, sweet Venus, with thy archer-son,
Is our applause: give me thy benison;
Bend my new mistress to accept my love—
She bowed in favour! Did you see her move?
Come, then, the goddess' promise ratify,
And you shall be the greater deity.
I swear by all this witness-train divine,
For all eternity I wish you mine.

But look, your feet are dangling: would you care
To put your toes up on the railing there?

Now for the chief event. The course is clear.
The praetor signs. The chariots appear.
I spot your favourite—certain of success:
The very horses seem your wish to guess.

* The procession started from the Capitol and came by the Forum and the Forum Boarium to the Circus Maximus, the whole length of which it traversed, while the ivory statues of the gods received applause especially from those whose patrons they were. On one occasion, in 45 B.C., the crowd withheld applause for the statue of Victory because it was accompanied by one of Caesar. Cicero expressed his delight at this in a letter to Atticus.

O agony! How wide he took the post!
What are you at? Your lead will soon be lost!
What are you at? You're ruining apace
My lady's hopes: pull at your left-hand trace!
We've picked a loser, sure;—but call them back,
Spectators, wave your togas round the track.*
See, back the togas wave them—Oh! Take care!
Here under mine there's shelter for your hair.

Once more the starting-boxes open wide.
Out fly the horses in a motley tide.
This time at least an open lead secure:
Make sure my lady's hopes, and mine make sure.

My lady's hopes have triumphed, mine not yet:
He gets his prize, but mine is still to get.'
She smiled, and shot a glance of promise fair.
'Enough for here: grant me the rest elsewhere.'

The way in which the wooer turns the favoured driver to account, first using him to establish a tie of common sympathy with the girl, then, when he is doing badly, contriving to shine by imaginary contrast, and finally exploiting her mood of enthusiasm when he wins, is as ingenious as it is true to life. It deserved to succeed.

Scarcely less witty and brilliant is the jealous lover's anticipation of a party (I, 4). Here the girl is officially the mistress of another, but has already given her favours to the poet:

Tonight your lover will be at the feast;
Your lover there! Would it may choke the beast!
So I'm to watch, a fellow-guest (no more),
Another clasp the girl whom I adore;
See you another's bosom nestling fill
And let his arm creep round your neck at will!
No wonder fair Hippodameia's charms
Made those wine-heated Centaurs fly to arms,
When I, no savage, no half-horse Yahoo,
Can scarce refrain from laying hands on you!

Yet may we scheme. Mark closely what I say,
Nor let the breezes bear my words away.
Be there before him; not that I can see
How that will help us—still, before him be.

* The spectators could by this means claim a fresh start.

When he reclines and you demurely go
To join him, touch my foot with covert toe;
Watch me, my nods, the language of my eyes;
Receive, return, these furtive gallantries;
Words without sound my speaking brow will sign;
Words framed with fingers note, or traced with wine.
When you recall the scenes our love has played,
On blushing cheek let tender thumb be laid;
Or if you would reproach me silently,
Hold with your hand your ear's extremity;
If what I say or do have favour found,
Finger your ring and turn it round and round;
Just touch the table, as men do in prayer,
To show you execrate that fellow there.

The cup he pours you bid him drink (take heed),
Then softly tell the waiter what you need.
The one you order I will first take up,
And where you'll drink my lips shall press that cup.
If he should give you food he's tasted first,
Spurn food once tasted by that mouth accurst.
Let not those arms upon your shoulders rest,
Nor lay your soft head on his bony chest;
From bosom and from tempting paps dismiss
His fingers. Most of all—allow no kiss;
For should you kiss him, I'd my love betray,
Cry 'those are mine' and hands upon you lay.

So much is all in view: where cloaks conceal,
There lie the roots of the blind fears I feel.
Then lay not leg to leg, nor thigh to thigh,
Nor let your soft foot press his hard foot nigh.
Much do I fear who much have wantonly
Performed: my own experience tortures me:
I and my lady oft beneath a dress
Have hastily achieved love's sweet success.
I know you won't; but lest you seem to have tried,
Come, lay that guilty-looking cloak aside.

Coax him to drink (though not to kisses' length),
And as he drinks add slyly to the strength.
When soundly sleep and wine his limbs entrance,
We'll take our cue from place and circumstance.
You'll rise, break up the party, homeward bound;
Remember, seek the densest crush around.

There will I find you soon, or you find me:
Touch me at any opportunity.

Alas, I plan what soon must be denied.
Night bids me sternly leave my mistress' side.
Her lover closets her; my tearful fate
To follow only to that cruel gate.
He'll take your kisses, more than kisses too;
What I may steal he can require of you.
But grudge it—that you can—and forced appear;
Breathe no endearments, let the rite be drear.
Pleasure for neither—that's the most I pray;
If less, for you no pleasure anyway.
But oh, whatever deeds the night may bring,
To-morrow swear to me you gave him not one thing.

This poem has an amusing echo in II, 5, where the poet's advice proves a boomerang. They are all three at the party, and the girl and his rival think he is in a drunken sleep; but he sees it all, the significant movements of the brow, the communicating nods, the speaking looks, the words framed with fingers or traced with wine, the prearranged code-signs. There can be no doubt, the correspondence in detail being so exact, that Ovid intended this irony, the laugh being against himself. There are other such cross-references in the *Amores*.

Sometimes the ironical twist occurs in the middle of the poem. The reader is invited to laugh at the poet's unguarded self-revelation. III, 4 begins with a sermon to a husband in a high moral tone. Why set a watch upon your wife, he asks:

Where fear leaves off, there chastity begins;
Who does not sin because she may not, sins.
Body in ward, the mind may wanton still:
Guard as you may, you cannot guard the will.

All the more outrageous is Ovid's wickedness, which does not reveal itself at first. From the sermon he goes on to prudential advice: by shutting her up you only suggest to rivals that she is particularly worth having, and everyone knows that forbidden fruit is the most tempting; in any case, a guard is degrading to a free-born woman. It is not until line 37 that his real intention slips out:

Only a boor minds if his wife betrays,
A country boor unversed in city ways.

Why marry a beautiful wife if you insist on having a faithful one? The two are incompatible. Come, don't be a puritan; cultivate all those friends her charms produce for you, and win a lot of good will with a minimum of trouble. How nice to be always asked by the young to their parties, and to see many presents in your home that others have had to pay for!

How shameless! But what fun! Just like Restoration comedy. And how pleasantly the theme is reversed in II, 19! There the 'husband' is spoiling the game by *not* forbidding the fruit. Ovid provides him with a list of suspicious circumstances which ought to put him on his mettle. And then, at line 47, comes a delightful twist: 'I give you due warning: unless you begin to set a watch on your lady, she will begin to cease to be mine'; and he proceeds to argue from his own feelings to the husband's, assuming that the latter needs him no less, to add a spice of piquancy to his conjugal love. The familiar complaints of lovers are neatly reversed, and he ends, 'If you want to keep me as your rival, forbid it'.

But for sheer, breath-taking impudence the pair of poems on Cypassis takes the palm (II, 7 and 8). Bursting with plausible self-righteousness, the poet shows Corinna how inconsistent and absurd her jealousies are. If he looks round in the theatre, or if a good-looking woman looks at him, she's jealous. If he praises a girl, it's obvious; if he decries one, it's suspicious. If he looks well, he must be indifferent to her; if he looks ill, he must be in love with someone else. And he hasn't even the consolation that the accusations are true! And now the last straw—he's accused of seducing Cypassis, the maid who does her hair. He hopes, if he has a mind to err, it won't be with a slave. Besides, is it likely he would risk an attempt on a faithful servant who is in favour with her mistress, with the prospect of both repulse and exposure? By Venus and her son he swears it is untrue!

Convinced by such unanswerable logic, we proceed to the next poem. It is to Cypassis. Ovid compliments her first on her hairdressing, and then on her technique in bed, and asks how Corinna got wind of their secret love-making. Hastily he forestalls any protest about his derogatory remarks on loving slaves with a recantation and a reference to Achilles and Agamemnon, and proceeds to chide her for having blushed when accused, contrasting the composure with which he had sworn by Venus ('may the goddess pardon the perjuries of an innocent heart!'). As a reward for this service he asks her to go to bed with him again that day. She shakes her head, and pretends to be afraid? But surely it is enough to win the approval of either, master or mistress. If she persists, he will confess and so betray her (with details so minute that they will both convince and enrage her mistress):

> Where and how oft we lay I'll tell to her,
> How many modes we used, and what they were.

Ovid's sly humour is seldom far away. In its less satirical form it appears at its best in the sentimental burlesque elegy on the death of Corinna's parrot (II, 6). The effect is achieved by following the set form of funeral elegy:* the bidding to mourners, the regrets—'Ah, what avails—', the outburst against the powers responsible with a list of those who could have been better spared, the deathbed scene, the hopes of a suitable future life, the committal. The parrot ends as a sort of Orpheus, charming with his talk an Orphic birds' paradise.

> The parrot, mimic bird from Indian skies,
> Is dead. All fowls, flock to the exequies.
> Go, faithful fowls, and beat the breast with wings
> And tear the cheek with claw-hooked harassings;
> Instead of hair, dishevelled plumage rend,
> And for the funeral trump your voices lend.
>
> Why, Philomela, wail for Tereus' crime?
> That plaint has long ago fulfilled its time.
> For this rare bird thy mournful dirges pour;
> Great was the loss of Itys, but of yore.
> Grieve, all that wing the limpid air above,
> But chiefly thou, devoted turtle-dove.
> Yours was a life of perfect harmony;
> Firm to the end was your fidelity;
> As Pylades to his Orestes clove,
> So to his parrot faithful was the dove.
>
> But what could faith avail, or gorgeous hues,
> Or voice of varied mimic sounds profuse,
> Or to have won straightway my lady's heart?
> Glory of birds, unhappy! dead thou art!

* Exemplified in his own Elegy on the death of Tibullus (*Am.* III, 9).

Thy plumes could dim the emerald's brittle pride,
Thy crimson beak in tawny saffron dyed.
For mimicry was never such a bird,
So well it lisped in echo of each word.

Not fighting, sure—fate's envy brought decease
To such a talker, such a friend of peace;
Pugnacious quails in constant strife engage
('Tis hence, maybe, they oft attain old age).
Thy wants were frugal: talking was so sweet,
Thy mouth had very little time to eat.
Nuts were thy fare, and poppy's drowsy seed;
For drink, the purest water all thy need.
The greedy vulture and the wheeling kite
Live on, and daws live on that rain invite;
The raven too, for all Minerva's hate:
Nine ages pass and scarce he meets his fate.
But gone that echo of each human sound,
The parrot, gift from earth's most distant bound
All that is best soon falls to envy's force;
The worst is suffered to run out its course;
Thersites saw Protesilaüs' urn,
And Hector's brethren watched his body burn.

Where are the vows my lady made for thee?
The gusty winds have swept them out to sea.
The seventh dawn, thy last to be, appeared,
And Fate stood over thee with distaff cleared;
And yet that tongue no langour stultified:
Dying, 'Corinna, fare thee well!' it cried.

Neath an Elysian hill a grove is found,
Dark ilex; ever green and fresh the ground.
There faith believes the good birds have their heaven,
And far from thence all noxious fowls are driven.
There spotless swans may feed at large, and eke
The long-lived phoenix, ever bird unique;
There Juno's peacock spreads his plumes abroad;
The pleasing dove kisses her eager lord.
Lodged in this grove amid these pious birds
The parrot draws them all to hear his words.

His bones a mound of fitting size inters,
With gravestone large enough to bear this verse:
MY LADY'S LOVE FOR ME THIS TOMB WILL TEACH.
MORE THAN A BIRD I HAD THE ART OF SPEECH.

Of course there is much in the *Amores* that is conventional and tedious *to us*. This is not always the poet's fault; his very success has helped to popularize his themes. Thus the motive

> I would I were the glove upon that hand
> That I might touch that cheek

has become a little hackneyed by now, so that we may do less than justice to the conceits of that charmingly phrased poem (II, 15) which accompanies the gift of a ring to his mistress. He envies it, and pictures how, if he could take its place, he would work himself loose and contrive to fall into her bosom; how she would moisten him at her lips before using him to seal wax; and wear him, he devoutly hopes, in her bath.

One of the troubles is that Ovid could rarely refrain from sowing with the sack instead of the hand, a fault which one at least of his own contemporaries noted. Having occasion to mention that even rivers have been in love, Ovid feels constrained to expend twenty lines in mentioning all the instances he can think of; and in III, 12 he takes twenty-two lines to give instances of marvels told by the poets, when two or three would have established the point. This is a fault from which other great Roman poets are not entirely free.

It is, however, true that genuine feeling can make a triumphant poem out of the most conventional forms, traditional details and rhetorical devices. The elegy on the death of Tibullus (III, 9) is as conventional as could be in form; it is full of traditional artificialities (so, after all, is *Lycidas*); and yet it pulses with indignation and pity. It is a passionate vindication of the value of poets in the world, all the more intense because it is the treatment of Ovid no less than of Tibullus that evokes it; just as Shelley's *Adonaïs* is a lament not only for Keats, slain by the Edinburgh reviewers, but also for Shelley,

> A herd-abandoned deer struck by the hunter's dart.

We may divine that one subject on which Ovid really felt strongly was the claims of *otium* as against *negotium*, leisure against practical activity. In this he is at one with Horace: leisure, so far from being disgraceful, is the only begetter of culture, including poetry, and the men of action are Philistines and enemies of the Muse.

The feeling of solidarity among poets comes out in the closing lines, where Tibullus is conceived as meeting in Elysium the great elegiac poets of the past, Catullus and Calvus, and Gallus whose tragic death was a recent memory. Can we doubt that there was also in his mind Gallus' friend Virgil, who is not mentioned, perhaps because he did not write elegy, but whom fate had snatched away in his prime, with his masterpiece unfinished, not long before Tibullus?

If for Achilles, if for Memnon slain,
Their goddess-mothers wept with human pain,
Mourn, Elegy, this wrong, and loose thy hair.
Alas too apt thy name shall now appear.*
Tibullus, bard and glory of thy lyre,
An empty corse, lies burning on his pyre.

Lo, Venus' son his quiver bears reversed,
His torch extinguished and his bowstring burst;
See how he goes with drooping wings distrest,
Beating with savage palm his naked breast.
Tears wet the locks that o'er his neck abound,
And from his lips the shaking sobs resound.
Thus, brother at Aeneas' funeral,
Men say he passed, Iulus, from thy hall.†
Nor less did Venus for this death lament
Than when the boar Adonis' body rent.

So 'sacred bards' and 'wards of heaven' are we,
And some would grant ourselves divinity!
Surely rude Death mars every sacred thing,
On all alike his murky hand doth fling!
Could e'en his mother Thracian Orpheus save,
His sire, his song that did the beasts enslave?
'Ah Linus!' in the forest that same sire
'Ah Linus!' mourned to his reluctant lyre.‡
And what of Homer, that Pierian spring
All poets' lips for ever freshening?
He too one day to dark Avernus came:
Only our verse escapes the insatiate flame.

* Deriving her name from the Greek for to cry 'woe'.

† Aeneas also was son of Venus, by Anchises, Iulus (= Ascanius) being his son and heir.

‡ Orpheus was son of Apollo and the Muse Calliope (Milton: 'What could the Muse herself that Orpheus bore, the Muse herself for her enchanting son?', no doubt thinking of this passage). Linus was another singer son of Apollo; Ovid accepts the derivation of the Greek cry of woe *ailinon* from *ai* ('alas') and his name.

By poets sung, the tale of Troy lives on,
And that slow web with nightly stealth undone;
So Delia, so shall Nemesis have praise,
Sung in Tibullus' first and latest lays.

Ah what availed Egyptian Isis' rites,
Her timbrels, and those chaste, unpartnered nights?*
When good men perish—may I be forgiven!—
By fate malign, I doubt of gods in heaven.
Live righteously—you die; those gods revere—
Death drags you from the altar to the bier;
Trust in good verse—Tibullus there lies cold:
All that remains a little urn can hold.
How could the flames devour thee, poet blest,
Nor fear to feed upon that sacred breast?
Flames that shrank not from such impiety
Could burn the temples of the gods on high!
The Queen of Eryx turned her face away,
Scarce able to restrain her tears, men say.†

Yet better thus than if Phaeacia's land
Thy nameless corpse had sunk in common sand;‡
For here thy mother closed thy swimming eyes
And gave thy ashes their last obsequies;
Thy sister here, her mother's grief to share,
Came with dishevelled, unadornèd hair;
And with thy kin to add their kisses came
Thy lovers both, and watched beside the flame;
Said Delia, parting, 'Happier didst thou live
As mine; while I enflamed thee, thou didst thrive';
But Nemesis, 'What is my loss to thee?
His hand in death declining clung to me.'

And yet, if aught survives but name and shade,
Tibullus, sure, dwells in the Elysian glade;
There, wreaths of ivy on their youthful brow,
Shall Calvus and Catullus greet him now;
Thou too, if falsely men thee traitor call,
Gallus, of life and spirit prodigal.§

* Tibullus' Delia, like Propertius' Cynthia, was a devotee of Isis, and as such observed periods of ritual abstinence from intercourse.

† Venus, who had a famous shrine on Mt Eryx at the western tip of Sicily.

‡ Corfu, identified with the Phaeacia of the Odyssey; Tibullus, taken dangerously ill there, prayed not to die away from his mother, his sister and Delia.

§ Calvus and Catullus, inseparable friends, occur here as writers of elegy; their successor Gallus, as first Governor of Egypt, committed suicide in 27 B.C. when summoned to answer some charge of disloyalty to his friend Augustus.

These are thy friends: if man hath any soul,
Tibullus, thou hast joined this blessed roll.
Peace for thy bones in quiet urn I crave,
And may the earth weigh light upon thy grave.

The motive that the poet, however poor, can give his lady a gift beyond price, the hope of an immortal name, had been used by Propertius, and occurs several times in the *Amores*. In the epilogue to the First Book of the *Amores* Ovid throws down the gauntlet to the Philistines, and in a splendid sweep of eloquence proclaims the triumph of poetry and his own confidence of immortality. As so often, the list round which the poem is built, here a list of poets, is too long; the temptation to bring in everyone, if possible with an echo of some words of theirs, proved too much for him. Nevertheless it is a fine poem, for once again sincerity breathes life into the dry bones (I, 15):

Why, rodent Envy, call my life a waste,
My verses, only idle wit misplaced,
Bid me go seek, ere feeble age forbid,
War's dusty prizes, as our fathers did,
Or memorize long laws, and mid the noise
Of thankless law-courts prostitute my voice?
Your aim is low, mine of transcendent worth—
Fame, to be ever sung throughout the earth.

Homer shall live while Tenedos shall stand
And Simoïs roll from Ida to the strand;
And Ascra's poet, while the vintage swells
And swathes of corn the curving sickle fells.*
Battiades shall every land resound:†
Though not in genius, great in art he's found.
Sophocles' drama need not fear decline;
Aratus lives while sun and moon shall shine.
While cheating slave, stern father, harlot smart
And bawd are with us, thou, Menander, art.
Ennius the rugged, Accius the sublime,
Have won a name that shall outlast all time.
The fame of Varro's Argo ne'er shall cease,
Of how Prince Jason sought the Golden Fleece.
Never shall perish high Lucretius' verse
Till one last day destroy the universe.
The Shepherd, Crops, Aeneid shall be read
While Rome remains the world's triumphant head.

* Hesiod. † Callimachus, son of Battus of Cyrene.

While Cupid lights his fire or aims his dart
Men will peruse Tibullus' polished art.
Gallus from East to West shall still be famed,
And with him his Lycoris shall be named.
Yea, flints with age may crumble, rust away
The ploughshare's tooth, but verse knows no decay.

Let kings and royal triumphs yield to song
Let Tagus yield that bears rich gold along;
Let baubles draw the vulgar, but to me,
Apollo, grant full draughts of Castaly;
Crown me with myrtle-leaves that shun all frost,
Fit reading for the lover tempest-tossed.
Envy the living gnaws; in death, it sleeps;
Then each his own deservèd honour keeps.
So I, when death my body gives to fire,
Shall live, and my best part survive the pyre.

CHAPTER V

THE 'HEROIDES'

THE dating of Ovid's earlier works, covering together about twenty-five years, presents insuperable difficulties, partly because their nature almost precludes topical references, partly because the *Amores* as we have them are a revised, rearranged and possibly supplemented selection, in three books published together, from five books originally issued singly. The *Ars Amatoria* as we have it is also apparently a second edition, in which Book III is an addition. We can do no more than conclude tentatively that by the year I B.C. Ovid had issued the first, if not also the second, edition of the *Amores*, and the first fifteen epistles of the *Letters of the Heroines* (*Heroides*), whether singly or in book form, and begun the *Ars*, this being the general order though there was some overlapping.

The nineteenth century laid arrogant hands on the work of many ancient authors. Large portions of the traditional texts were bracketed as interpolations simply because a particular editor felt them to be unworthy of the author, subsidiary 'arguments' being easily discovered *a posteriori*. The *Heroides* have received much attention of this kind. But there is really no evidence sufficient to discredit the authenticity of any poem as a whole. Nos. XVI–XXI differ from the *Heroides* proper in that they consist of pairs, letters from heroes with the heroine's replies. They contain a few metrical peculiarities, but these do not amount to much. To anyone not on the look-out for evidence of spuriousness they seem anything but inferior to nos. I–XV. I propose to treat all twenty-one poems as Ovidian, and deal with them together.

Although Ovid may write about women often with amused cynicism, he seems to have had an unusual inclination to see things from their point of view. He had a masculine and Mediterranean conviction that any woman could be had for the asking—'she is chaste whom no one has asked'—but he had also a tender side to his nature which gave him an interest in the weaker sex and a certain insight into what their feelings might be. As Sellar well remarks, he treats the love of a woman for a man as serious, but not *vice versa*. Nevertheless, he can see that men are often cads when it comes to relations with women, and in their way the *Heroides* may have served to make some of his male contemporaries search their consciences.

Thus the predisposition was there; but in view of the extent to which Ovid was influenced, both in detail and in choice of subjects, by his friend Propertius, it is probable that the idea of writing elegiac letters from deserted heroines was suggested by Propertius IV, 3, an imaginary letter in which a real person, under the name of Arethusa, is conceived as writing to her husband, who has gone to the wars, under the name of Lycotas. There had been poems entirely concerned with legendary heroines before, and imaginary letters may possibly have been used already as a literary form at least in the rhetorical schools. Ovid's claim to originality was for having combined the two, or for having seen the possibilities, such as they were, of developing Propertius' charming invention into a genre.

The choice of the epistolary form for what are really tragic soliloquies was not entirely happy. Of course it gives an opportunity for a certain amount of 'business', especially at the beginning and end. Penelope tells Ulysses not to reply, but to come back in person; she does not know his address, so must hopefully give a copy of her letter to every traveller who touches at Ithaca. Any blots are attributed to tears, or even to the anticipated effects of a suicide's life-blood. Poor Briseïs, a captive from Mysia, can hardly write Greek at all. Grief makes lettering unsteady, and pens drop from nerveless fingers. Leander's having to write is in itself sufficient proof that the sea is unsafe for swimming; only one sailor could be found brave enough to embark from Abydos with his letter. And Cydippe, plighted irrevocably to Acontius through inadvertently reading an oath aloud, begins her reply with telling effect:

> Trembling I read your note without a sound,
> For fear my tongue by some new oath be bound.

But in general the letters make little attempt at realism, and the shackles of the fiction are easily cast aside.

One drawback is the necessity of choosing a point in the story when it would be plausible for a letter to be sent. This prejudices the letter from Laodameia to Protesilaüs (XIII). According to the story, an oracle had said that the first man of the Greek army to touch Trojan soil would straightway be killed. Protesilaüs leapt ashore first and was promptly slain by Hector. On hearing of this his wife Laodameia prayed, and was granted, that his shade might visit her for a short while. Her devotion and refusal to be separated from him cost her her life. She became the type of wifely devotion, and both Catullus and Propertius had shown the imaginative possibilities of this beautiful tale. Now the whole interest begins with Protesilaüs' leap, and the great moment is the return of his shade; but in order to make the delivery of a letter plausible, Ovid had to envisage Laodameia as writing it when the last news was that the fleet was still detained at Aulis. He can portray her wifely devotion, but with regard to the subsequent and unique parts of the story he must confine himself to elaborate tragic irony.

But the intrinsic objection to the *Heroides*, from our point of view, is one which a modern might more easily anticipate than an ancient. We are much more interested in originality of content, and much less in form, than the Romans. How could anyone, we ask, hope to make a series of poems readable which should represent the feelings of a number of not very markedly differentiated characters in a situation which, for all the variety of circumstances, was emotionally the same, even granted that they were originally circulated one by one? If such a poem is to be moving, it must convince. The poet must feel genuinely for the suffering woman, and must beguile us to enter into his feeling. He may succeed once, but when he solicits out sympathy for one woman after another, we begin to suspect his. And this suspicion is increased when, for instance, the supposedly naïve Phyllis comes out with a verbal conceit such as this (II, 25–6): 'Demophoön, both promises and sails you gave to the winds: I complain that your sails are unreturned, your promises unkept.'

The sources used for the *Heroides* range throughout Greek and Latin literature. The letter from Briseïs to Achilles (III) brilliantly develops hints from the *Iliad*. But more often than epic, Greek tragedy provided Ovid with his sources. There were extant then many more of these dramas than now, and he speaks of them with enthusiasm and apparent familiarity at *Tristia* II, 381–406. Indeed, as far as their spirit goes, the true ancestors of these outbursts are in Euripides. He, like Ovid, had tended to see things from the woman's point of view, and although he was accused of maligning the sex, he was the harbinger of its emancipation in the Hellenistic age. An obvious case in point is the speech of his Medea when confronted with Jason, which directly influenced Ovid's treatment (XII); and there are other speeches in Euripides by women who have been wronged in one way or another which are similar in conception. The fine and moving outburst of Andromache in the *Troades* comes near in places to Ovidian-style rhetoric. But Euripides can carry it off where Ovid cannot. His heroines' outbursts do not occur until the progress of the drama has heightened the tension, so that we do not feel them to be overstrained. His Andromache ends in a wild rhythm of frenzy now beyond the reach of the compact, end-stopped elegiacs of the Roman, in which one couplet will make a point, and the next few develop it, and then the poet's unflagging fertility will produce another point—everything in neat and water-tight compartments.

Whatever their origin as an idea, and whatever their varied sources, in treatment the *Heroides* were influenced by the school-exercise called *ethopoeia* (characterization). It is they, no doubt, which have given Ovid the reputation of being more rhetorician than poet. The situation is given, and the former star of the declamation-school, assuming the character of the heroine, proceeds to make every point that can be made. The familiar commonplaces are pressed into service, supplemented by motives peculiar to the particular story. The literary sources are scrutinized for any hint, and the circumstances of the heroine and hero, their life and their family connexions, are fully exploited. The heroines are mainly concerned with scoring points, whether argumentative or emotional. Ovid makes little attempt to conceive them as belonging to a more primitive civilization (what ancient writer would?). In so far as they are not embodiments of *das Ewig-Weibliche*, they are Roman women of his own day.

So much we may plausibly ascribe to the influence of the schools; but Ovid himself seems to have had a fundamental trait in his own psychology which pushed its effect to extremes. He was 'puzzle-minded'. He loved to set himself a problem and then treat it exhaustively, fitting in all the pieces provided by the subject. He cannot select; he must go on to the end, even if it spoils his poem. Deïaneira must recite all the amours of Hercules, not excluding the grotesque story of his obliging the fifty daughters of Thespius, and follow this with a complete catalogue of his labours, of which he was no doubt even now boasting to her rival! He cannot let well alone, as Seneca remarked. Nearly all the *Heroides* are too long; the shortest extends to 116 lines, and the average is about 190.

With our modern background we expect such poems to be moving individually, or at least collectively to provide penetrating psychological studies of how various women would behave in a similar situation. It is true that Ovid takes some pains over both *pathos* and *ethos* and varies his *color*, yet the heroines are little differentiated except to the extent that their situations differ. Psychological subtlety is not one of the characteristic excellences of ancient literature, though Ovid excels many predecessors in this respect. We may be fairly sure that his audience read these poems as connoisseurs of rhetoric; they did not weep for Ovid's Dido as Augustine was to weep for Virgil's. They would derive particular pleasure from recognizing the details in the traditional story and observing how dexterously Ovid had made use of them; they would burst into applause at a telling couplet; and of course they would delight, as modern practitioners do, in the easy mastery of the verse, the ingenious tricks and periphrases, the grace, the inevitability. The *Heroides* were probably not intended to move; they are a display of virtuosity designed to entertain. We can at least appreciate the terse, quotable aphorisms; the fine expressions of *ethos*; the irony when Hypsipyle says she thought of sending her two children by Jason as envoys to him, but was deterred by the thought that Medea might kill them—Medea who was to kill her own children; the double irony when Penelope imagines Ulysses telling some love that his wife is 'rustica' and only fit to stay at home and weave, whereas she is preserving her fidelity to him precisely by the trick of her weaving, while in reality he for his part is even now telling a goddess that he wishes to leave her for home because he prefers his wife, homely though she be by comparison. We can admire (not without a smile) the verbal jugglery of such couplets (far neater in the original) as

> If none in beauty not a match for thee
> Shall be thy love, then none thy love shall be,

or

> Nor Paris nor another blame I can
> Who, to obtain a wife, has played the man.

But such conceits can be incongruously absurd, as when Medea complains that, though she could put a dragon to sleep, she cannot put herself: and we can only laugh outright when Ariadne says that she is not surprised that the horns of the Minotaur (whom she insists on calling her brother) could not pierce Theseus' breast, his heart is so hard. There are, indeed, plenty of examples of what we should consider bathos or bad taste, if we were to take these letters seriously; such as Hero's suggestion that, if Leander feels he cannot manage the double journey, she will swim out and meet him half-way to kiss on the crest of a wave. Nor are the heroines too miserable to make puns. I feel sure that in the *Heroides* Ovid, a baroque spirit before his time, was prepared to risk seeming comic if only he could seem clever.

Here and there, amid the desert of debating points, we do come across cases of what seems genuine feeling or pathos, when the poet forgets himself and his audience. Canace, doomed to die herself for her incest with her brother Marcareus, laments for their newborn child, exposed to die on the mountains, as many an innocent mother must have lamented in times when this barbarity was the normal form of birth-control:

> My son, your mother's sorrow, born this day,
> Born and cast out to ravening beasts a prey,
> My son, poor pledge of love, alas, unblest,
> This day your first, this day shall be your last.
> With no due tears may I your body lave
> Nor bear shorn locks in mourning to your grave,
> Nor may I kiss your cold lips, bending o'er:—
> Wild beasts are tearing what my body bore.

Medea, rejected by Jason, vividly describes her anguish:

> Thrust from our home, I took our children two,
> And, ever present still, my love for you.
> Sudden the wedding-song assailed my ears,
> I saw the wedding-torches through my tears;
> The pipes began to sound your marriage-lay,
> More drear to me than funeral-trumpets they.

Foreboding much, yet disbelieving still
In guilt so black, my heart with fear ran chill.
The crowd approaching 'Hymen, Hymen' sing,
The nearer they, the worse my suffering.
My slaves in corners strive to hide their tears,
None willing to confirm such hideous fears;
I too strive fondly not to know 'tis true,
And yet my heart is rent, as though I knew;
When, eager for the sight, our younger boy
Placed at the door, calls out to me with joy,
'Mother, come here! A great procession, led
By father: all in gold he drives ahead!'

Hermione tells of her bewilderment in her girlhood when her mother Helen left Sparta with Paris, and of her embarrassment when she was brought back, ten years later, after the fall of Troy:

I scarce recall—and yet I do recall:
Foreboding, grief and fear were over all;
My mother's father, sister, brothers there
Were weeping; Leda sought her Jove in prayer.
Myself, with girlish tresses torn in woe,
Cried 'Mother, will you leave me, leave me so?'...

My mother gone, my father with the host,
Though both yet lived, I felt that both were lost.
Your baby, mother, never in your ears
Lisped the sweet prattle of her tender years;
No little arms around your neck I threw
Or climbed upon your lap to comfort you.
You did not bring me up, you were not there
The promised bride for wedlock to prepare.

When you came back I met you on the shore,
But, truth to tell, remembered you no more,—
Yet knew you straight for Helen, none so fair,
While you must ask, 'Which is my daughter here?'

These three passages have one element in common, they all introduce children: the innocent, unconscious baby of Canace, the naïve little boy of Medea, the lonely child Hermione. Ovid's attitude to women, even suffering women, might sometimes be equivocal, but the pathos of childhood touched him as it had touched the Alexandrian poets.

The passage about Medea derives its effect also from his exceptional skill in narrative. The heroines are far more pathetic when they simply tell their story than when they utter strings of reproaches and arguments, regrets and lamentations. The story of Ariadne, told against a romantic background of shore and cliffs and trees, is one of the best things in the whole collection.

It was the hour when earth is glistering
With rime, and leaf-hid birds begin to sing.
Scarce half awake as I lay on my side,
My drowsy hands to clasp my Theseus tried—
In vain! I drew my hands in, tried again,
Stretching my arms to sweep the couch. In vain!
Fear shook off sleep; I sat upright in dread
And flung myself from the deserted bed,
Beat on my breast with palms resounding deep,
And tore my hair still disarranged from sleep.

The moon is up. I search if I can spy
Aught but the shore: shore only meets my eye;
Now here, now there, I run, and all unplanned;
My tender feet sink deep into the sand;
And 'Theseus!' all along the beach I cry;
'Theseus!' the rocks and hollow caves reply;
Oft as I call, they call in sympathy,
As if to aid me in my agony.

A hill there is, crowned with a fringe of trees,
Its side a cliff carved out by angry seas.
Strong in my frenzy I ascend, and sweep
With searching eyes the wide-unfolded deep,
And thence—for e'en the breezes are unkind—
I spy your sail flying before the wind.
Then at that sight, which ne'er did I deserve
To see, I freeze like ice, unstrung my nerve;
Yet pain allows no rest; I spring upright,
Spring up, and 'Theseus!' shout with all my might,
'Where are you fleeing? Wicked man, turn back:
Reverse your ship for one her crew doth lack!'

There is one touch here that jars, to my feeling: the fine conception of inanimate nature sympathizing with Ariadne's plight is blurred by the rather trite parenthesis about the winds being heartless as her lover. But how many touches there are which are fresh and true! Her gradual awakening, her sleep-dishevelled hair, her feet sinking in the sand, the hill so vividly pictured in a few strokes.

The plight of a deserted heroine can indeed inspire a moving and beautiful poem if these elements that Ovid used all too sparingly—narrative, romantic setting and pathos—are given their due place, and reproaches (wherein lies the danger of excess) are not multiplied till they become tedious. Tennyson has demonstrated this in his *Oenone*, a poem which may have been suggested by *Heroides* v and certainly takes some hints from it, but which is steeped in romanticism. But one can scarcely imagine Ovid sustaining, or wishing to sustain, such a level of romantic and lyrical beauty throughout a whole piece. His genius was for wit.

It is not surprising that we feel a certain relief when we come upon a piece in the *Heroides* which is not one more version of the now familiar complaint. If we cannot be moved, we may perhaps be amused. The specious arguments of Phaedra in IV, designed to allay the scruples of Hippolytus, are worthy of the bawd Dipsas in *Amores* I, 8. Ovid is here once more in his element, the poet of amorous intrigue and brazenness:

> Do not, because I seek my stepson's bed,
> Let empty names put fears into your head;
> Such antique scruples' days were numbered when
> Old Saturn still enjoyed his rustic reign;
> Jove, ruling that what pleased could not be sin,
> Sealed it by marrying his next of kin.
> The bond of kinship cannot firm remain
> Where holy Venus has not forged the chain:
> Why strive to veil our passion? Where's the need,
> When kinship's name can cloak the guilty deed?
> Embraces seen will praise on both confer:
> I'll pass for a devoted stepmother.
> Not yours to force a husband's bolted door
> In darkness, or deceive a janitor:
> One house has held, one house shall hold us still,
> Openly have we kissed, and kiss we will.
> No blame will you receive, but praise instead,
> Safe at my side, and even in my bed.
> Only make haste and straight our union seal,
> Ere you, like me, be broken on Love's wheel.

How shall we assess the *Heroides*? It is undeniable that they have been highly popular throughout the centuries. But taste has changed considerably in the past hundred and fifty years, and it is most important that traditional judgements should not be accepted without question. The classics have suffered because their exponents have too often felt it their duty to be propagandists, with the inevitable result that unprejudiced readers are disappointed and become sceptical. The proof of the pudding is in the eating. To me the single *Heroides* (I–XV) are a uniform plum pudding with a fair admixture of glittering rings and sixpences. The first slice is appetizing enough, but each further slice becomes colder and less digestible, until the only incentive for going on is the prospect of coming across an occasional ring or sixpence. It seems a pity that so many schoolboys should first be introduced to Ovid through this work. One suspects that the choice is due to the unobjectionableness rather than the interest of the subject-matter. Yet even with this restriction one would have thought the *Fasti* or *Metamorphoses* more suitable.

It is with palates almost ruined by long draughts of the bitter lees of love in the *Heroides* proper (I–XV) that we come to the living wine in XVI–XXI, three letters from heroes with the heroines' replies. Here the passion is either awakening or at its height. The epistolary fiction is maintained, but instead of 'half a dialogue' we have something approaching a love scene. It is a considerable improvement. Hero is waiting in her tower for Leander as he swims the Hellespont by night, and the setting is no less romantic than that dawn on Naxos:

While thus, or nearly, to the moon I spoke,
The friendly water yielded to my stroke;
The billows gleamed with her reflected light
Which clear as day illumed the silent night.
No sound, no murmur to my ears there came,
Save where the surface rippled as I swam;
Only the halcyons, still on Ceÿx bent,
Seemed to be uttering a sweet lament.
At length, with effort of my arms distressed,
I reared myself upon a billow's crest,
And saw far off a light that made me cry,
'My flame's own light on yonder shore I spy!'

Narrative skill and the pathos of childhood excitement before a catastrophe combine again to move us in the account Cydippe of Athens gives of her visit to Delos, surely inspired by recollections of the poet's own youthful tour. Acontius, a handsome youth, saw

Cydippe at a festival on Delos, and straightway fell in love with her. Having no hope of winning anyone so inaccessible by ordinary means, he followed her to Artemis' temple, and rolled in her path an apple on which he had written in verse, 'I swear by Artemis that I will marry Acontius'. Her nurse picked it up and, being illiterate, handed it to Cydippe to read; and she, reading aloud as even adults normally did in antiquity, pronouned the fatal oath before she could realize its import.

Fired by its fame, to Delos I would go;
So keen I was, my ship seemed all too slow.
How oft impatiently did I deplore
The niggard canvas and the sluggish oar!
Myconos, Tenos, Andros now were past
And shining Delos hove in sight at last.
'Island', I cried, 'Why do you flee from me?
Are you once more adrift upon the sea?'

I landed when the day was well-nigh done,
Well-nigh unyoked the horses of the sun.
Soon as they did with daylight reappear,
My mother woke me, bade me dress my hair;
Herself the robe upon my shoulders laid,
Gems on my fingers, gold upon my head.
Then forth we go, the Island's deities
With gifts of wine and incense to appease;
She with a victim's blood the altars dyes
And heaps the flames with solemn sacrifice;
I with my nurse to other shrines repair
And wander through the hallowed places there,
Now pace the colonnades, now in amaze
At royal gifts and countless statues gaze,
Gaze at the altar made of myriad horn,
The tree neath which Latona's twins were born,
And all the rest—I can no longer, no,
Will not recall what Delos has to show.

Acontius, as I looked, you looked on me,
Sure you could prey on such simplicity.
To the high steps of chaste Diana's fane—
Where should be safer?—I returned again.
An apple to my feet came rolling, thus
Inscribed—but stay! those words are perilous!
Nurse picked it up, and wondering, 'Read it', said,
And, mighty poet, trapped by you, I read.

Perhaps more interesting than this struggle against destiny is the struggle within the soul of Helen in XVII, a rare opportunity for the poet who formulated the dilemma 'I see and approve the better course, yet choose the worse'. Though here again there is the sanction of a goddess in the background, we are less conscious of it. Helen is depicted as a young and innocent wife. Paris has come to Sparta and been hospitably received. Taking advantage of a temporary absence of Menelaus, he sends his hostess by the hand of a servant a passionate love-letter (XVI). She begins her reply with splendid scorn, answering point for point, and continues so for sixty-four lines; then a slip betrays her real feelings, and gradually she begins to waver until she becomes hopelessly involved:

The bounty that your letter promises
Might move indeed even the goddesses;
Yet were it in me to transgress my laws,
Yourself had been a more compelling cause;
Either I'll keep my honour ever true
Or follow, not the gifts you bring, but you;
Not that I scorn them; gifts are then, I know,
Most precious when the giver makes them so;
Far more I prize your love, your toil for me,
The hope that brought you leagues across the sea.

Your wanton signs at table in the hall,
Try as I may to feign, I mark them all:
Now you transfix me with lascivious look
Whose urgency my eyes can scarcely brook,
And now you sigh, now take the cup from me
And drink where I have drunk it pointedly.
Oft have your fingers, oft your brow conveyed
Signs clear as any speech could e'er have made.
Oft have I feared lest Menelaus see,
And blushed at gestures made too openly;
Often 'twas on my lips or in my mind,
'This man is shameless'; and 'tis true, I find.
Upon the table-top, my name above,
I read traced out in wine the words 'I love',
But, not believing you, my eyes said 'nay'.
(Alas, that I have learned to speak that way!)

These are the charms, had I the mind to sin,
That might seduce me, these my heart could win.

Nay, I confess it: perfect is your face;
Well might a woman long for your embrace.
Let her who may with honour have that joy;
No stranger shall my chastity destroy;
Learn you, like me, to admire and leave alone;
What else is virtue but delight forgone?
How many youths have prized what you now prize?
Have you alone discriminating eyes?
Not more perception have you, but less grace,
Have no more heart, but only show more face.

She wishes she had been unmarried when he came, but warns him against thinking she would leave Menelaus, even if she longed to go as his bride to Troy, adding a moving appeal,

Cease, I implore, to tear this breast apart,
Nor, if you truly love me, break my heart.

She doubts his story of his judging between the three goddesses, and having modestly added that at least she would never have been chosen as Venus' reward, confesses that she is flattered by praise from such a quarter, and finally apologizes for her initial incredulity! Yet still she wavers and struggles, now dwelling on the hopelessness of his plan, now deploring her inexperience in deception:

Happy the seasoned lover! I, untaught,
Fancy the path of sin with perils fraught.

Her mind is in utter confusion. She feels all eyes are upon her, and confesses that rumours have come to her ears:

But you, deceive them—if you will not cease!—
Why cease, though, when you can deceive with ease?
Make love, but watch! With Menelaus flown
More, but not perfect, liberty we own.

She now admits more than she did before. When Menelaus left and they were exchanging farewells, he told her to look after the house and their Trojan guest; whereat she could hardly restrain her laughter, and could only murmur, 'I will'. And yet she is afraid, for the very fame of her beauty makes Menelaus anxious, and she herself recoils before the untried:

I yearn and fear and know not what I will;
My heart is doubtful and I waver still;
For he is absent, and you sleep alone;
I by your beauty, you by mine, are won;

> The nights are long, our talks are intimate,
> You such a tempter, and within the gate:
> Why, everything invites me to proceed,
> And yet some fear restrains me from the deed.
> To tempt's unfair: I yearn for fair duress:
> Force should have purged me of my prudishness.

But she returns again to thoughts of how to get over her passion. And so it goes on to the end, where she refuses to see him, but agrees to continue negotiations through her handmaids. The whole piece, 268 lines long, is a psychological study presented with masterly wit and insight.

Perhaps it was the study of Greek tragedy for purposes of the *Heroides*, and in particular of Euripides' *Medea* for XII, that inspired Ovid at this period to his only effort at drama.* He heralds it at *Amores* III, 1, 29, 'Now, Roman Tragedy, may I win fame by you'. That poem depicts a struggle for his soul between the Muses of Tragedy and Elegy, at the end of which the former grants him a short respite: 'Moved, she gave me indulgence—let the tender Loves hasten, while they have time; a nobler work is pressing on their heels.' The tragedy he did produce attained a great reputation in antiquity. Tacitus asserted that no work of Pollio or Messalla was so celebrated as the *Medea* of Ovid; and Quintilian remarked that it seemed to him to show how much that poet could have achieved if he had only chosen to discipline rather than indulge his genius. Only two lines of it have come down to us, and we have no means of assessing its merits. If it achieved contemporary success, it is surprising that Ovid made no further attempt. Quintilian was discussing literature with an eye to oratorical education. We may accept his statement that this play was free from perverted ingenuity; but in Ovid's day the taste of theatre audiences had long been debased, and it may not have come into its own until drama intended for reading had been established in fashion by Seneca.

At *Metamorphoses* VII, 1–424 Ovid tells Medea's story in full *except* for her expulsion from Corinth and the murder of her children. The natural inference is that these last events had been dealt with in his tragedy, as in its predecessors. The Epistle (XII) is conceived as being written at a moment just before the tragedy (at least in Euripides'

* It could, of course, have been the other way round.

version) begins. It precedes any interview with Jason, which would have rendered it superfluous, and *a fortiori* the murder of the children, which would have overshadowed everything and shut her out of the line of pathetic and injured heroines. It is, in fact, a sort of introduction to the drama, which may already have been planned, or even composed. She ends with vague but awful threats, not yet envisaged. 'I will do such things—what they are, yet I know not.' Unlike Lear, she still has power to hurt, and the audience knows it and shudders.

CHAPTER VI

THE 'ARS AMATORIA' AND 'REMEDIA AMORIS'

AT some time during Ovid's early period he tried his hand at didactic poetry of the most prosaic kind—versification of a technical treatise. Precedents for this went back for two or three centuries, and it would seem that Romans in Ovid's day had written verse treatises, for instance, on games of various kinds, on etiquette, on dyeing fabrics and on making pottery. The subject he chose was cosmetics (*medicamina faciei*), and after fifty clever and spirited lines of introduction he plunges into a series of versified recipes, presumably taken from some prose treatise by a professional pharmacologist. It is hardly a matter of regret that after a further fifty lines our manuscripts break off. One would like to think that Ovid broke off too. He tells us that the book was small, but he also indicates that it was published; and the ending as we have it is too abrupt to be an intentional close. What can have induced him to embark on such a poem? He was not a tasteless bore. One may guess that what amused him was, not the subject-matter itself, but the idea of writing a didactic poem on a subject connected with his speciality, love, and in elegiacs, the metre of love-poetry. His unusual tendency to see things through the eyes of the opposite sex, already exemplified in the *Heroides*, would help to account for his choice.

There was also the irresistible temptation *épater le bourgeois*. Cosmetics, then as now, were considered in strait-laced circles to be a shade unhealthy or improper, though nothing would induce the girls to give them up—at any rate the girls whose main business was to attract men, though Ovid also implies that this work at least is also intended for respectable ladies. Even Propertius, whose primary objection was that such adornments suggested a desire to attract others besides himself, took a high line about them to reinforce this: 'So now you are madly imitating the painted Britons, and flaunting foreign dye upon your hair? As nature made it is all beauty best: Belgic dye is a disgrace to Roman faces.' It is the recurrent cry that nature is right and art wrong, which, sooner or later, is bound to produce a revolt. 'Art', said Oscar Wilde, 'is our spirited protest, our gallant attempt to teach nature her proper place.'* The 'nineties in England were such a period of revolt, and when they become self-conscious and articulate in the first number of *The Yellow Book* (1894), it is no surprise to find a provocative, bantering article by Max Beerbohm in defence of cosmetics. Ovid, similarly *fin de siècle*—indeed *fin d'ère*—without knowing it, had said much the same in *his* defence of cosmetics, the prologue to the *Medicamina Faciei*: the age of Sabine matrons is passed, who preferred to cultivate their ancestral acres rather than themselves; now women go in for every kind of adornment, and do their hair carefully even in the depths of the country; the bridegroom is himself groomed with no less care than the bride—and rightly. One can imagine him at some party conceiving and throwing out the bright idea that he should write a didactic poem on cosmetics; his friends delighted, and pressing him to do so; and alas, the stifling of what had promised to be a lively squib in the sand-dunes of the intractable material.

But the previous generation at Rome had seen the appearance of didactic poems that were utterly different from these, the *De Rerum Natura* of Lucretius and the *Georgics* of Virgil; and elegy itself suggested a subject which could be developed in a true work of literature. Tibullus had shown the way with a witty poem in which the cynical Priapus gave hints on how to win boys; Propertius had passed on for the use of others some fruits of his experience with Cynthia; and Ovid himself had instructed his mistress on the conduct of their affair at a party, and had let us overhear the bawd Dipsas putting her worldly wise. Virgil had demonstrated how didactic material could be diversified and made readable. The *Georgics*, indeed, are only pseudo-didactic; in effect they are the first great descriptive poem; and perhaps Ovid's *Ars Amatoria* should also be classed as pseudo-didactic, since it was more likely to be enjoyed by sophisticated readers as satire and the comedy of manners are enjoyed than used as a handbook by young lovers. It had no comparable predecessor, otherwise Ovid would have mentioned it for

* The nineteenth-century revolt was led by Gautier and Baudelaire, and continued by Huysmans and Wilde. It was, significantly, Ovid himself who coined the phrase about Nature imitating Art, in describing a grotto of Diana.

certain in his *apologia* (*Tristia* II). It is not a parody, yet its dealing at length and systematically with such a subject in a form associated with serious instruction, and not without verbal echoes of serious poetry, inevitably generates a pleasing atmosphere of burlesque; and I feel sure that Ovid knew it would.

By now he was in his forties. He was, in fact, exactly as old as Horace was when he published his first three books of Odes. Both are middle-aged—sympathetic but amused and detached observers, sometimes affecting to be singed in the flame but certainly never on fire, giving advice to the young from the maturity of their experience. Here is no reading for the passionate romantic, 'trained to sing nothing but Calvus and Catullus'. There is no sentiment: love is an elaborate game, in which all's fair, a chase which is exciting for hunter and hunted alike. It is assumed that, to begin with at least, the hunter is not in love, for he is advised to act as though he were; but it is equally assumed that the woman's object is to make him fall in love (I, 611–20). The outrageousness, the blasphemy against conventional sanctities, that we found in the *Amores* is still the salt of the *Ars Amatoria*. It is not, however, a pornographic work. The prurient will read on with increasing disappointment, and may never reach their first meagre reward at the end of Book II. It is, in fact, an Art of Courtship or Gallantry, and hardly touches on the act of love itself. When it does, Ovid feels the need at least to feign bashfulness, and he avoids direct language.

He is at pains to emphasize that his poem has nothing to do with married or 'respectable' women. The *demi-mondaines* concerned, mostly freedwomen, do not differ essentially from the Corinna of the *Amores*. They are potential friends and companions, not common prostitutes. Even before he embarks on his minute recipes for cosmetics, Ovid reminds his pupils that habits, character, goodness, are the foundation of lasting love, far more than a pretty face. But the girl must be accomplished as well as good, able to sing an air from the theatre, to mime an Egyptian ballad, to play the lyre and harp, and to dance; she must know her poets (not excluding Ovid); and the young suitor in turn had best be not only a good talker, but in Greek as well as Latin—a talker, not a declaimer, for no one but a fool addresses a tender girl like a public meeting. The nature of Book II is sufficient indication that Ovid is thinking of fairly permanent liaisons.

The first book tells where to find a mistress and how to win her; the second, how to keep her affections. These two form a complete whole, and the third, instructing the girls in turn how to catch and keep their man, was an afterthought, though it was characteristic of Ovid to see the other side of the picture. When talking to the men Ovid stresses the importance of good character in both parties, whereas when talking to the women he puts all the emphasis on personal appearance and the arts of seduction; for in psychological matters he was nothing if not a realist.

The artistic problem was, how to create, out of what was bound to be a miscellaneous collection of precepts, a full-scale didactic poem (its ultimate length was 2330 lines) which should be readable. We soon discover one device of embroidery which he was to employ throughout—the old device of mythological parallels. The first four lines of the poem state the principle that love must be controlled by art; then—was not Automedon a famous charioteer, Tiphys a famous steersman? Venus has made Ovid tutor to her boy; he will be the Automedon and Tiphys of Love. The next couplet tells us that, as befits his years, Love is wild, but also malleable; then—did not Chiron, tutor to Achilles, tame his fierce nature by teaching him the lyre?

This 'business' occupies eighteen lines, and then we meet the second main form of embroidery, the parallel from nature, generally from animal nature. Does not the ox allow its neck to be subdued to the plough, the horse accept the bridle? The fact that in love the female may take the initiative is illustrated by two parallels from the animal kingdom and ten from mythology. Time and again such passages occur throughout the poem, till Ovid himself sighs at last, 'Why detain you with precedents, the host of which wearies me?' Occasionally one may admire the ingenuity with which the poet finds his parallel, but many are obvious enough; and, however neat the expression may be, it is undeniable that the monotony tells on the modern reader, who begins to feel he knows just what is coming next.

Fortunately Ovid had other resources. Set pieces had been one of the main features of Virgil's *Georgics*, as of Lucretius' *De Rerum Natura*, and Ovid has a dozen passages that deserve to be so called. A hundred lines from the beginning we come upon an admirable example. He has been describing how all the smartest women flock to the theatre (like trains of ants, inevitably, or like swarms of bees), where one may find girls for every purpose—love, flirtation, a single bout, a long affair—when suddenly he plunges into a delightful burlesque of the Callimachean *aetion* or story told to account for the origin of something; it is the famous legend of the Rape of the Sabine Women by the Roman soldiery at the instigation of Romulus, which took place (Ovid would have us believe) during a theatrical performance. The story is told in the swift, vivid manner which was later to characterize the *Fasti*. The diversely violent scene, depicted with perfect artistic control, invited the emulation of many a painter of the Renaissance, through whose eyes we are apt to look as we read. Ever since then, says Ovid, love and the theatre have been connected. And he archly adds an aside: 'Romulus, *you* knew how to give gratuities to soldiers; if you offer me such a gratuity, I will turn soldier.'

Another good opportunity for meeting girls had been, he says, a pageant organized recently (2 B.C.) by Augustus, a reproduction of the Battle of Salamis on a specially excavated lake at the foot of the Janiculan Hill. This leads naturally into a set piece about the forthcoming expedition to the East of young Gaius Caesar, son of Agrippa and Julia (on which he was in fact to die of a wound). Just when we begin to think that this rhetorical digression has wandered too far and too long from the subject Ovid deftly brings us back to it, with an anticipation of the joyful scene at the boy's return, and the masque with symbolical figures (still a feature of Italian carnival processions) that will accompany his triumph.

> Mingled with girls shall happy youths look on;
> That day shall every barrier be gone;
> And if some girl inquire, 'What kings are these,
> What places, mountains, rivers, if you please?'
> Tell her; and if she ask not, tell her too,
> And if you do not know, pretend you do:
> 'Euphrates this, with reeds upon his brow;
> Those dark green locks—that must be Tigris now;
> Call these Armenians; Danaë's Persia this;
> Some city of Achaemenus, that is;
> There goes a sheik, and there'—trot out a name,
> Real or plausible, it's all the same.

Sixty lines later we have another famous story, of how Pasiphaë loved a bull, and produced the Minotaur. The predilection of Hellenistic poets for stories of monstrous or forbidden love, which sometimes affected Ovid, may seem perverse, but as a psychological phenomenon it is by no means unparalleled. We may find a clue in W. B. Yeats' *Autobiographies*, where he is talking of similar predilections among the poets of the 'nineties with whom he associated in his youth. 'Is it not most important', he says, 'to explore especially what has been long forbidden, and to do this not only "with the highest moral purpose", like the followers of Ibsen, but *gaily out of sheer mischief, or sheer delight in that play of mind*?' The words I have italicized seem to me to express perfectly what I take to have been the mischievous spirit of Ovid. There was something absurdly piquant in imagining just what a woman would do in this unlikely situation, on the assumption that she would treat the bull like a man, *mutatis mutandis*. Pasiphaë's royal hands undertook the unwonted task of cutting the choicest grass for her love, who for his part was disappointingly unappreciative of her fine apparel. She wished she too had horns, and looked jealously upon the more beautiful cows; she was mortified when she found that some heifer clumsily capering before her lord obviously won his favour, and straightway had her separated from the herd and set to ploughing, or even sacrificed her to the gods with vengeful jubilation.

Several other legendary stories are told at length. A shorter passage of great charm reinforces the lesson that good talk can compensate for indifferent looks. We know how Desdemona 'fell in love with that she feared to look on', hearing Othello speak

> of most disastrous chances,
> Of moving accidents by flood and field,
> Of hair-breadth 'scapes i' the imminent deadly breach,

and so forth. Ovid's Ulysses held the love of the divine Calypso by telling her of his part in the Tale of Troy, with diagrams drawn on the sand.

But most of the poem is naturally occupied with advice. Usually a general precept will be enunciated, followed by details of how to apply it. What should the suitor do if he is rebuffed? He must be patient and submissive. There follows the inevitable reminder that lions and tigers can be tamed, and bulls broken in, by patience; and that Milanion, the stock example of a patient lover, won Atalanta after prodigies of endurance. The equally patient reader is then rewarded with a lively list of instructions:

> Yield to rebuff: yielding will win the day;
> Just play whatever part she'd have you play:
> Like what she likes, decry what she decries,
> Say what she says, deny what she denies.
> Laugh when she laughs. She weeps? Be sure you weep.
> Let her dictate the rules your face must keep.
> When, at her whim, you throw the ivory dice,
> Throw ill; if she does, bid her throw them twice;
> At dominoes claim not the forfeit due.
> Make sure the deuces always fall to you.
> When in the Soldier-game your marbles go,
> See your man falls before his glassy foe.
> Yourself hold up her parasol outspread;
> Yourself through crowds make clear her path ahead;
> Gladly the footstool at her sofa put,
> And put the slipper on or off her foot.
> Often her hand, though stiff yourself with cold,
> To warm within your bosom you must hold;
> Nor think it base (to please her, what is base?)
> To hold the glass yourself, Sir, to her face.

And now some good advice to women:

> You're anxious I should take you out to dine;
> There too you bid me teach you how to shine.
> Come late. By lamplight enter gracefully:
> Lateness enhances—grand procuress she.
> Though you be plain, their cups will lend you grace,
> And night itself your blemishes efface.
> Eat daintily. Good table-manners please:
> No dirty fingers smear your cheeks with grease.
> Don't nibble first at home, but stop before
> You're sated, when you could perhaps hold more:
> Had Paris seen fair Helen eat with greed,
> Revolted, he'd have rued his famous deed.
> Drinking is more becoming to the fair:
> Bacchus and Cupid are no ill-matched pair—
> This too, so long as head and brain and feet
> Are sound: ere things look double, call retreat.
> A fuddled woman is a shameful sight,
> A prey to anyone, and serve her right.
> Nor is it safe to drowse when table's cleared:
> In sleep there's many an outrage to be feared.

At times the precepts merge into satire. What is this but satire on the character of *demi-mondaines*?

Her birthday hold a day of strict taboo:
All giving-days must be black days for you.
Vain all your schemes to dodge: a woman's stealth
Can always fleece a lover of his wealth.
Some vulgar salesman calls while you are by
And spreads his wares before her spendthrift eye;
She'll ask your judgement, as a connoisseur,
Then kiss you, then suggest you buy for her—
One thing for years her soul will satisfy,
Just what she needs, and now's the time to buy.
No use to plead you have no cash in sight:
You'll sign—and curse the day you learned to write.
Now she'll solicit with a birthday-cake,
Born when it suits her whim the date to fake,
Now feign a loss and shed a touching tear—
A precious earring fallen from her ear.
She borrows much, but won't repay, of course:
You lose, and get no credit for your loss.
Ten tongues, ten mouths—still could I not convey
The unholy tricks that all such women play.

Here, on the other hand, satire merges into the comedy of manners:

Yet there are cultured girls, a breed most rare,
And girls not cultured but who wish they were.
Both should be praised in song: a pleasing voice
Can make the meanest poetry sound choice.
Burn midnight oil: both may accept an ode
To her, in lieu of a small gift bestowed.

But what you mean to do in any case,
Contrive she ask, then do it as a grace;
If you have promised freedom to a slave,
Make him this favour through your mistress crave;
Or if some punishment you would remit,
Contrive she plead, and owe you thanks for it:
Yours be the gain: to her the credit pay,
And, losing nothing, grant her fancied sway.

But whoso would a mistress' love retain
Must act as spellbound by her beauty's chain.
Praise Tyrian, if in Tyrian she's drest;
Or if in Coan, Coan suits her best;

If she's in gold, then more than gold's her price,
But if in woollens—'woollens are so nice!'
Stripped to her shift—'you set my heart aflame!',
And then, 'be sure you don't get cold!' exclaim.
Her hair is neatly parted? Praise it thus.
Curled with hot irons? Curls are marvellous.
Her limbs in dance, her voice in song, adore,
And when she stops, complain, and ask for more.
Even the joys of night, her blissful ways
In bed, may be the subject of your praise.

No chance of a paradox, a joke, an aside escapes the witty, resourceful, irreverent mind of the poet. In the very exordium, where conventional poets were wont to claim the inspiration of a god, Ovid disclaims any such thing. He will not lie about having been taught by Phoebus or meeting the Muses on Helicon: 'experience is my prompter: trust a poet who knows'. At the end of a string of injunctions about caring for one's mistress in sickness, he adds: 'There are limits however: don't be the one to cut down her diet, and see that your rival administers any unpleasant medicine she has to take.' The outrageousness of the *Amores* is still in evidence. Ovid blasphemes unconscionably against Homeric sublimity, rebuking the old priest for officiously prejudicing the golden future of his daughter Chryseïs as Agamemnon's concubine, and asserting that the king himself, having rightly enjoyed Briseïs, rightly also swore by his sceptre that he had not done so (a sceptre being no god). To the girls he recommends a lover's funeral as a good occasion for finding another lover: walking in tears with hair let down is rather attractive.

As in the *Amores*, the intricate play on words brings out the intricacies of love's psychology—the mixture of fear and desire in a girl: 'What she asks she fears, what she does not ask, she desires—that you persist: press on, and soon your prayer will be fulfilled.' Never give up hope of a girl, however cruel: 'even she you might believe unwilling will prove willing'; one should even pray to be the man 'without whom she could not live, but wishes she could'. There are epigrams, such as 'quarrels are a wife's dowry', and 'to-day is always the best day for breaking free', and 'who says too often "I am not in love", is'. What could more neatly express the dual purpose of girls in attending the theatre than 'they come to watch, and to be watched they come', or the effect of wine on love, than 'and Venus in their wine is fire in fire'?

The third book gives Ovid a chance to show us the reverse side of things, as he loved to do. After a few words on the degradation and unfairness of defeating an unarmed foe, he goes over to the woman's side and gives her advice with remarkably sympathetic insight. Not until line 577 does he affect consciousness of how completely he has betrayed the citadel of his fellow-males, but by now it is too late: he can only go on to the end; 'and let me be constant in my faithless treachery'. There follow some amusing precepts on how to keep a man on the boil. Don't make things too easy. Create an atmosphere of danger. Though the door may be quite safe, make him climb in at the window; and look apprehensive when he appears. Let your maid burst in and cry 'we're undone!', and then hide the trembling youth somewhere.—But let him enjoy you sometimes without alarm, or he may think your nights not worth the candle.

The reverse side from another point of view is given in the *Remedia Amoris*, with which Ovid completed his erotic cycle in A.D. 1.* We should expect him to enjoy turning the precepts of the *Ars Amatoria* inside out, but in fact he only does this to a limited extent. There were all sorts of sources available: for instance, many of the precepts to be found in Ovid had occurred in a passage in Cicero based on a Stoic treatise, and he certainly had in mind a famous section in Book IV of Lucretius. The remedies for unhappy love are supposed to be for women as well as men, though the pretence sometimes wears thin. Besides the obvious advice there is some quite penetrating psychology. For instance, do not explain why you wish to separate; do not air your grievance, but nurse it. If you recite her offences, she may clear herself; you may even find yourself helping to excuse her. He who is silent is firm; he who reproaches a woman is asking to be satisfied.

A single specimen of some length will give a fair impression of the work at its best. One can see that the poet is at least as much intent on amusing the reader as on curing the unhappy lover. (The passage

* It is fantastic to suppose that Ovid wrote the *Remedia* as 'a sort of recantation' of the *Ars*, to appease hostile criticism. He goes out of his way to deride his critics. It is a burlesque of didactic poems about remedies, and a piquant pendant to its predecessor.

here about making a rose smell less sweet by calling it by another name is a characteristic reversal of a well-known commonplace about the euphemisms with which men palliate the defects of those they love, which he had used himself in the *Ars*.)

Often your heartless mistress' crimes recall:
The wrongs she did you, oft rehearse them all.
'This thing she took, and that, nor sated yet
She forced me sell my home to pay my debt.
Thus did she swear, and thus herself forswore.
How oft she made me lie before her door!
Others she cares for, but my love disdains:
The nights I forfeit are a salesman's gains!'
Let all this rankle and pervade your sense:
Brood on it all, and breed your hatred thence.
Would you had words to vent your odium!
But hug your pain and eloquence will come.
Lately my thoughts upon a girl were bent
Who was not well-disposed to my intent.
A sick physician, my own herbs I tried
(Shamefully sick, it cannot be denied).
Intently on my mistress' faults to dwell
Helped me, and oft repeated, made me well.
'How ugly are the woman's legs!' I thought,
Though, in all conscience, ugly they were not;
'How far from beautiful the arms of her!'
Though, in all conscience, beautiful they were;
'How dumpy!' (slander); 'How rapacious she!'
(That proved my sharpest spur to enmity.)

Some virtues verge on vices: tip the scales
And even a grace disparagement entails;
So where you can her qualities misprize,
Just cross the borderline and criticize.
If buxom, call her fat; swarthy, if dark;
If slender, on her skinniness remark.
Be she not simple, she's a forward miss,
But be she virtuous, simpleton she is.
Observe, again, her worst accomplishment
And press for that with wheedling compliment:
From her that cannot sing demand a song,
A dance from her whose movements will be wrong.
She has an accent? Let her talk away.
Call for the lyre she has no skill to play.

Her gait's ungainly? Make her walk. Her pair
Of breasts immense? Remove her brassière.
Tell funny stories if her teeth are bad:
Eyes apt to run? Then let your tales be sad.

It helps to pay a sudden call at morn,
Ere she has time her person to adorn.
Adornment wins us: gems and gold hide all:
Of her ensemble she's but a fraction small.
One gropes for what one loves 'mid all that show;
Rich Cupid dazzles with his aegis so.
Come unannounced, catch her without those arms:
Ah, her defects will banish all her charms.
But here of over-confidence beware,
For beauty unadorned can oft ensnare.
Go when she smears concoctions on her face,
Go and observe, and don't feel out of place:
Boxes you'll find with myriad varying hues,
And see strange juices down her bosom ooze.
Those drugs recall old Phineus' fabled slime:
Their stench has turned my stomach many a time.

Finally, there is for us an adventitious pleasure in the glimpses of Roman life that these poems afford: the new marble colonnades, adorned with old pictures and with statues, where girls could be picked up; the hot sulphur baths of Baiae; the famous grove of Diana at Nemi; the statues in the theatres, of wood covered with gold leaf; the cushions that relieved the hard seats of the Circus; the wax-tablets on which it was sometimes possible to decipher the previous letter; the girl whose clothes have been stolen by a pretended lover of feminine tastes, shouting 'Stop thief! Stop thief!' all over the Forum; the newer Forum Julium with its temple of Venus Genetrix, who laughs to see even the lawyers below caught in the toils of love; the crowds on the Jewish Sabbath; the women thronging to the Lament for Adonis and the mysteries of Isis.

We hear of women's fashions. An oval face calls for a plain coiffure with a parting ('Laodameia' style); a round face should have a small knot on the top of the head, allowing the ears to show; some may prefer to let their hair hang down on either side ('Apollo the Lyre-player'), some to sweep it back ('Diana the Huntress'), some wear it loosely bobbed, some tightly bound, some held by a tortoiseshell comb, some waved, and, finally, some artfully dishevelled. There are German hair-dyes, and wig-stalls like that in the Circus in front of the Temple of Hercules and the Muses. There are powder, rouge, eyebrow-pencil, patches, mascara, saffron and cosmetics of all kinds.

A man, in Ovid's opinion, should be spruce and bronzed by exercise in the Campus. His teeth and nails should be clean, his hair and beard neatly trimmed, his nostrils free from hair, his breath and armpits from smell. His toga should fit well and be spotless, his shoe close-fitting with unwrinkled tongue. Whatsoever is more than this cometh of vanity—leave it to wanton girls. And do not curl your hair either, or smooth your legs with pumice—leave that to Cybele's eunuchs. It might be Beau Nash speaking. Elsewhere we have a vignette of a dandy—hair sleek with scented oil, shoe-tongue tucked in, fine-spun toga, more than one ring. The loosening of the toga seems to have been a sign of desire to attract a woman.

A passage giving advice to girls on how to elude their male-chaperone is full of sidelights on Roman life:

> You wish to write? Then cheat your escort-spy
> When bath-time comes to give you privacy.
> Tablets a friend can take on your behalf,
> Tucked in her bosom underneath a scarf;
> Notes in her garter bound she can conceal,
> Or hide your billet-doux beneath her heel.
> Should he suspect, bid strip your go-between
> And write your message on her back unseen.
> Fresh milk's an ink that's safe and cheats the eye
> (To read, a touch of charcoal-dust apply);
> Or use as pen a stalk of moistened flax:
> Letters can lurk beneath the virgin wax.
> Close watched Acrisius lest his daughter err:
> He failed, and found himself a grandfather.*
>
> Poor escort! Theatres the city fill,
> And chariot-races she can watch at will.
> At Isis' sacrifice with timbrel sit,
> And go where male companions are not fit,
> Where the Good Goddess' temple bans the sight
> Of men—save those *she* chooses to invite.

* He immured his daughter Danaë, but could not prevent Jupiter from having access to her in the form of a shower of gold.

Often the escort keeps her clothes outside
The bath, while she makes merry unespied.
An artful friend will sickness feign at need
(She's not too sick her double-bed to cede).
Do master-keys not mistresses imply?
Are doors the only way to reach you by?

Read by themselves, the *Ars* and *Remedia* may be accounted brilliant and entertaining works. Read after the *Amores* and *Heroides* they are apt to suffer. Quite apart from the sameness of tone, there is too much *rechauffé* fare. Surely we have heard before, and more than once, of lovers communicating by writing on the table in wine, exchanging glances and signs, drinking from the side of the cup where the other has drunk, and touching hands; and how could the author of the brilliant monologue at the races in *Amores* III, 2 bring himself to introduce a garbled summary in didactic form? The trouble was that in his previous work Ovid had introduced themes which would have a rightful place in any *Ars Amatoria*, and whose omission might have made it seem incomplete. Had he known at the time that he was going to write the *Ars*, he would perhaps have avoided them. As it is, we feel before the end that his erotic vein is now worked out. Perhaps he felt the same. After all, he was now in his forty-fifth year.

CHAPTER VII

THE 'METAMORPHOSES'

It was natural that Ovid, now in the fullness of his powers, should aspire to create a *chef d'œuvre*. He might have essayed an epic of adventure. Happily he did not; for Virgil had now set a new standard for epic, infusing it with philosophic import, and Ovid was no philosopher. What he did decide to do was more within his powers. He had already shown that he had a genius for imaginative story-telling: he would retell a number of legends, many of them not well known, after the manner of those Hellenistic poems which we call epyllia, but sustaining a more epic tone than the Hellenistic writers.

He might simply have recounted the stories in succession, without connexions or setting; but instead his ingenious mind wove a continuous narrative in which there are some fifty stories long enough to rank as epyllia and some two hundred others that are treated more cursorily or merely referred to. Beginning with the Creation, he ends with the apotheosis of Julius Caesar and the amazing metamorphosis on which Augustan poets loved to dwell, that of Rome from a little village into the capital of the world. The idea of linking such stories had already occurred to Callimachus and Nicander; and that of arranging them chronologically had also occurred to others. What was new, so far as we know, was the systematic *combination* of these two features in one work, and that a work of poetry. Together they succeed in creating an illusion of 'one world', an imaginative world dominated by the surprises of magic, but none the less convincing and self-consistent.

Why should he have restricted himself to stories of metamorphosis? The truth is, he did not. We have not far to read before we come to a major episode without such justification, that of Phaëthon, which is obviously introduced for its own sake, since we cannot suppose that its three hundred and fifty lines are simply a prologue to the briefly told transformation of his sisters, the Heliades, into poplars; and the same is true, for instance, of the picturesque story of Meleager, the

Rape of Proserpine, the Rending of Pentheus and the Death of Achilles. But there were few legends that did not contain a metamorphosis at some point, which incidentally gave scope for the poet's penchant for the grotesque. Besides, others before him had produced collections of such stories in verse, among them his own friend Aemilius Macer.

Into the labyrinthine question of Ovid's debt to his predecessors for material I do not propose to penetrate. Since it would seem that Ovid used various sources, sometimes even for the same story, and we have grounds for thinking that he did not hesitate to invent if it suited his purpose, it really does not matter much where he found this or that detail or idea. In any case, the works whose titles would lead us to suppose that they might have been his chief sources have almost entirely perished. Probably he relied on a good memory of wide reading as much as on source-books unrolled before him as he wrote, and he was nothing if not inventive himself. If we knew for certain where he was innovating, it would often be instructive: as it is, we must simply deal with the poem as we find it.

The organization of this immense work (longer than the *Aeneid* or *Paradise Lost*) must have been a great labour, but we may be sure that it had a fascination for the author, solving his jigsaw puzzle, far greater that it can have for us, who merely survey the completed picture. The ostensible basis is chronological—'from the beginning of the world down to my times'. But of course many of the legends have no place in time. Some of these are disposed of by letting them be told by some character in a gathering, of spinners or feasters or loungers or soldiers in a tent at evening; a mother-in-law and daughter-in-law exchange stories, and tales are woven into tapestries, or embossed on a bowl. Some are associated antithetically, after the manner of contemporary wall-painting—the wicked Erysichthon and the pious Philemon, the accursed love of Byblis and the blessed love of Iphis.

For some reason or other it was fashionable to insert in an epyllion a secondary tale which might have no bearing on the main theme. Indeed, nearly all extant epyllia dating from before Ovid have such a digression. Of some fifty episodes in the *Metamorphoses* which are long enough to rank as epyllia about a third contain one. It is apt to irritate us, like the ramblings in our early novels: we lose the thread, forget the situation or who is speaking to whom.

After the Introduction (the Creation and the Flood) the poem falls into three roughly equal parts, dealing respectively with Gods, Heroes and Heroines, and 'Historical' Personages, the whole being framed between a very brief personal Prologue and Epilogue;* but there are many digressions that blur these classifications. From the Flood down to the end of Book XI the only basis for chronological sequence is such as the ancient genealogies might suggest, save that the legends in Part I are mainly primeval, whereas those in Part II belong to an era which may be called that of Hercules, conceived as being not much anterior to the Trojan saga. For the rest we have grouping round certain themes, places or personalities.† In the course of Book XI we enter the twilight before history, where there is a traditional sequence of events, from Priam's Troy and Aeneas' wanderings to Romulus' Rome. Not until the last book do we emerge into the full daylight of Roman history.

In his choice of legends Ovid was eclectic, though it is remarkable how many he fitted in, losing no occasion to mention a metamorphosis. Stories that were similar, and also different versions of the same metamorphosis, were well spaced out. Where a well-known poet had treated the same story, he tended to accept the main outline and vary the details, passing over what had been elaborated before, and *vice versa*. For instance, in the tale of Orpheus he does not throw into relief his second loss of Eurydice, the central theme in Virgil's treatment, but dwells on his death, of which Virgil had told only briefly. It is also interesting to see how he modifies his treatment in the case of stories he has himself told elsewhere. Thus Deïaneira's complaints are confined to eight lines, presumably because they had been fully vented in *Heroides* IX.

Quintilian remarks once: 'There is a frigid and puerile affectation in the rhetorical schools of making even a transition score a point and expecting applause for this conjuring trick; Ovid plays in this way in the *Metamorphoses*, but he has the excuse of being obliged to knit most diverse topics into the semblance of a whole.' Transitions were, in fact,

* Prologue, I, 1–4; Introduction: The Creation and Flood, I, 5–451. Part I. Gods, I, 452–VI, 420; Part II. Heroes and Heroines, VI, 421–XI, 193; Part III. 'Historical' Personages, XI, 194–XV, 870. Epilogue, XV, 871–9.

† For example, Loves of the Gods, I, 452–II, 875; Thebes and Bacchus, III, 1–IV, 606; Revenges of the Gods, V, 250–VI, 420; Athens, VI, 421–IX, 100; Hercules, IX, 101–449; Loves of Heroes and Heroines, IX, 450–XI, 84.

I have here made use of the handy table of Dr M. M. Crump, *The Epyllion*, pp. 274–8.

a large part of Ovid's game. Friendship or relationship between heroes was one link, identity of time or place another. Any chance association would serve; or an association could be invented, as at v, 489 ff., where he makes Arethusa (not the Sun, as at *Fasti* IV, 583–4) tell Ceres where Proserpina is, perhaps as a convenient way of introducing the story of her metamorphosis. The only occasion on which he shirks his self-imposed task is in the last book, when there are other indications that his zeal was flagging. The end of a story rarely coincides with the end of a book. He will even begin a new one within the last few lines. This is partly the time-honoured device of the serial writer to whet the reader's appetite for the next instalment; but it is also an indication of the continuity of the work, which should not have been divided into books at all were it not that its length necessitated a number of rolls. We thus get the impression of a real, coherent world, in which there is interaction between events that had generally been thought of in isolation.

For metre he chose the hexameter of epic and epyllion. But Ovid's hexameter is unlike Virgil's. The gravity, variety of rhythm and expressiveness of Virgil's verse were due largely to heavy elision, but also to variation of pauses in the line and to free use of spondees, whereas Ovid dispensed as much as possible with elision, tended to pause at the caesura or at the end of the line, and was in general more dactylic, sacrificing everything to lightness and speed. His are the hexameters of an elegist. (In English therefore the effect is probably best rendered by retaining the couplet but allowing free enjambement, following the tradition of Chaucer rather than Dryden.) He also tightened up the rules for elision and caesuras, and denied himself exceptional licences. One must admit the justice of Dryden's criticism: 'Ovid, with all his sweetness, has as little variety of numbers and sound as [Claudian]: he is always, as it were, upon the hand-gallop, and his verse runs upon carpet-ground. He avoids all synaloephas [elision]...so that, minding only smoothness, he wants both variety and majesty.' Yet may not Ovid perhaps have been right, for the purpose in hand? The essential thing was that the reader should glide easily on without pausing to reflect. For his purpose in writing was clearly to entrance, and nothing more. It was something in the post-Platonic world that a poet should have the courage to disregard the puritan critics. Instead of disparaging him for not displaying the intellectual passion of a Lucretius, the religious patriotism of a Virgil or the moral purpose of a Horace, we should be grateful that he realized his own limitations and chose a subject in which the qualities he did have could find scope. But both his merits and defects will come out more clearly if we consider various aspects of his work with illustrations.

(I) SPIRIT AND TREATMENT

When we take up a book, we usually have some idea of what pleasure or profit we may expect to derive from it. If it is a long poem, we soon discover its general tone, whether it be *The Faerie Queene* or *Paradise Lost* or *The Prelude*. But it is not so with the *Metamorphoses*. Sir Harold Nicolson has put clearly the dilemma of the ordinary reader:

> The difficulty in appreciating at its true value this compendium of *Myths, Ancient and Modern* is that we are unable to assess Ovid's own point of view. Was he poking covert fun at his gods and goddesses? Was he compiling merely a useful Companion to Literature? Was he collecting an anthology of these already fading fables? Or was he just using the stories as vehicles for his fluent narrative pen? It is hard to believe that a man so convivial, urban and disrespectful can have approached these myths with any reverence. It is as if some bright young man of the twenties had composed a long poem in fifteen books, in which he had interwoven such disparate themes as the Garden of Eden, The Ten Commandments, Samson and Delilah, King Alfred and the cakes, Drake's drum and the death of Nelson. We should be at a loss to decide whether he was writing ironically, allegorically, symbolically or simply with some perverted antiquarian purpose. We should be perplexed by our inability to define his state of mind.

Now here is a case where it certainly helps to know the antecedents of a poem. For it is safe to say that the *Metamorphoses* would not have been what they are but for the example of that perverse but brilliant Alexandrian whom most Roman poets admired so much, Callimachus. When Callimachus set out to tell of the origins of obscure customs and names (*Aetia*), he apparently decided not only to make his poem a continuous whole by linking the stories with narrative, but to turn his great versatility to account, sustaining the interest by variations of mood and tone, and by every sort of trick and surprise. Even from the scanty fragments we can gather some idea of his method, which he kept up for two of the four books. This was not merely an *ad hoc* device: it arose from his own nature, as we can see from the Hymns, which survive complete. Thus in no. III, to Artemis, he slips insensibly from burlesque or *genre* into romance, from romance and beauty into pedantry, all within the framework of the traditional hymn-form.

Now we know that Ovid studied Callimachus, as every elegiac poet did. It may well be that it was the example of the first two books of the *Aetia* which incited him to make his a single poem with ingenious transitions; and, like Callimachus, he seeks to sustain interest by introducing every variety of literary form and mood. To those who are familiar with Callimachus, there is nothing novel or unique about the spirit of the *Metamorphoses*.

Here, then, is a partial answer to Nicolson's question. We must approach the poem with no preconception about what we are to get out of it, taking each episode as we find it, letting 'the most capricious poet', as Touchstone called him, lead us on through romance, burlesque, splendour, horror, pathos, macabre, rhetoric, genre-painting, debate, landscape-painting, antiquarian interest, patriotic pride—wherever his own fancy leads him. Of course we must know our Ovid first, but surely his other poems make him familiar enough. That done, if we clear our mind of watertight compartments, we can at least hope to sense the chameleon variations of this masterpiece of Greco-Roman baroque art.

'Baroque' is not a word to use lightly in a metaphorical sense without some qualification. It has for some time been recognized that there are affinities between Hellenistic and baroque culture. In both periods an outburst of exuberance succeeded an age of classic perfection, this having been the only immediate alternative to fossilization and the dull repetition of formulae. Baroque art tends to be grandiose, arresting, theatrical; full of restless and exuberant vitality, it strives after variety, strangeness and contrast—now fantastical, now playful, now picturesque. Indifferent to truth, it claims the right to exaggerate or deceive for artistic ends.

Is there not something baroque about the description of the palace of the Sun with which Book II opens?

> High-pillared rose the palace of the Sun;
> With glittering gold and flaming bronze it shone;
> The roof above was ivory gleaming white,
> Silver the double doors' refulgent light.

More wondrous still its art, for Vulcan's hand
Had graved the Ocean coiled about the land,
The whole round earth, and sky o'erhanging all.
Sea-gods were in those waves, the musical
Triton, the changeful Proteus, Aegaeon,
His arms around huge-backed sea-monsters thrown,
And Doris' daughters—swimming some were seen,
Some perched on rocks to dry their tresses green,
Some riding fish, their faces not the same
Yet not unlike, as sisters true became.
The land had cities, forests, beasts and men,
Rivers and nymphs and gods of field and glen;
And crowning all was heaven's resplendent floor,
With signs of zodiac, six on either door.

And look at that Triton in Book I, blowing the retreat for the waters of the Flood:

Seas rage no more. The Lord of Ocean's tide,
To soothe the surge, his trident lays aside,
And calls the sea-green Triton, from the swell
Emerging, shoulders thick o'ergrown with shell,
To wind his echoing conch and sound retreat
To waves and rivers. He his trumpet great
With hollow spirals ever-widening takes,
Trumpet that, blown far in mid-ocean, wakes
Earth's utmost bounds from rise of sun to set.
So when those lips and beard all dripping wet
Touched it, and breathed, and gave the ordered sign,
'Twas heard by every water, fresh or brine,
And hearing each did straight his flood confine.

And what of Phaëthon's headlong career in Book II? When he came face to face with the Scorpion's claws, in terror he dropped the reins. The horses plunged, and left the well-known path. The moon wondered to see her brother's chariot beneath her, and the clouds were singed and smoked. The higher regions of the earth caught fire and great cracks appeared. Vegetation first turned pale and was then burnt up; whole cities and nations perished. The mountains were on fire, even many-fountained Ida and Rhodope, bereft at last of her snows. Phaëthon gasped the stifling air and felt the chariot grow hot. Enveloped in smoke and falling ashes he could not see around him. Then was the Ethiopians' blood drawn to the surface of their bodies, and their skins went black. Then did Libya become a desert, and nymphs with dishevelled hair wandered looking for their springs and lakes. Rivers seethed, the gold in Tagus melted and the birds in Caÿster were boiled. The Nile fled and hid his head, which is hidden to this day, leaving seven dry valleys in his delta. Earth gaped, and light penetrated to the underworld, terrifying Pluto and Proserpine. Seas contracted and dried up, revealing the mountains they had covered. Fish sought the depths, the dolphins could not leap, and dead seals floated on the brine. Nereus with his daughters lurked in tepid caves, Neptune himself dared not emerge from the waves, and the Earth-mother, lifting her head and shielding her eyes with her hand, uttered an agonized protest to Jupiter.

The polychrome celature of the palace of the Sun suggests some fantastically ambitious design of Benvenuto Cellini; the Triton blowing his conch may be seen in Raphael's fresco of *Galatea* in the Villa Farnesina at Rome. It was from such works that the inspiration of baroque art was derived. As for the Earth shielding her face with her hand, one is reminded of the gigantic figure of the Nile on Bernini's Fountain of the Rivers in the Piazza Navona, shielding his eyes with his hand in order, it was said, that he might not see the rival Borromini's façade of Sant'Agnese in Agone.

Yes, the *Metamorphoses* is 'baroque' in conception with its huge extent of ceaseless movement, its variety, its fantasy, its conceits and shocks, its penchant for the grotesque and its blend of humour and grandiosity. But one must not press the comparison too far. It is eminently classical in expression, with its clear and simple diction and versification; and for all its straining after variety, the bulk of the poem consists in straightforward narrative untrammelled with excess of detail.

Myths are apt to consist of a bare sequence of events, because they arise from a love of symbolism or aetiology, from something at any rate which is other than desire to tell a good tale. Ovid's method is to take the traditional story and 'play it straight', to imagine what would, as a matter of fact, have happened in the circumstances, human nature being what it is, and gods and demi-gods only human in their emotions. We are accustomed to this literalness in the treatment of the Bible stories by medieval artists. But Ovid is anything but naïve: he is pseudo-naïve, bent on exploiting the varied effects of literalness. Let us go ahead and see what happens, he seems to say. Some parts will prove pathetic, some grotesque, some stark, some comic—in fact, a great deal of the essential variety of tone will result automatically.

(2) GROTESQUENESS, HUMOUR, WIT

The treatment of the act of metamorphosis itself claims first consideration. In Homer transformation takes place instantaneously, but in Hellenistic art as well as poetry we are invited to observe the process. Thus in Apollonius, and after him in Ovid, we see the warriors springing from the dragon's teeth at various stages of emergence. On Pompeian wall-paintings of Hellenistic inspiration we see Actaeon with horns only, or with a stag's head only, not yet completely changed. We see laurel branches sprouting from the head and shoulders of Daphne. Of course the effect is grotesque, but a taste for the grotesque was characteristic of the jaded palate of Hellenistic decadence.

Is there some fascination, subtler than meets the eye, in the idea of metamorphosis which haunts the folklore of almost all nations? The lively imagination of primitive peoples invents a story to account for a natural feature which looks like something else, or for a name which sounds like something else. The resemblance between human character and that of various animals may also give rise to legends. But why should they appeal to sophisticated people? Whence the success of Garnett's *Lady into Fox*? Anything weird, of course, appeals to the part of us which enjoys fear that is unaccompanied by danger, the feelings we titillate by reading ghost stories. But Fränkel, who cites an imaginative experience of childhood recounted by André Gide, may possibly be right in suggesting that there is ultimately something sexual about them. If so, however, the springs are deep in the well of the subconscious. With what modest restraint Ovid, so often referred to in tones that suggest he was salacious, describes the changing of Iphis from a girl into a boy!

Daphne, even as a laurel, retained her beauty's sheen: Lycaon, turned to a wolf, had still his grey hair, his fierce look, his flashing eyes, his savage appearance. The churlish rustics, changed by Latona into frogs for refusing to let her drink, 'even now exercise their ugly tongues in wrangling, and shamelessly even under water still try to curse, their voices hoarse, their throats swollen and their mouths distended with incessant quarrelling'. Ovid likes to suggest thus the origin of the myths.

Nothing could be more grotesque than the metamorphosis of Scylla by Circe. 'She waded waist-deep into the water, when suddenly she saw her loins disfigured with barking monsters; and at first, not realizing they were part of her own body, she tried to flee and drive them off and feared the savage muzzles of the dogs; but as she fled she carried them with her, and feeling for her thighs and legs and feet she found only gaping jaws as of Cerberus in place of them.'

On this side the grotesqueness of realism merges into horror. When Homer describes carnage we may not like it (after boyhood), but we recognize that this is something which belongs to his age; he is not self-conscious about it. Disgusting sights are inseparable from war. But in the tender Virgil and the good-natured Ovid of Augustan Rome such descriptions jar. Granted that in their Rome even the educated classes were familiar with the slaughter of the arena, if not also of war, the elaborate squalors described on occasion by these two poets strike one as conscientious attempts at Homeric realism. No doubt Ovid felt that his patchwork would be incomplete without a battle-piece or two, which would also give him an opportunity to include the emotion of shock among those with which he strove to vary the appeal of his poem, and there would be some at least among his audience whose jaded taste would respond to any novel sensation of gruesomeness he could inflict, like twentieth-century Parisians at the Grand Guignol. How these must have relished the flaying of Marsyas by Apollo!

On the other side grotesqueness merges into humour. The monstrous Cyclops, fallen in love with Galatea, begins to care about his personal appearance, combing his matted hair with a rake, trimming his beard with a pruning-hook, and using the reflexion of a pool for the purpose of composing and titivating his features. Mercury, bent on putting the hundred-eyed Argus to sleep, sits down patiently, detains him in lengthy conversation, and then pipes to him till some of the eyes go to sleep; but the monster struggles to keep a quorum awake, until the god, having plunged into the story of Pan and Syrinx, sees the last eye finally close and forthwith cuts off his head.

There is a kind of humour that evokes the response 'How charming!'

rather than 'How funny!' English has no good word for describing it, but the Greeks used *charis*, recognizing that there is an element of neatness and grace involved. Most of Ovid's humour is of this kind, and it pervades the *Metamorphoses*. Often there is an element of burlesque. It is delightful to see Circe presiding, like any Roman matron, over her household. The busy scene is familiar, but with a difference. The girls in her service are Nymphs and Nereïds, and they are not employed in the usual task of carding and spinning wool: they are assistants in an efficient enchantress' botanical laboratory, sorting out flowers and herbs into baskets, while she superintends, well skilled in the use of each leaf and in blending them, and carefully weighs out the correct quantities.

The story of Erysichthon, condemned to perpetual hunger for cutting down the grove of Ceres, gave ample scope for humour. Callimachus had treated it in a spirit of broad farce in his Sixth Hymn. Ovid chose instead to dwell, in a light and charming vein, on his final expedient, the selling of his daughter to buy food. The spirited girl refused to gratify her new master; and as she fled before him she prayed to Neptune (who had ravished her once) to save her, whereupon he changed her on the spot into a fisherman:

> Spying her thus her master cried, 'Ho there!
> Fisher with rod and line and baited snare,
> So may your sea be calm, your fishes naught
> Suspect nor sense the hidden hook till caught,
> Say, where is she in rags with streaming hair
> That trod this shore but now?—I saw her there
> With my own eyes, and here the footprints cease.'
> She, comprehending her divine release,
> And smiling that he asked her, where was she,
> Answered, 'Excuse me, sir, whoe'er you be:
> Bent on their task my eyes have never stirred
> From this same pool; but you may take my word
> (So help me now the Sea-god!), but for me
> No man has trod this foreshore recently,
> Nor woman neither.' Turning in his track
> The dupe retired. She changed to maiden back.
> Perceiving then her mutability,
> Her father sold her many a time, and she
> As mare, or bird, or cow, or hind was freed,
> Compounding fraud to gratify his greed.

Wit and pathos mingle in the story of Narcissus, who loved only himself, and Echo, who pursued him but could speak only to the extent of repeating the last words of others:*

> Narcissus roaming through the forests she
> Beheld, and burning followed stealthily;
> The closer he, the warmer her desire,
> As on a torch quick sulphur will aspire
> To anticipate and snatch the kindling fire.
> How oft she yearned to approach and woo the lad
> With soft, entreating words! Nature forbade:
> Begin she may not, but this much she may—
> Catch any sounds, and words thereto repay.
> It chanced that, severed from his friends, he cried
> 'Anyone here!', and Echo 'Here!' replied.
> Amazed he darted glances all about;
> Then 'Come!' he shouted: she returned his shout.
> He looked, and no one came, protested 'Why
> Avoid me?', and received the self-same cry.
> He stood, and by the answering voice deceived
> Said, 'Here! I want you'. Never more relieved
> To answer any sound, Echo averred
> 'I want you!', and to implement her word
> Forth from the wood she came and ran to throw
> Her arms around that neck desirèd so.
> He fleeing cried, 'Hands off and let me free:
> I'll die before you have your will of me!'
> She answered only, 'Have your will of me!'

Ovid's wit abounds in conceits of every kind. There is the reversal of literary cliché, as when the Bear, proverbial in Homer for not dipping in the Ocean like other constellations, seeks to plunge into the forbidden waves at the scorching of Phaëthon's chariot; or when the Sun, who is proverbially all-seeing, has no eye for anything but his beloved Leucothoë. There are verbal conceits, especially where paradoxical characters are involved. Here we have the Ovid of the elegiac poems, 'in love with his own genius'. There are the conceits which presage the epigrams of Lucan. And finally, there is often wit in the ingenuity of the transitions. Sometimes distant relationship forms the link. Ovid

* Ariel uses echo in this way to tease Ferdinand in the Dryden–Davenant version of *The Tempest*.

shows himself a Proust-like connoisseur of the Olympian Jesse-tree, with its endless ramifications. Ulysses' reply to Ajax is worthy of M. de Charlus:

Since Ajax claims to be great-grandson of Jupiter, let me say that Jupiter is the founder of my family also, and I am the same number of generations removed from him. For Laërtes is my father, Acrisius was his, and he was the son of Jupiter—and this line contains no exiled criminal. I have also through my mother a further claim to noble birth, from Mercury: I have divine blood on both sides.

(3) NARRATIVE AND DESCRIPTION

The bulk of the poem, however, consists of straight narrative. The acknowledged excellence of Ovid as a narrator depends in fact on economy and consequent swiftness, but more on his eye for significant detail, the quality we associate with 'good reportage'. 'If you look for Helice and Buris, once cities of Achaea, you will find them under the waves, and sailors will still show you the sloping towns with their walls engulfed.' Here it is the word 'sloping' that makes the picture vivid; peering with the sailor into the depths, we see the shapes in refracted light. How delightfully true to life is the description of young Icarus watching his father make the wings: 'The boy was standing by and, unaware that he was handling his own ruin, with smiling face now caught at feathers floating in the draught, now moulded the yellow wax with his thumb, and with his playing hindered his father's wondrous work.' And when later they soar, we see the whole scene: 'a man angling for fish with quivering rod, a shepherd leaning on his staff, a ploughman on his plough-shaft, beheld them and stood amazed, thinking they must be gods, that they could fly through the air'.*

Now here, now there, darts the eye of the poet's imagination. It does not always follow a story consecutively. For instance, when Triton blew retreat to the Flood, the result is described as follows: 'The rivers subside, and hills are seen to emerge; now the sea has a shore: the channels contain the swollen streams; the earth arises; as the waters decrease, places increase; and after all those days the woods show their uncovered

* It has been suggested that this passage may have inspired the works of art at Pompeii depicting the scene. P. Brueghel's well-known picture at Brussels, 'The Fall of Icarus', shows the fisher, shepherd and ploughman going on with their tasks again unheeding, as Icarus, a minute figure, strikes the water. It may well be that Ovid's description suggested to him this treatment.

tops again, with mud still clinging to the leaves.' Lessing remarked that these events are not described in the order of their occurrence; the hills should appear first, and so forth. In fact, the poet is showing us jumbled lantern-slides, not a film. But generally the slides are so well chosen that we can imagine the rest.

The freshness of Ovid's vision (or maybe his skill in exploiting the vision of predecessors) is particularly evident in his similes. These rarely extend beyond three lines, and are often shorter, for we must not be distracted for a moment from the story; but they are as apt as they are picturesque. Narcissus beats his breast till red patches show, like apples that are partly rosy and partly pale, or unripe grapes in a cluster beginning to purple; and Arachne flushes for a fleeting moment, as the sky grows crimson at dawn and anon pales again with the sunrise. Apollo is inflamed by Daphne as hedges burn with fire a traveller has brought too near or left at daybreak unextinguished; and at sight of Coronis' pyre he groans as a cow groans when before her eyes the hammer, raised to the butcher's right ear, descends with resounding blow to dash out the brains of her suckling calf. In the story of Hermaphroditus and the nymph Salamacis there are six comparisons in thirty lines.

Ovid does not hesitate to use similes taken from his own times. The Maenads attack Orpheus, flocking round him like birds in daylight mobbing an owl, or hounds harrying a stag to death some morning in the arena. (Here again a single word, 'morning', imparts reality to the scene.) Atalanta's body flushed as she ran, as when a crimson awning stretched over a white courtyard colours it with borrowed hues. Particularly good is the likening of the warriors that arose from the dragon's teeth to figures embroidered on a theatre curtain rising (in Roman fashion) from the ground: 'Even so, as in the festive theatre the curtain is raised, figures of men emerge, showing first their faces, then little by little all the rest, till at last, drawn up with steady motion, their whole forms are revealed and they plant their feet on its lowest edge.'

It is easy to see how it came about that Ovid had such an immense influence on Renaissance art. There is a plastic quality about his work. He catches the significant moment or attitude or gesture and imprints it on our mind. Interesting attempts have been made to identify his own debt to particular works of art, or to distinguish their influence from that of literature or first-hand experience. These have been criticized, but one may plausibly guess that works of art seen on his visit to Athens at an impressionable age, and those plundered or imported from Greece which adorned the colonnades, temples and palaces of the city which Augustus was turning under his eyes from brick to marble, coloured his whole imagination. Many of the best narrative episodes are too long for quotation here in full; but Arethusa's account to Ceres of her pursuit by the river Alpheüs in human form, being fairly short, may serve as well as any to illustrate Ovid's genius at its best:

Returning tired from the Stymphalian chase—
And doubly hot with toil and sun I was—
I found a stream that smooth and silent ran,
Clear to the bottom, so that you could scan
Each pebble there; it hardly seemed to move.
Wild silvery willows shaded it above,
And poplars that by rivers nurtured grow.
I approached, I tried the water with my toe,
Then to the knee, nor yet content, undressed
And o'er a curving willow flung my vest,
And dived all naked in. I swam and plunged
And tossed my arms a thousand ways and lunged,
When suddenly beneath the pool I heard
A sound, and climbed the nearest bank afeared.
'Stay, Arethusa!' from his depths there cried
Alpheüs: 'stay!', again he did me chide.
I fled, just as I was and all unclad
(Ill chance, the other bank my clothing had).
Fired, he pursued my open nakedness:
The more I ran, more fiercely did he press.
As pigeons flee a hawk on fluttered wing
And hawk pursues the pigeons fluttering.
Right past Orchomenus, Psophis, Cyllene,
Maenalus, Erymanthus, did I flee,
And Elis' land, nor swifter yet was he.
Ill-matched, I could not long sustain that pace,
Accustomed he to endure a lengthy race;
Yet over fields and mountains forested,
O'er rocks and stones and pathless wastes I fled.
With sun behind I saw preceding me
A shadow huge—or terror made me see—;
I heard his dreaded footfall, that I swear,
And felt his breath beat on my braided hair,

Fordone, 'O help, or I am caught!' I cried,
'Dictynna,* help the maid who at thy side
Oft chosen bore thy bow and quiver's load!'
The goddess hearkened, and forthwith bestowed
A cloud for covering. In quest of me
The river roamed, groping bewilderedly.
Twice circled he my hiding-place about,
And 'Arethusa!' twice did loudly shout,
'Ho, Arethusa!' Ah, how felt I then?
As lamb that hears the wolves about the pen
Howling, or hare that, lurking in the brake,
Dread muzzles sees nor motion dares to make.
He moved not on, for further went no trace
Of footsteps—only watched the cloud and place.
Sweat from my leaguer'd limbs began to well,
And watery drops from all my body fell;
Each footstep left a pool, each tress a fount,
And sooner than I can the tale recount
I was a spring. But still the river knows
His love, and now his human shape forgoes,
To mingle with me turning back to waves.
Diana cleaves the ground, and through dark caves
To Ortygia, that bears her blessed name,
I pass, once more the daylight to acclaim.

However much at home Ovid may have felt in the sophisticated society of the capital, he must sometimes have longed, like Horace, to escape to the hills and streams, far from 'the smoke and wealth and din of Rome'. The *Metamorphoses* is undoubtedly a poem of escape. It wafts the reader into a world where the geographical features may be familiar, but the actors, divine and human, move hither and thither with the swiftness of the wind, from Babylon and the Sun-god's palace beyond the Ethiopians to Sicily and the banks of Po, and look down on the earth as man could do only in imagination until eighteen centuries after Ovid wrote.† Its true centre, the abode of Rumour, in mid-air, commands a view of the whole. Naturally this primeval world is not urbanized: with rare exceptions we move among mountains, valleys, rivers, forests, seas.

* Diana of the hunting-nets.

† Cf. *Fasti* IV, 561–72, and Chaucer's dream of being carried aloft by an eagle, *The Hous of Fame* II, 896 ff.

To us it is a romantic world, quite apart from its inhabitants. Its very wildness makes it so. But are we importing modern sentiment if we attribute such feelings to Ovid? Let me put the point more concretely. J. H. Newman's words

> O'er moor and fen, o'er crag and torrent, till
> The night is gone,

though they are only a list of natural features, and indeed are ostensibly but symbols of the difficulties of our earthly journey, evoke strong romantic feelings in readers conditioned by Wordsworth and his successors, for whom 'over the hills and far away' is the essence of poetry. When Ovid wished to describe some character traversing his world, he similarly used lists of natural features, as in 'passing o'er hills, o'er dales, where chance led' or 'yet through fields, o'er forest-covered mountains, o'er rocks and stones and pathless places I ran', and here again romantic echoes are raised in our minds, though it is difficult to say how he could have expressed himself more plainly and realistically. An ancient poet has only to mention natural features of the countryside for modern critics to scent the poetry of romance.

Nevertheless, it is well known that after the urbanization of society in Hellenistic times both poetry and the visual arts began to view nature in a spirit not much different from ours; and I believe that when Catullus addressed Diana as born 'to be mistress of the mountains and the green forests and the hidden glades and the sounding rivers' his feeling was indeed romantic; nor do I see any reason to doubt that Ovid had similar feelings. If he rarely indicates them expressly, it may be because of the nature of his genre; the early epyllion was objective; it did not dwell on the emotions expected of the reader, as the idyll and the later epyllion were apt to do. Ovid is sparing of comment, even the comment of epithets; he may suggest, but he does not exclaim.

Let us take a salient example. The miraculous beauty of the dawn has never ceased to challenge the descriptive powers of poets. One has only to think of Shakespeare. The first dawn in the *Metamorphoses* is a colourful allegorical picture which is said to have inspired Guido Reni's once celebrated Aurora Pallavicini:

> Lo, Aurora, waking from the ruddy east, opened the crimson doors and the halls full of roses: the stars fled away, marshalled by Lucifer, who last of all

departs from his post in the sky. When the Sun-god saw him setting and the world growing red, while the slender horns of the moon seemed to vanish away, he bade the swift Hours yoke his steeds. Quickly the goddesses obeyed his command, led forth the steeds, filled with ambrosial nurture and breathing fire, from their lofty stalls, and fixed their jingling bridles.

But after this, while we cannot doubt the poet's impressionability, his daybreaks are indicated in sparing language, for the narrative cannot wait: 'as the first sunlight struck the peaks'; or 'Lucifer had marshalled the host of the stars on high'; or 'when next Dawn, borne on her saffron car, shall bring back the day'; or at most, 'the next Dawn had banished the torches of night, and the sun's rays had dried the rimy grass'. Nevertheless, the feeling for beauty is there; in the last example, as so often with him, one word, 'rimy', is enough to bring the picture to life.

It is the same with descriptions of scenery: Ovid rarely dwells on them in the idyllic manner. But there is one exception so striking that we may be justified in assuming that he is indulging an enthusiasm of his own. The reader cannot fail to have been struck by the lifelike beauty of the reach of the Alpheüs which tempted Arethusa to her fateful bathe. There are a dozen extended descriptions of natural scenery in the poem, and practically all of them centre round water, cool, calm and shaded. Mountain ridges and cliffs are not described; nor are valleys, forests or meadows, save as a setting for water; and the water is not generally cascading or hurrying, but gentle or calm and translucent, shaded by trees or overarching rocks. Cool streams and fresh grass, we remember, are what Ovid in his mind's eye associated with the countryside of his boyhood home amid the Apennines.

Here is a good example:

> Thick set with pines and cypress-spires the glade
> Gargaphië lay—Diana loved its shade—
> And in its deepest nook a woodland grot,
> Not of man's art, but artfully begot
> By nature's genius, that from tufa soft
> And living pumice carved its arch aloft;
> Hence to the right a rivulet clear as glass
> Spread purling into pools begirt with grass.
> Oft would the Goddess, wearied in the hunt,
> Refresh her virgin limbs in that pure fount.

In the same book (III) there is a copious spring in a low-arched cavern, thickly surrounded with bushes and saplings, in the depths of a primeval forest, and again a clear pool of silvery-bright water, untouched by shepherds or by mountain-grazing goats or any other beast, undisturbed by bird or wild animal or falling branch, with fresh grass round the edge and a fringe of trees that fend off at all times the heat of the sun. Sometimes there are flowers too, like the crimson water-lotus on the shelving bank of the myrtle-crowned pool into which the nymph Lotis had been turned. And of course they abound near the swan-lake of Enna whence Pluto seized Proserpina. Soft damp moss on the floor, and variegated shells on the roof, were the interior decoration of the dark cave of pumice and tufa where the river god Acheloüs dwelt.

Sometimes it is sea water that makes the scene, like the favourite bow-shaped pool of Scylla on the Calabrian coast; or the height on the same coast on which she turned to face Glaucus, where the mountains gather to a wooded peak hanging far out over the deep; or the lonely shore of Euboea, its grass ungrazed by cattle, sheep or goats, its flowers unrifled by bees or human hands, its hay unmown, where Glaucus sat counting his fish before he ate the fatal herb that drove him into the sea. And there is the lovely spot where Peleus found Thetis.

> On the Thessalian coast there curves a bay
> With jutting arms; a haven, you would say,
> Were but the water deeper; o'er the strand
> Shallow it spreads; around, the solid sand
> Records no footprint, checks no step, nor lies
> With seaweed strewn. A myrtle-wood there is
> With variegated berries hung, and close
> A cave, by nature made or man—who knows?—
> By man most like. Whereto, naked, astride
> A harnessed dolphin, Thetis oft did ride.

One of the first landscapes we come upon in the poem is wilder and still more romantic. 'There is a glen in Thessaly shut in all round by forest-clad steeps. Through it the river Peneus flows with foaming waters from its source beneath Mount Pindus; its heavy falls concentrate a mist that drives fine vapours up to scatter spray on the tree-tops, and deafens the surroundings, near and far, with its thunder.' For two centuries at least Romans had been familiar with 'picturesque' landscapes in the Hellenistic manner painted on the walls of rooms. From about 40 B.C. dates the romantic series illustrating the *Odyssey* now in the Vatican, with its arched or overhanging rocks. Ovid's contemporary Vitruvius gives instances of what such landscapes might represent, as painted in colonnades—harbours, capes, shores, rivers, springs, straits, temples, groves, mountains, flocks, shepherds—adding that there are sometimes large pictures portraying the gods, or scenes from mythology unfolded in order, likewise the Tale of Troy, or the Wanderings of Ulysses.

Grimal draws attention to a passage in the *Metamorphoses* which, he rightly claims, might be taken for a description of some landscape-painting at Pompeii:

I had driven my weary herd down to the bay when the sun was high in the middle of his course. Some of the cattle had lain down on the yellow sand and were gazing out on the broad expanse of sea; some were slowly ambling up and down, while others were swimming out and standing with their heads reared above the surface. A temple stood by the sea, not resplendent with marble and gold, but made of heavy timbers and overshadowed by an ancient grove.

He also shows that Ovid freely varied traditional features, whether provided by literature or visual art. We may fairly conclude that he was influenced by both of these, but that his own experience gave life to his pictures of traditional or conventional scenes.

Among the descriptive passages in the *Metamorphoses* are several that portray the surroundings of a personified abstraction in an allegorical way. We are shown Envy in her hideous abode, Famine in the waste land of Scythia, the House of Rumour and the Cave of Sleep. These elaborate conceptions, none of them new, are forerunners of the medieval and renaissance allegories. The Cave of Sleep is perhaps the most worth quoting, and as it is the ancestor of one of the most famous passages in the *Faerie Queene*, an attempt to translate it into Spenserian stanzas may at least bring out the affinity:

Near the Cimmerians, in a mountain deep
  Hollowed, where morn nor noon nor evening pries,
There lurks a cave, the abode of drowsy Sleep;
  Dark vapours from the ground and shadows rise
  Murky; nor there the wakeful cock with cries

Summons the dawn, nor noisy vigil keep
  Watchdogs aroused, nor geese than dogs more wise;
No rustling trees are heard, nor bleating sheep,
Nor howling beasts, nor men that one another clepe.

There Silence reigns, save that from nether floor
  Of rock up wells the river Lethe's spring,
Whose whisper lulls to rest; and all before
  Poppies abound and herbs past numbering,
  Whose juices Night distils, and scattering
Puts the dark world to sleep. There is no door
  In all that house on creaking hinge to swing,
No janitor; and in the midst doth soar
An ebon couch of down with dusky pall spread o'er.

Here lies the God himself, with limbs asprawl
  In slumber....

When Euripides brought the hero Telephus on to the stage disguised in rags and introduced 'familiar things such as we use and live among', he created a scandal in fifth-century Athens, but he also began a movement which had a profound influence on Hellenistic taste. Gods and mythological personages alike were brought down to human level and into the light of the present day; and further, both in the visual arts and in poetry there developed a love of depicting ordinary people realistically, not without affectionate sympathy, and also detailed scenes from everyday life. Ovid shared this taste for 'genre' to some extent; at any rate, it could be one contributor to the variety of his patchwork. But it comes in most appropriately in the story of Philemon and Baucis. This tale of how an old peasant couple 'entertained angels unawares' is located in Phrygia. It may well have been a local tradition of this visit of Jupiter and Mercury to mortals which suggested to the people of Lystra that Barnabas and Paul were those gods come down in the likeness of men. Wherever Ovid may have found it, he perceived that it had affinities with Callimachus' *Hecale*, the story of an old woman who entertained Theseus, and from that famous poem he borrowed both the idyllic colouring and the idea of painting a genre picture of peasant life, as well as several direct hints. The result is one of his happiest creations, and the description of the meal deserves quotation at some length:

So when the gods came to this dwelling poor
And stooping entered through the lowly door,
Philemon brought a bench for them to sit,
And bustling Baucis spread a rug on it,
Stirred on the hearth the ashes scarce alive,
Yesterday's fire with bellows to revive,
Fed it with bark and puffed it into flame;
Chopped sticks, dry branches, from the roof the dame
Brought down, and broke, and placed beneath the pot,
And next the cabbage, from the garden-plot
Picked by her husband, stripped. He with a fork
Reached and unhooked a smoky side of pork
From a blackened beam, and from this treasured spoil
Cut a small piece and put it on to boil.
Meanwhile they both beguiled the time with talk...

...a mattress soft of river-sedge
Laid on a bed with willow legs and edge;
O'er this a quilt reserved for festal days
They drew, but cheap and old in truth it was
And no ill match for that old willow bed.
The gods lay down. Baucis the table laid,
Girt up and trembling. One leg of the three
Was short: a tile restored stability.
The top thus levelled she with mint did wipe,
Then set Minerva's olives clean and ripe,
Cherries of autumn-tide preserved in lees,
Endives and radishes and thick cream cheese,
And eggs cooked lightly on the gentle fire,
All served on earthenware. No metal higher
Than this the encrusted wine-bowl dignified
And beechwood beakers lined with wax inside.
Nor was it long before the hearth sent up
Its steaming dishes. Then they filled the cup
With wine of no great age. A little space
Was cleared, and these to nuts and plums gave place,
And wrinkled dates, and open baskets decked
With fragrant apples, purple grapes fresh-picked,
And last a honey-comb; but better still
Their kindly looks and bountiful goodwill.

Space forbids quotation of the rest of this charming story—how the gods performed with the wine-bowl the miracle of the widow's cruse; how the old couple were so impressed that they prepared to kill their only goose, but proved unable to catch it; how the gods then sent them up a hill, so that they escaped from a flood which drowned their less hospitable neighbours; how their house was turned into a marble temple, and their prayer was granted that they should be priests in it for their lives and in death be not divided. In the end they were turned into trees on which the pious put wreaths.

'I see Baucis and Philemon as perfectly before me', said Dryden, 'as if some ancient painter had drawn them.'

(4) THE GODS

What was Ovid's own attitude to the Gods? Probably few educated Romans believed in their actual existence, but for some they were at least symbols or representatives of a divine power in which they believed, although for others they were simply traditional machinery without which epic poetry at least was unthinkable. Here again Ovid has provided a clue. In a famous passage of the *Ars Amatoria* he gives a wholly irreverent defence of perjury in love:

> Jove swore to Juno falsely by the Styx:
> Now he aids those who imitate his tricks.

After which he proceeds to announce his *credo*. This has been so often quoted in the first sentence only, and even misconceived by some who have quoted the rest, that we should make sure what he means. His words may be paraphrased as follows:

> It is expedient there should be gods, and this being so, let us suppose they exist. For the good of society we should keep up the traditional religious ceremonies, and use the gods to enforce the commandments: 'Thou shalt live innocently, for the gods are not remote or indifferent.' 'Thou shalt pay back what is entrusted to thee'; 'Honour thy father and thy mother'; 'Thou shalt not defraud'; 'Thou shalt do no murder'.

In other words, religion is a useful sanction for social morality. To take 'a deity is at hand' as a statement of the poet's own view would be absurd; it is meant to be in inverted commas; this is what we have got to tell people, he is saying. In the *Metamorphoses* his real convictions are not in any case involved. Heinze says rightly, 'The question how this mythical world of the gods should be represented by him in his poem was not one of belief, but of style, and he answered it differently for the *Metamorphoses* and for the *Fasti*'. It would have put everything out of gear if he had not accepted the mythological gods along with the legends. He treats them very much in the manner of the epic tradition he was following, disregarding the higher criticism that had begun in the sixth century. He hardly ever even affects surprise in this poem, as he does in the *Fasti*, and while he is not averse from retailing stories in which deities are worsted, he preserves his adopted attitude of orthodoxy by putting these into the mouth of their enemies.

Nor are the gods of the *Metamorphoses* the factitious guardians of morality whose usefulness he proclaimed in the *Ars Amatoria*. Far from it. If they cannot frustrate Destiny, they are otherwise free to gratify their whims, which they do without scruple. Their chief motives are lust (especially in the males) and revenge for slights (especially in the females). Only on the rarest occasions is one divinity thwarted by another; for the rest, their control is complete. Their only sign of compunction is in the grief they display for the loss of those they have loved. It would have been out of keeping if Ovid had raised the question which Virgil himself raised only to drop, 'Can there be such anger in celestial hearts?'

The Creator with whom the poem opens belongs to a different category. He is the Zeus of the philosophers, and has nothing to do with the mythological line which culminated in Jupiter. We will deal with him in a different context. For the rest Ovid consciously follows the epic tradition; but he goes further in the direction of irreverence, influenced no doubt by the Alexandrians, who took particular pleasure in making gods and heroes behave just like ordinary people of the day. The sophisticated no longer believed in their literal existence, and we cannot doubt that they were amused at the aroma of burlesque which anthropomorphism produced when pushed to extremes. Ovid's Jupiter, even when he addresses the gods on his son Hercules' apotheosis, lacks something of the remoteness that makes the Homeric gods impressive for all their escapades. He behaves on that occasion rather like the Emperor seeking senatorial approval for something he intends to do in any case, as the conferring of some signal honour on a member of his own family, relieved to find that there is general support, and confident that Pollio and the die-hards will swallow it with as good a grace as possible.* Indeed, the very first appearance of the Olympians in the *Metamorphoses* is at a very Roman council summoned to 'the Palace of great heaven'. This is approached by the Milky Way, a Palatine Slope off which open the mansions of the noble gods, their doors wide open and their halls thronged. The plebeian gods live elsewhere: in this quarter the right honourable (*clari*) and influential deities have set up their *Penates* (aristocratic gods revering household gods of their own!). This passage in itself is sufficient intimation that we need not hesitate to accept as burlesque any future treatment of the gods that appears to be such.

The myths being what they were, the gods had frequently to be represented as loving nymphs or mortals, nor would this be uncongenial to the poet of the *Amores*. The aristocrats among them were generally irresistible. What chance had Proserpine,

> Within a trice seen, loved, and raped by Dis?

But the circumstances were seldom dignified; for

> There's no concordance or companionship
> Twixt majesty and love.

At the outset we have Apollo, hybristic in his triumph over the Python, jealously reproving Cupid for usurping his weapon, the bow; whereupon Cupid asserts his supremacy by wounding him with a shaft of love for Daphne. Thereafter we are shown the gods, one after another, in amorous situations which can only be called comic. The domestic life of Jupiter and Juno was food for amusement already in Homer. Ovid loses no time in introducing it. In the first book we find Jupiter enticing Io into the woods with disingenuous offers of protection from wild beasts, and then, when she tries to flee, impeding her with a thick mist and so ravishing her. Juno, perceiving this preternatural darkness, instinctively looks round to see where her husband has got to, suspicious from bitter experience. Not finding him, she glides down to earth and dissipates the fog. But already Jupiter has foreseen this and changed Io into a cow. Even in this form she is still beautiful, and Juno, regarding her with grudging admiration, inquires with feigned innocence who

* There was almost a riot when Hebe was allowed to restore Iolaüs to youth: each deity clamoured for her favourite to be rejuvenated, Aurora for Tithonus, Ceres for Iasion, Vulcan for Erichthonius, and Venus (with an eye to her *future* amour) for Anchises.

is her owner and what her herd. Jupiter, to stop her awkward questions about ownership, answers that she is sprung from the earth itself, whereupon Juno promptly asks for her as a gift. Caught in a cleft stick, Jupiter can only comply. But Juno, still suspicious, sets the hundred-eyed Argus to watch her, and when Mercury kills him at Jupiter's instigation, sends a Fury to drive her across the world, till she prays to Jupiter for release, whereupon he throws his arms round Juno's neck and begs her—successfully—to relent.

The episode of Phaëthon follows, but no sooner is that over than Jupiter, touring Arcadia to inspect the damage, spies the nymph Callisto, lying weary and all unguarded in the depths of a forest. 'Surely here is an intrigue my wife will never find out', he says; 'or if she does—this, oh this, is well worth any railing!' Straightway he puts on the guise of Callisto's mistress Diana, rouses her, and not put off by her response, 'Hail, deity, greater in my judgment than Jupiter, as I would say to his face', ravishes her and so betrays himself. Full of shame, she rejoins the train of Diana (after making sure the goddess is not Jupiter in disguise again). The other nymphs (sophisticated after much experience of satyrs) perceive by a thousand signs that something has happened, but the virgin goddess remains innocently unaware until on one occasion, now nine months gone with child, the blushing victim is constrained by her companions to join them in a bathe.

Surely all this is sheer comedy, in the spirit of the *Amores*. Before the book is out Jupiter has gone off after Europa, changing himself into a bull of immaculate beauty, whose points are described in detail. When the princess holds out flowers to him he takes the opportunity to kiss her hands, hardly able to control himself, and leaps sportively about in the grass; and so little by little entices her to the famous sea-voyage.

Things reach such a pitch that poor Juno falters pathetically in the proud threat she has always made when angry: 'if I am queen to Jupiter, and both his sister and wife—sister at least for sure'. When she was succeeding by 'sympathetic' magic in preventing Alcmena from bearing her son to Jupiter, the lie of a servant-girl trapped her into breaking the spell. Her bitterness was tersely colloquial when she heard about Semele: 'and to cap it all, she's with child!' It was the last straw when she found that, just as she was about to catch her husband with nymphs on the mountain-sides, Echo had been in the habit of detaining her in idle conversation till they got away.

Yet there were moments of conjugal truce. On one such occasion Jupiter, mellowed with nectar, put cares aside and bandied good-humoured badinage with her, saying: 'I maintain that you females get more pleasure than we males do.' Juno denied this, and the only way of reaching a conclusion was to summon Tiresias, who had been both in his day. Needless to say, Tiresias supported Jupiter, and Juno (how feminine!), taking too seriously a matter of no consequence, blinded him for life, a penalty which Jupiter could only mitigate by giving him the gift of prophecy.

Much of this by-play is not necessitated by the stories at all. Nor is it only Jupiter and Juno who are affected: most of the major deities contribute to the comedy. We have already encountered the virgin unawareness of Diana. Her brother Apollo, victim of Cupid's nemesis, is ludicrous enough as he pants out a long speech while vainly pursuing Daphne. He is terrified that she will hurt herself, and offers to run more slowly if she will too!* That failing, he launches into fifteen lines of self-recommendation, qualified by regrets that his arrow is not after all the most potent and his art of healing cannot cure love. Mercury, desiring to seduce Herse, does not seek to disguise himself; such is his confidence in his looks. Nevertheless, he thinks it prudent to smooth his hair, arrange his cloak to hang neatly, with all the border and gold embroidery showing, hold his wand gracefully and see that his feet are clean and his winged sandals polished—for all the world like a Greek dandy. In the contest of weaving between Arachne and Pallas we expect the goddess to win; but in the event neither she nor Envy can find any fault in Arachne's work, and out of sheer pique and jealousy she tears the web and beats her rival over the head with her shuttle till she takes refuge in hanging herself. Only then does the goddess relent, so far as to let her hang on alive in the form of a spider.

Sometimes the anthropomorphism produces charming effects, as when Pallas calls on the Muses on Helicon in order to inspect the miraculous new spring of Hippocrene. She admires their home and

* Like the Cambridge proctor's 'bulldog' who protested, 'If you don't run faster, sir, I shall have to catch you.'

says they must be happy in their surroundings and their pursuits. In reply one of them, after modestly remarking that the goddess would be a welcome member of their band if her valour had not marked her out for more important work, agrees that they should be happy, if only they could feel secure; but lately, for instance, being caught in a storm while on their way to Parnassus, they had been invited to shelter in his house by the usurping king Pyreneus, only to find when the rain stopped that he would not let them go, so that they had had to put on their wings and fly for it. Further, they had been challenged to song by the Pierides, and had felt bound to accept. The nymphs were appointed judges, took the oath by their own streams, and seated themselves on benches of living rock; whereupon instead of drawing lots for first innings, the eldest Pierid rudely began. After summarizing her offensive song the Muse begins to recount their own reply, then politely breaks off—'But perhaps you are in a hurry and have no time to hear what we sang?' 'Not at all', replies Pallas, sitting down in the shade; 'Please tell me in order everything you sang.' The modesty of the Muses is as delightful as the graciousness of the *grande dame*.

Some of the stories have more in common with folklore than with the Olympian mythology. To this category belongs the story of Midas, with the delightful incident of his slave who, in his capacity of barber, could not help knowing the secret of those ass's ears concealed beneath the royal turban. Bursting to tell it but fearing the consequences, he dug a hole, muttered the story into it, and filled it in. But whispering reeds sprang up there, which in due course betrayed the secret when rustled by the breeze. In the story of Phaëthon the Sun, though called Phoebus, is the all-seeing god of folklore, having his palace not at Delos or Delphi but in the mystic realms beyond the Ethiopians.

As for the lesser divinities—rivers, mountains, nymphs and so forth—they are generally innocent and attractive. Ovid plays characteristically with their ambiguous form—natural object and personification at the same time. Tmolus, where Pan was singing to the nymphs and daring to challenge Apollo, is presented as a mountain towering and steep, looking far out to sea, with one slope running down to Sardis and the other to Hypaepae. A few lines later he has been chosen to judge the contest: 'The aged judge took his seat on his own mountain-top and shook his ears free of trees.'

The nymph Cyane originally lived in the pool in Sicily to which she gave her name. Rising from this she protested to Dis, as he passed, against the rape of Proserpine. He thereupon smote her pool with his sceptre and opened a path to Hades. In grief at this she melted into her own pool; hence she had no voice to tell Ceres, when she came, where Proserpine had gone, but she could give a clue by showing on her surface the girdle the latter had dropped. It all depends on what the poet finds effective for the moment; for a few lines later Arethusa, though she is a spring, has green locks which she brushes back from her brow, and her waters keep silence while she speaks. What she tells Ceres, indeed, must rank among Ovid's most beautiful imaginings, culminating in two unforgettable lines:

O thou distraught
Mother of fruits and of that maiden sought
The wide world over, rest, nor angry be
With faithful, innocent earth. Unwillingly
She opened for that rape. 'Tis not my land
I plead for, brought from Elis to this strand,
From Pisan home; yet Sicily I love,
Though foreign-born, all other lands above;
Here have I, Arethusa, made my home.
Spare it, most merciful. Why I did come
Displaced beyond such wide expanse of sea
To Ortygia, that will I presently
Tell thee in timely hour of better cheer.
Earth gave me way through cavernous depths, till here
Emerging I beheld the stars again.
On Hades' Stygian flood as I was then
Passing, these eyes your Proserpine espied,
Still sad indeed nor yet unterrified;
Aye, but a queen, supreme in that dark land,
Dowered with the might of Pluto's royal hand.

(5) MORTALS

The world of the *Metamorphoses* has something of the quality of *A Midsummer Night's Dream*. It conveys an impression of freedom and clarity combined with a sense that we are temporarily detached from the realms of ultimate seriousness, of normal logic and moral values:

Al was this land fulfild of fayerye.

The distresses of the actors, more frequent than their joys, are often made less real by the pervading atmosphere of miracle. They are pathetic for the moment, but not tragic; and in any case we witness them for too short a time for our sympathies to be more than superficially engaged. Who weeps for the divine Calypso deserted by Homer's Odysseus?

It is in keeping with what we know of Ovid's character that interest is concentrated on the women more than the men, as in the story of Pyramus and Thisbe, one of the most delightful in the whole work. No one knows where Ovid found this romance. The setting is in Babylon, and its ultimate origin may have been in some ancestor of the *Arabian Nights*. The daughter of Minyas, who tells it to her companions over the wool, hesitates between choosing it and other tales of the East, that of Dercetis of Babylon, or of her daughter Semiramis, or of a Naiad of the Indian Ocean, doubtless from the same source.* The story of the wall with a crack through which they had perforce to make love, of their tryst at Ninus' tomb forestalled by a lioness, and of the tragic misunderstanding that brought both to suicide, is familiar from Shakespeare. Ovid is here at his best. In short, staccato sentences he tells the exciting story, with romantic touches to set the scene and frequent soliloquy to keep it alive. It is a purely human story: the aetiological motive, the changing of the mulberry into a blood-red fruit in memory of their death, is merely incidental. There are many vivid touches: the chink in the wall wide enough for them to converse, but not to join kisses; Thisbe stealing out, terrified the hinge will creak; the lioness seen by her far off in the moonlight, as she waits under the mulberry tree by the tomb. But it is a pure romance of incident: the feelings of the lovers are as simple as they are strong, and they are taken for granted.

The companion piece of Cephalus and Procris is equally good, but more complicated psychologically—a tragedy of jealousy and misunderstanding which leads to the death of Procris. Unlike Pyramus and Romeo, Cephalus did not himself commit suicide, and the story is made more poignant through being recounted by him. The experience

* The tale of Leucothoë (IV, 190–233) is apparently of Persian origin. It looks as though Book IV is particularly oriental in origin. The tale of Myrrha also has an oriental setting, Araby being the proverbial land of myrrh.

of being ravished by Aurora against his will (a proceeding rather difficult to envisage) begot in him suspicions of the faithfulness of his newly married wife; he disguised himself and laid siege to her chastity, only to find misery when she began to yield, and to lose her when he revealed himself. He begged and won her back, there was a blissful period of married love, and then another tragedy of misunderstanding, all the more bitter because now it was Procris who lost faith.

The story of Ceÿx and Alcyone, one of the best in the *Metamorphoses*, is moving in the same way as that of Cephalus and Procris or Protesilaüs and Laodamia, because it deals with deep conjugal affection, which Ovid does not hesitate to call 'fire'. Here is a sequence of events only too real to us—the wife left at home while her husband goes overseas, the ship gradually passing out of sight, the counting of the nights, the preparations for his welcome home and prayers for his safety and fidelity; and then the vivid dream bringing conviction that he is dead, and the grim reality of finding his corpse washed up on the self-same beach on which he had said good-bye. The story is long enough for us to enter into Alcyone's feelings, though much of it—too much—is occupied with the brilliantly vivid picture of the rise and fury of the storm at sea.

Here again the miraculous element, the metamorphosis of the pair into halcyons, only intrudes incidentally, at the end. But there is also a peculiar, wistful pathos in some of the stories in which it plays an integral part—in Io, for instance (here the pathos is tinged with humour), starting in terror at the sound of her own lowing, or at the sight of her bovine face reflected in the familiar pool, and following her sisters and father in the hope of caresses; then later, when restored to human form again, afraid to speak lest she moo, and hesitatingly trying out words so long unused; or in Callisto, changed to a bear, when she comes face to face with her hunter son Arcas, fixing on him eyes that seemed to recognize him, so that he shrank back full of uncanny fear and poised his spear when she tried to approach him.

Ovid's interest in psychology comes out especially in the five soliloquies expressing a conflict in the soul of a woman about to commit a crime. In the days when Socrates was teaching that virtue was a matter of knowledge Euripides had made his Phaedra utter words which Ovid latinized and put into the mouth of the young Medea as 'I see and approve the better course, yet choose the worse'. Indeed, the chief ancestor of his soliloquies of this kind is probably the famous speech in which Euripides' Medea deliberates whether to kill her children. This barbaric woman, with her power of magic and her intolerable grievance, who twice had to make a terrible decision, obviously fascinated Ovid. Having envisaged her in the *Heroides* and in his lost tragedy, he devotes more than half of *Metamorphoses* VII to her. There is a piquant touch of irony when Jason begs her use her magic to transfer part of his life to his father Aeson: his filial devotion suddenly makes her ashamed of her own disloyalty to her father Aeëtes, which had nevertheless saved Jason's life: 'she was moved by the devotion of the pleader, and the thought of Aeëtes abandoned stole into her heart, how different from his!'

Love is the chief theme of the *Metamorphoses*, and in most cases it is quite normal; but on occasion Ovid deals with a story of abnormality such as fascinated the Alexandrians and figures largely in the summaries of later compilers. Here alone does he abandon his attitude of objectivity and adopt, or affect, a moral standpoint: 'Byblis is a warning that girls should be lawful in their loves.' This much said, he tells with unmistakable gusto the story of the girl who loved her twin brother, Caunus. He keeps 'on the right side of the law', but one may doubt whether he is in fact much concerned about propriety, as can be seen from the jaunty tone of the warning he prefixes to the still more scandalous story of Myrrha, who loved her father: 'This is a dreadful tale; keep far off now, daughters and fathers; or if my songs charm you, do not believe this one; or if you must believe it, believe also in the punishment of the deed.' On the other hand, anyone familiar with Alexandrian literature must be struck by the infrequency and restraint with which Ovid deals with homosexual love. He mentions the tradition that such practices were introduced into Thrace by Orpheus, touches on Jupiter's rape of Ganymede, and tells at no great length of the passion of Apollo for Cyparissus, who became a cypress tree, and for Hyacinthus, who became a flower. But these last two episodes, involving as they do well-known instances of metamorphosis, are the only ones he chose out of a large number such as he could find in his probable source, the *Loves* or *Fair Youths* of Phanocles, a whole volume of elegiac poems on the subject. In passing from Phaëthon to Cycnus in Book II he says they were linked by kinship and still more by like-mindedness, avoiding reference to their love, which seems to have been known to Virgil. All this is consonant with Ovid's own disposition, as we have already noted in the case of the elegiac poems; in view of Greco-Roman tradition and practice it suggests a positive attitude rather than mere indifference.

Two of the most haunting episodes of the whole poem deal with abnormal sexuality of a slightly different kind, those of Narcissus and Hermaphroditus. As to the former, we have already glanced at his rejection of the pathetic Echo, the beauty of the pool in which he gazed, and the conceits for which his nature gave Ovid such good opportunities. The story of the latter is said by its narrator to be unfamiliar; it is an *aetion* for the reputedly enervating quality of the spring of Salmacis in Caria. The son of Hermes and Aphrodite is a beautiful boy who roams the world for the sheer joy of seeing new country. Wandering from his birthplace on Mount Ida through Asia Minor he came upon one of those beautiful pools that Ovid loves to describe. 'The spring was clear right to the bottom. No marsh-weeds grew there nor clogging sedge nor spiky rushes; the water was translucent; but the margins were fringed with fresh turf and evergreen grasses.' Here dwelt the naiad Salmacis, the only one who never followed the train of Diana the huntress. At most she bathed from time to time and did her hair in the mirror of her own pool before lying down in a shimmering dress on the grass, or picked flowers, as she was doing when she saw and fell in love with Hermaphroditus. Eager as she was to approach him, she collected herself first, tidied her clothes, composed her features, and 'deserved to seem beautiful'. Then she boldly accosted him with expressions of admiration and prayed to be his wife or paramour. The passage that follows is remarkable for its succession of vivid similes:

> She said no more. He blushed, too young to tell
> What love is, and the blush became him well;
> So apples redden in the sun, and so
> Stained ivory, and neath her pallid glow
> The moon, when bronzes clash their aid in vain.*
> As the nymph begged again and yet again

* The clashing of bronze was supposed by the superstitious to aid the moon in struggling against eclipse.

If but a sister's kiss, and sought to embrace
His ivory neck, 'Hold, or I leave this place—
And you!' he cried. Salmacis trembling said,
'I leave the place to you, young sir', and made
As if to go, yet oft looked back, and mid
Some neighbouring bushes closely crouched and hid.
The boy, alone, unwatched, as he did deem,
Paced in the grass, and in the lapping stream
His toes at first and then his ankles dipped;
Lured by the water's coolness, swift he stripped
His delicate garments from his body's grace.
Then Salmacis did burn and in amaze
Long for his naked form, her eyes alight,
As when the sun's clear orb exceeding bright
Shines from a mirror with reflected ray;
Scarce can she wait and scarce her joys delay,
Mad with desire his dear embrace to essay.
He clapped his body with his hollow palms,
Swiftly dived in and with alternate arms
Swam: like an ivory through the water clear
Or lilies cased in glass he did appear.
'I have won and he is mine!' the Naiad cried,
Flung off her clothes and plunged into the tide,
Clasped as he struggled, as he fought caressed,
Slipped her hands under him to feel his breast,
This side and that the unwilling boy confined
And, as he strove to free himself, entwined;
Even as a snake, caught up into the air
By an eagle, writhes its tail and hanging there
Tangles the head, the feet, the flapping wings;
Or as the ivy to the tree-trunk clings,
Or octopus its prey beneath the tide
Grapples with tentacles on every side.

Hermaphroditus struggled, but Salmacis prayed that no day might ever separate them and her prayer was granted, for they became merged in one ambiguous body; whereupon he in turn prayed that whoever entered the pool as a man should emerge but half a man.

Somewhat similar is the story of Iphis, whose father told his expecting wife he would put her child to death if it proved to be a girl. (It is startling to remember that this was quite common practice in the Greco-Roman world.) Isis appeared to her in a dream and told her to preserve the child whatever its sex; so when it was born a girl she gave out that it was a boy, and called it by the equivocal name of Iphis. Trouble came when Iphis, now thirteen, was betrothed to Ianthe and fell in love with her; in a long soliloquy Iphis enlarges on her plight; till her mother takes her to Isis' temple to pray, whence she emerges as a boy, and duly marrying Ianthe, lives happily ever after.

Finally, there is the famous story of Pygmalion, who could only love the ivory statue of a woman which he had made. It is tempting, especially to the Teutonic mentality, to intellectualize these myths; to see in Pygmalion, for instance, the eternal seeker after ideal perfection, dissatisfied with the world around him; but we must not force such interpretations on stories which, whatever their mythological origin, are surely told by Ovid for their own sake, and for the psychological paradoxes which intrigued him. He was certainly conscious of the protagonists as types of sexual abnormality, as he shows, for instance, by emphasizing the vanity of Salmacis, which would emerge as a trait of the fused Hermaphrodite; but they are only that, not symbols of something wider. Ovid's Narcissus may be the *Urnarzissist*, but he is not presented as a symbol of self-love in general.

Had Ovid pity for such psychological misfits? He could in any case hardly express it directly, having adopted the role of detached spectator, though once he makes dramatic use of a familiar rhetorical figure of speech, when, as though unable to stand aloof any longer, he breaks in to warn Narcissus against his reflexion:

> Naught in itself, with you it came, it stays:
> With you 'twill leave—could you but go your ways!

At least, as their soliloquies show, he was capable of imaginative understanding of how they would feel.

One word more. Ovid shows a sympathetic understanding of young people. It is no mere conceit when he makes Proserpine, in the moment of her abduction, distressed also for the loss of the flowers she has been gathering. And when young Phaëthon, having boasted of being the son of Apollo, is told by his companion Epaphus that he should not believe all his mother tells him, his reaction is as charming as it is probable:

He blushed, shame choking down his anger, and took Epaphus' words to his mother: 'and what will hurt you more, mother, I who am always so quick-tempered and free of speech said nothing. I am ashamed that any one could have so insulted us and that I could not refute him. But if indeed I am sprung from heavenly parentage, give me some proof of my noble birth to assert my divinity.'

(6) PHILOSOPHY

If it is a mistake to philosophize the legends of love and metamorphosis, what are we to make of the two openly speculative portions of the poem, the exordium recounting the Creation, and the exposition of Pythagorean doctrine near the end? It cannot be said that Ovid ever gives the impression of being a philosopher; indeed, he sometimes displays an indifference to truth which was characteristic of the average Roman. But it would obviously suit the artistic form of his poem if he could start with an account of how the world began and rise at the end to a plane of thought which had something in it of the 'sublime'. He would choose the accounts which seemed to him most suitable and poetic. He had obviously studied at least the less technical parts of Lucretius, and may have wished to emulate him here, while lacking his intellectual passion and integrity.

The precise pedigree of his eclectic cosmology cannot now be determined, but it smacks most of Posidonian Stoicism. His 'this strife God and kindlier Nature dissolved' seems to identify God and Nature in Stoic fashion, while later he contents himself with a non-committal 'whichever of the gods it was'. Lafaye is surely right in his comment, 'On dirait qu'Ovide est surtout jaloux de mettre tout le monde d'accord.' Why quarrel about metaphysics? The Creator is assumed to be benevolent:

> That demiurge, source of a better world;

and his supreme work is man, made from divine seed to be lord of creation; or was it Prometheus who moulded man out of clay which still retained something of its heavenly origin? Ovid, like the Book of Genesis, presents us with alternative versions and leaves it at that. Prometheus moulded man in the image of the almighty gods and made him stand erect by contrast with the beasts:

> To man he gave to hold his forehead high,
> Bade him look up and view the starry sky.

So Ovid expresses an old Socratic fancy already latinized by Cicero. It is his mastery of verse and language that gives value to this second-hand exordium, which all the time was leading him on, through the Fall of Man, to two great events which would give full scope to his powers of grandiose description, the Deluge and the Conflagration.

But he gives us even before the Deluge one foretaste of what was to come, a story of metamorphosis due to divine vengeance (Lycaon turned to a wolf); and before the Conflagration two stories of metamorphosis due to divine lust (Daphne and Io); and thereafter we are in the main stream of the poem. Not until the last book do we come into touch with philosophic speculation again. There, by what Ovid must have known to be a glaring anachronism, the Roman king Numa is made, in accordance with tradition, to imbibe from Pythagoras at Croton his doctrines, which are expounded for the space of four hundred lines.

Was Ovid a neo-Pythagorean? Surely not. It is true that for two generations the sect had been in vogue at Rome, but it was characterized on one side by a mysticism, not untinged with quackery, alien to his rational temperament. It is easy to see why he should choose nevertheless to expound it here: its doctrine of the transmigration of souls, which made no distinction between human and animal forms, provided an imposing climax to the stories of metamorphosis. It also invested this make-believe world with the semblance of a logic of its own. Indeed, it is hard to think of any other philosophy which could have been brought in here without disrupting the thread of the whole poem.

We need not discuss here the theories about what secondary sources he may have used. His Pythagoras begins with the injunction against eating meat, a straightforward topic which at once allowed the poet to indulge in conceits after his own heart:

> To bury flesh in flesh! O dreadful deed!
> With body's meat to fatten body's greed,
> And life by theft of other's life to feed!

Then he launches into an impassioned plea based in the first instance not on the doctrine of transmigration but simply on the sentiment of kinship between men and animals, such as we find in Virgil's *Georgics*. There is nothing here which might not come naturally from a modern vegetarian. Ovid's capacity for putting himself in the position of others, already seen in his soliloquies, is here extended with moving effect to the ox. He may not have been a vegetarian himself, but he was a born advocate who in this case had at least a strong sympathy with his brief:

Poor sheep, what harm do you, a placid tribe,
Born to serve man, whose nectar we imbibe
From udders full, who wool for clothing give,
Less useful if you die than if you live?
Oxen, what harm do you, beasts without guile,
Innocent, simple, born for honest toil?
Thoughtless, nor worth the bounty of the plough,
He who his partner of the fields, but now
Unyoked, can bear to slay, with axe to rive
That toil-worn neck that often did revive
His stubborn fields and make his harvests thrive!
Nor is this crime enough: they implicate
The gods themselves, and fancy that the great
Immortals joy in patient bullock slain.
A noble victim, perfect without stain
('Tis death to please), stands at the altar there
With gold and fillets decked, and unaware
Hears the priest pray, sees sprinkled on his brow
The barley-meal he laboured for. And now
Those knives, perchance glimpsed in the pool, descend
And redden with his blood. Forthwith they rend
His entrails from his living breast, to scan
In them, forsooth, the gods' intent for man.
Hence, mortals, (so you crave unhallowed meat!)
You dare to feed. Ah, do not, I entreat.
Tasting bull's flesh, reflect that you devour
Your own familiar country-labourer.

The incidental rejection of augury here prepares us for the transition to the second part, an eloquent passage in the high Lucretian manner on the delight and novelty of the doctrine about to be expounded. Indeed, the opening words of the exposition might have been written by Lucretius himself:

Ah, race whom fears of chilly death appal,
Why dread ye Stygian shades, mere fables all,
Perils by poets feigned fantastical?

But then comes the surprise: it is the certainty, not of the dissolution but of the immortality of the soul, through transmigration, that is to banish fear of death. Lucretius had said of atomic dissolution, 'all things are changed, nothing perishes'; Pythagoras says it of metempsychosis.

From transmigration the theme widens to embrace the doctrine that all things are in flux. Even here there is still a superficial connexion at least with the main theme of the poem, since the metamorphoses as described take place so fluently as to suggest that the identity of species is less hard and fast than we think; but it is tenuous enough, and in essence literary rather than philosophic. There is still no effort of thought involved. The poet simply does what other Roman poets had done: he takes a Greek generalization and enlarges on concrete illustrations of it. It was not hard to marshal a series of natural phenomena, inorganic and organic, up and down the world, which involved change, such as springs that are alternately hot and cold, and the recital of them would be picturesque. 'I myself have seen—' says Ovid, using the formula which so often introduced a tall story. (The ancients no doubt found sea-shells far inland, but did they ever really find an old anchor on a mountain-top?) The recital finally modulates into a higher key with the thought of the rise and fall of famous cities.

From time to time in the course of the poem there have been passing reminders that the poet is a citizen of no mean city: the amber into which the tears of Phaëthon's sisters are changed is 'destined to be worn by Latin women'; Apollo, still in love with Daphne when she has become a laurel, foretells among her honours that she will be the pride of Roman generals proceeding in triumph to the Capitol, and guard on either side the civic crown of oak-leaves before the door of Augustus; and the long roll of the rivers affected by Phaëthon's fires is made to culminate in the Tiber, 'to whom dominion over the world had been promised'. Pythagoras now prophesies the future greatness of Rome: 'Even so in these days fame has it that Trojan Rome is rising, which beside the waters of Apennine-born Tiber is laying its foundations under a weighty charge: so is she by growth being transformed, and shall one day be the head of the whole wide world.' This, he adds, is no new prophecy, for Helenus foretold to Aeneas at the fall of Troy that a better Troy would arise, 'greater than any is, or shall be, or has been seen in former years'.

(7) ITALY AND ROME

We have anticipated, however, for much has been heard of the Romans before we come to Pythagoras. Towards the end of Book XIII Aeneas leaves Troy on his fateful journey. Hitherto, as we have passed from one saga-group to another, the tide of time has flowed and ebbed beyond the horizon of history. Now the principle of chronological sequence takes charge again; it is 'after that' rather than 'meanwhile' that sustains the illusion of reality. From now onwards Ovid would be dealing not only with Greek legends which might or might not be familiar to his Roman audience (those in some of his Greek sources covered Sicily and south Italy—*Magna Graecia*), but also with events which were believed to be semi-historical and which had been dealt with by Latin writers of towering genius and repute, Ennius, Virgil and Livy, not to mention Propertius and some famous antiquarians. He interweaves Greek and Roman legends cunningly, so that we never feel there is a complete break in the texture and continuity of the poem; even in the latter part of the last book he contrives to introduce the Greek Hippolytus, restored to life as the Italian Virbius, telling of his death on the shore at Troezen in the Peloponnese.

The passages which are a mere summary of the *Aeneid* must have been irksome to Ovid as they are to us, but how else could he cross over from Greece to Italy? Aeneas' arrival at the Straits of Messina gives occasion for two famous stories: Galatea tells Scylla how she was wooed by the Cyclops Polyphemus, and Scylla herself, for rejecting the advances of the marine deity Glaucus (who also tells her his story), is transformed by Circe into a monster. Thirty lines suffice to cover the diversion to Carthage, and the journey on again as far as the coasts above Naples. Here there is another interlude, while two sailors left behind by Ulysses tell each other what has happened to them since; Achaemenides enlarges on his terror-stricken life among the Cyclopes before Aeneas rescued him to Macareus, who in turn recounts the story of Circe.

Circe brings us very near to Rome; her island, now a rugged mountain-peak joined to the mainland by the drained Pontine Marshes, is visible from the neighbourhood of the Campagna; and while she was dallying with Ulysses, Macareus had heard from one of her nymphs the story of Picus, the mythical king of Italy, who loved the nymph Canens, born on the Palatine to Janus and Venilia, and was changed by her rival Circe into a woodpecker. By such easy stages does the Greek world melt into the Italian. We are borne as on a tide which, as its waves advance and recede, yet almost insensibly gains ground. The events of the second half of the *Aeneid* are briefly told, and then, with the interlude of two stories, one Latin and one Greek, we pass to those of the *Annals* of Ennius, and his famous scene of the council of the gods at which Mars claimed the apotheosis of his son Romulus. Like Hercules', Romulus' mortal part was dissolved, and he received a new form worthier of his heavenly home.

The first half of the last book is taken up with Pythagoras' speech, the teaching imbibed by Numa. This is followed by the legend of Hippolytus-Virbius, and the Roman story of Cipus. Roman indeed this is, for here first in the poem is sounded the true note of patriotism which we hear in Livy. Cipus was a praetor who suddenly grew horns, and on being told by an Etruscan augur that this portended that he should be king if he returned within the walls, went into voluntary exile rather than subject the city to a monarchy. It is a far cry from the *Naturkinder* of the dawn of the Greek world to this stoical Roman, the forerunner of Regulus.

Cipus takes us at one bound into Republican times, more than a century beyond Numa. Ovid does not even try to carry us over the next bound to the year 292 B.C., when we assist at the migration of Aesculapius to Rome; and there is only the connexion of contrast to bridge the next two hundred and fifty years and bring us to Julius Caesar. It looks very much as if his delight in invention was flagging, as well it might be by now, so that he made haste to his designed conclusion. Roman legends were more stereotyped than Greek, and they tended to be moral rather than imaginative; and he himself was treating them simultaneously in the *Fasti*, a very good reason for skating over them here. But this decline really began with Book XII, in which we are aware of a conscious effort to raise the poem into a 'higher', more serious strain. There are fine things in the last four books, such as the contest of Ajax and Ulysses, and parts of the speech of Pythagoras, itself hardly justified save as part of an attempt to give the poem a serious climax. But only occasionally, as in the idyll of

Polyphemus and Galatea and the tale of Vertumnus and Pomona, is there a touch of the old whimsical humour. Aesculapius is brought all the way from Epidaurus to Rome in the form of a snake with complete solemnity (so it seems to me); to have exploited the ample opportunities for burlesque would no doubt have been too near the knuckle. We have passed insensibly from the mythology of Greece to the religion of the Roman state for which the Emperor was concerned to restore respect. The Island of Aesculapius in the Tiber was a sacred place, and many readers would resent any aspersions on its sanctity.

Ovid's Polyphemus idyll, based on Theocritus VI and XI, is obviously written with one eye on Virgil's *Eclogue* VII. Theocritus' Cyclops addresses his love with four complimentary comparisons; Virgil's deemed four one too many; but Ovid's launches into no less than fifteen, and before we can recover, adds fifteen uncomplimentary ones. This is obviously burlesque, not a case of 'being unable to let well alone'; but it is not critical burlesque. Here, as elsewhere, there are many instances of his borrowing from Virgil, 'openly imitating with intent that it should be recognized', in the words of Gallio. In dealing with the events covered by the *Aeneid* he shows dexterity in avoiding competition, enlarging where Virgil only hints or sketches, and *vice versa*. Nevertheless, it was inevitable that his style should be cramped, his genius rebuked, by his greatest predecessor.

We must remember, however, that while our interest may flag the nearer he gets to Rome, that of his Italian readers would become more intense. To hear legends told of familiar places, and told in literature that has the stamp of immortality, is an inspiring thing. The 'Gathering of the Clans' in *Aeneid* VII would not be an anticlimax after the Descent into Hades to the Italians of Virgil's day, as it may seem to us; it was their Magna Carta, the seal of their right to a share in the glory of Rome. With something of the same feelings they would hear how Aesculapius

> won through the Sicilian Sea and the Straits of Pelorus, sailed by the islands of King Aeolus and the copper-mines of Temesa and made for Leucosia and the rose-gardens of mild Paestum. Thence he skirted Capri and Minerva's promontory and the vine-clad hills of Surrentum, Herculaneum and Stabiae and Parthenope made for leisure, and on to the temple of the Cumaean Sibyl. Then he came to the warm springs and Liternum with its mastic trees, the Volturnus

rolling much sand beneath its stream, Sinuessa thronged with white doves, sultry Minturnae and her whom her foster-son buried (Caieta); and on to the home of Antiphates, and Trachas beset by marshes, Circe's land and the hard sands of Antium.*

It is said that as Mommsen passed through Italian villages a local patriot might be heard boasting, 'Ha parlato bene del nostro paese'—'he spoke well of our village'.

And now Ovid gathers up the threads of his poem. In the first book, when Jupiter revealed the treason of Lycaon, the gods 'all clamoured and with eager loyalty demanded the man who had dared such a plot; even so, when an impious band was mad to quench the name of Rome in Caesar's blood, the human race was stunned by the terror of such a catastrophe and the whole world trembled; nor is the devotion of your people, Augustus, less comforting to you than the gods' was then to Jupiter'. And as the end of the poem was approaching Pythagoras had prophesied:

I see Troy's offspring found a city home
Greater than was, or is, or is to come;
Leaders from age to age shall build her might,
Only a Julius raise her to the height
Of world-dominion; him, when earth has known
His bounty, heaven shall claim and call her own.

At last the climax has come: 'Caesar is a god in his own city.' The idea that mortals might be transformed into stars or constellations was inherent in the very names of many of these, and in the third century the celebrated Eratosthenes had made a collection of aetiological stories about them, a source-book for many writers. Several such metamorphoses have occurred in Ovid's poem, as that of Callisto and Arcas, and now comes the greatest of all, an event fresh in the memory of men. Suetonius describes it as follows:

Julius Caesar died in his fifty-sixth year and was received into the company of the gods, not only by the decree of the Senate, but also in the conviction of the populace. For at the first games which his heir Augustus was giving in his memory a comet shone for seven nights continually, and this was believed to be the soul of Caesar translated to heaven; for which reason a star is placed over his forehead on his statue.†

* Aeolus' Island may be Lipari; Surrentum = Sorrento, Parthenope = Naples, Caieta = Gaeta, Antiphates' home = Formiae, Trachas = Tarracina, Antium = Anzio.

† Virgil's fifth Eclogue (Daphnis) may refer to this. The effect of the coincidence on popular credulity can readily be imagined.

But Julius must not outshine Augustus; so Ovid hastens to say that his chief title to divinity was neither his military nor his civil triumphs, great though they were, but his offspring. He does not hesitate to use words of real paternity, culminating in a conceit worthy of Lucan: 'that Augustus might not be sprung from mortal seed, it was right that Julius should be made a god'—though all the world knew that Augustus' father was Gaius Octavius, and Julius only his adoptive father! Flattery could hardly go further, and when all allowance is made for differences of convention, we cannot help being alienated. There is nothing in Virgil or Horace, especially after the settlement of 28 B.C., that affects us quite as this does.

It is also unfortunate that he should have followed this with a description of the portents that preceded the murder of Julius; for eloquent though the passage is, it challenges comparison with one of the greatest in Virgil, the close of the first Georgic, and cannot stand it. In reply to Venus' appeals to avert the tragedy Jupiter reveals to her the decrees of fate, engraved on everlasting adamant, the deification of Julius, the conquests of Augustus and his domestic reforms. It is strange to find Ovid writing in the serious vein of the Augustans: 'When he has given peace to the world, he shall turn his mind to civic justice and be a most righteous author of laws, and shall guide morality by his own example; and looking to the age of posterity and the generations to come shall bid the son of his revered wife to bear his name and his burdens alike.'* When Jupiter ends, Venus at his bidding enters the Senate-house unseen, snatches the soul of Julius from his body as he is stabbed and translates it as a comet to heaven, whence he looks down and agrees with fame in setting Augustus' deeds above his own.

Once more Ovid challenges Virgil, with a variation of the great prayer to the ancestral gods that closes the first Georgic, and adds to Horace's his plea 'Late may your return to heaven be'. When Virgil uttered that appeal and Horace composed his second Ode the whole future was at stake; it was uncertain whether the young Octavian would be allowed to heal the wounds of the civil war; there was a motive of desperate urgency which was lacking when Ovid wrote under the ageing Emperor, and we feel this, as well as discomfort at the garbling of a great and familiar passage, as we read what Ovid intended

* The son of Livia is Tiberius.

to be his grand finale. The last hundred and thirty lines of the *Metamorphoses* are as eloquent as a master of language could make them; but the sap of the Augustan spring, like the dew of the Hellenic dawn, has dried up, and the autumn leaves are falling, gorgeous still in their way and reminiscent of past glories, but faded and tarnished and rather melancholy.

(8) DRAMA, RHETORIC, WORDS

Dryden, discussing the wit of the Ancients in his *Essay of Dramatic Poesy*, gives his opinion that 'he of them who had a genius most proper for the stage was Ovid; he had a way of writing so fit to stir up a pleasing admiration and concernment, which are the objects of a tragedy, and to show the various movements of a soul combating betwixt two different passions, that, had he lived in our age, or in his own could have writ with our advantages, no man but must have yielded to him'. He cannot believe that 'he who in the epic way wrote things so near to drama as the story of Myrrha, of Caunus and Byblis and the rest, should stir up no more concernment where he most endeavoured it'. We may grant that the author of *Aureng-Zebe* may not be an infallible critic of drama, but his opinion is at least interesting. Had there been a healthy stage and a judicious audience in Augustan Rome, Horace might have written for it successful Terentian comedy, and Ovid successful Euripidean psychological melodrama. In monologue and messenger speech at least he would have excelled, as abundant passages in the *Metamorphoses* testify, and perhaps also in dialogue. (One of the things which keeps the poem alive is the abundance of directly reported speech.)

Some critics may reply that he is rhetorical, thereby betraying lack of sincerity, and that this is fatal. But is not sincerity an equivocal term to use of a dramatist? His business is, not to express his own emotions, but to imagine other people's; and surely in this Ovid excels. If his characters sometimes speak rhetorically, this may be because rhetoric was ingrained in the Romans, making them speak, even in moments of passion, in a way more likely to sound artificial to an Englishman than to an Italian or to a Frenchman nurtured on Corneille and Racine. Even in Euripides the influence of the new art can already be felt.

For a century or so it has been axiomatic in England that Ovid has no genuine feeling. Here is Sellar, whose account of him is in general admirably just and perceptive: 'He has little power over the springs of pathos....A great sorrow, a great affection, a great cause or a great crisis, awakens in him little corresponding emotion.' This may possibly be true of the cause or crisis, but is it so of the sorrow or affection? The sorrow of Cephalus, or the affection of Alcyone? Dr Crump is very severe on the deliberative monologues: 'None of these speeches has any real note of passion. The heroines state that they are the victims of emotions which they cannot control, and the reader accepts the statement as necessary to the story; but the emotion is not felt.' 'All, though voicing a real mental process, are incapable of rousing the sympathy of the reader.' It was not ever thus, and one wonders whether we are now reading Ovid without prejudice. The opinion of Dryden may come as a shock:

> Though [Virgil] describes his Dido well and naturally, in the violence of her passions, yet he must yield in that to the Myrrha, the Byblis, the Althaea, of Ovid; for, as great an admirer of him as I am, I must acknowledge that if I see not more of their souls than I see of Dido's, at least I have greater concernment for them: and that convinces me that Ovid has touched those tender strokes more delicately than Virgil could.

I would agree with this only up to a certain point: I find Dido's outburst as 'rhetorical' as anything in Ovid—until the supreme moment when her pride breaks down and with it all her fine rhetoric—'if only some tiny Aeneas...'; yet I do find myself 'concerned' for Myrrha and Byblis and Althaea, despite their occasional conceits.

As for the 'rhetoric', Heinze is mainly right when he says that 'not a slightest track leads us to the supposition that Ovid for his pathetic monologues of deliberation can have learnt anything from the rhetorical schools more than the art of speech in general, the sharpening of thought into effective words'. There are, however, some passages in the *Metamorphoses* in which the influence of those schools may be suspected. There are speeches on what were probably already stock subjects for *Suasoriae*; there are conceits or epigrams which are known to be borrowed from his admired Porcius Latro; and Cepheus' speech to Phineus, who is about to attack Perseus, the rescuer of his betrothed Andromeda, suggests at least a typical theme for *Controversia*: 'A man rescues a girl from imminent death, and on being offered the reward of his choice, requests to marry her. Should her betrothed give way, on the ground that but for the rescuer she would not be alive?'

The thirteenth book opens with a grand debate on a time-honoured subject, the contest between Ajax and Ulysses for the arms of the dead Achilles, which were awarded to the latter. The story is assumed as known in the *Odyssey*, and it had its place in the Epic Cycle. What gave the event its lasting interest was the contrast between two types of character. In Homer Ajax is the tower of strength in battle, the man of stolid, unquestioning courage and huge physique. Denigration of him begins only with the later epics of the Cycle and Pindar. In Sophocles' *Philoctetes* and in Euripides he has become the prototype of the post-Periclean politicians, Cleon and the rest, consumed with ambition, fascinated by cleverness. Meanwhile the Sophists got busy, Gorgias' *Defence of Palamedes* disparaging him and Antisthenes' *Ajax and Odysseus* paradoxically coming to his defence. Nor, in due course, did the rhetoricians of Rome overlook so promising a subject for debate; a declamation by Porcius Latro upon it gave Ovid the idea for his line 121. One can guess where Roman sympathies would lie—not with the know-all Greekling. In this they had on their side the dominant tradition, echoes of which we find in Virgil. We can say with some confidence that when Ovid saw to it that Ulysses won heavily on points, he was taking a positive stand against the tide. His 'blockish' Ajax is the dull-witted soldier little respected by the bright elegiac poets of love, while Ulysses is the man of genius, the clever, subtle thinker and speaker. As the poet warms to his task he leaves no doubt as to his own feelings. He is hitting back at that 'gnawing Envy', which reproached him in his youth with not seeking martial glory. The idea of making Ulysses say that Ajax would in any case not appreciate the marvellous engravings on the shield described by Homer must have given him particular pleasure.

Erudition is not obtrusive in the *Metamorphoses*. Ovid does not speak in riddles, as the Alexandrians often did, though he sometimes throws out hints that he knows many more stories than he tells. Sometimes also, to add yet one more ingredient to his hotch-potch, he will rehearse a catalogue in the Hesiodic manner revived by the Alexandrians. We have noted already his unfortunate passion for being exhaustive: he destroys credibility in his description of Hercules' end by making the hero in the midst of his agony recall each one of his twelve labours; Sophocles knew better, and achieved twice the effect by making him mention only half of them. Ovid has not indeed the face to recite the names of all Actaeon's hounds (Hyginus knew eighty-five), but he does go so far as thirty-three (Aeschylus thought four enough) before relenting with an 'and others tedious to relate', and is careful a few lines later that the three mentioned as first leaping on the victim should not be from among those already named.

No one who appreciates Milton will maintain that catalogues of names cannot be poetic, provided at least that they are not unduly prolonged. The panorama of peaks that burned in Phaëthon's conflagration is magnificent in sound as well as imagination. The epithets and touches of literary allusion are just sufficient to relieve monotony; and the same applies to the catalogue of rivers which follows shortly after. (The mention of so many geographical names should not, however, lead us to suppose that Ovid worried about geographical accuracy.) Cicero, quoting an old line, remarked that it was 'lit up by the splendid place-names'.

It might be expected that a poem so pictorial as the *Metamorphoses* would abound in onomatopoeia, or 'expressiveness', as I would rather call it. This is notoriously an effect to which some are far more sensitive than others, and there is a strong element of subjectivity involved. I can only say, *pace* Mr Higham, that I find surprisingly little in this poem compared, for instance, with the work of Virgil, who is admittedly one of the great masters of the art. The croaking of the frogs at VI, 376 is admirable, but this is one of the few examples that I should admit, though I have read through the poem on the look-out for it. Poets vary as readers do in the value they attach to this quality. Those who, like Virgil or Wordsworth or Tennyson, concentrate on the object and try to convey it as vividly as possible to the reader, will naturally pay great attention to so helpful a device; while those who are chiefly concerned to create beauty or convey thought will care less about it. The fact that Ovid sacrificed the expressive flexibility of Virgil's hexameter for a more regular rhythm of lightness and speed in itself suggests that he did not regard it as of prime importance.

(9) CONCLUSION

To the Romans, who had as yet no novels, these stories must have given a delight beyond what we can recapture. They had mostly been told in Greek, but the time had come when only a new language and the fresh outlook of a different race could bring them to life again. They continued to give this delight in the Middle Ages and well after the Renaissance. The first eleven books are the best, when Ovid's fancy is freer. As soon as he begins to aspire to epic seriousness, he comes into competition with poets who surpass him in this vein; one feels one is passing from carefree youth to careful middle age. But taken as a whole the poem gives an effect of completeness. On his way to exile Ovid, charging a friend with its publication, insists that he would have emended it if he had had the opportunity. He says that on his departure from Rome he burnt the manuscript with his own hand—a gesture doubtless challenging comparison with Virgil's dying request to his executors to burn the *Aeneid*, but a 'rhetorical' one in any case, since friends had copies, and he must surely have known it at the time. Even supposing that the poem lacks the final touch (though it is hard to say where, given its general nature), it bears no such traces of incompleteness as the *Aeneid*. There are no apparent faults of construction, and, for Ovid, remarkably few faults of taste; and, indeed, if he had recognized any later, he might still have kept them in, for did he not say that a poem, like a face, was the more attractive for having a mole somewhere? One cannot but suspect that he is seeking to safeguard himself against criticisms, or simply to enhance his reputation, in a way reminiscent of Pope, by suggesting that even a masterpiece was not his best. At all events there is no sign of dissatisfaction in the epilogue as we have it:

> So ends my work, that not Jove's wrath, nor flame,
> Nor steel can vanquish, nor devouring age.
> Let come that day, which o'er this mortal frame
> Alone has power, to end my pilgrimage,
> Yet shall my better part have heritage
> Among the stars, indelible my name.
> Wherever Rome extends her sway my page
> Shall there be read; and if what bards proclaim
> Has truth, throughout all time I shall survive in fame!

How amply this prophecy was fulfilled shall be told in due course.

CHAPTER VIII

THE 'FASTI'

THE last two books of the *Metamorphoses*, as we have seen, dealt in part with legends of Rome, a subject which was occupying Ovid at the same time in a major work in elegiac couplets. We do not know when he began the *Fasti*, but he had composed six books by the time of his exile, half of a poem which, if completed, would have run to about ten thousand lines. Each month has a book to itself, beginning with a discussion of the significance of its name and then following the almanack of the Julian year: 'I sing of occasions, with their origins, spread throughout the Latin year, and of the rising and setting of constellations.' So Ovid introduces his poem, a jumble of astronomy, history, legend, religion, superstition, scholarship, guesswork and antiquarian lore. The ingenious transitions of the *Metamorphoses* are not attempted, but the right to pass over one item and elaborate another at whim is maintained. Roman legends connected with the festivals are interwoven with Greek. Why do the Luperci run naked? We are told first that Faunus, the deity concerned, is the naked Pan of primitive Arcadia, where men lived naked as the beasts (besides, it is easier to run naked). Then follows a Greek legend of how he was deceived by a change of clothing, and a Latin one of how Romulus and Remus, when the alarm was raised that thieves were stealing their cattle, ran naked as they were to intercept them. Greek also are the myths of the origin of the stars.

The choice of such a subject would be easily accounted for by reading, and no less easily by environment. The literary grandparents of the *Fasti* are, on the aetiological side, the *Aetia* of Callimachus, admired of all Roman elegists, and on the astronomical side the no-less admired *Phaenomena* of Aratus. Their father is clearly the last book of Propertius. In it the self-styled Roman Callimachus claims to have set out to emulate his hero, 'I shall sing sacred rites, and days, and the ancient names of places'. It looks as though he intended to write a separate elegy on each topic; but he completed only four, and the introductory poem of his last, miscellaneous collection that contains them is a whimsical apology for not having persevered.

There were other reasons besides poetic emulation why Ovid should have taken up the task that Propertius had abandoned. The Romans had long been interested in the origins of their customs and the early legends of their people. More learned writers had recently entered the field, and finally Augustus, in his efforts to restore the old Roman virtues, was attempting not only to revive the old religion but also to kindle an admiration for the old worthies of Rome, whose statues he set up round his new forum. Among poets Virgil, and eventually Horace and Propertius also, had written in sympathy with this movement.

The idea once conceived, Ovid set to work. He chose as metre the elegiacs of the *Aetia* rather than the hexameters of the *Phaenomena*, probably because he felt most at ease in them. The basis of the poem was to be the calendar as reformed by Julius Caesar and inaugurated on 1 January 45 B.C. This reform had led to a widespread setting up of Fasti on tablets in public and private places all over Italy, and it is from remains of these that we are able to reconstruct the Roman calendar. This skeleton Ovid proceeded to clothe with flesh. Of his Greek fables the majority were no doubt derived from Hellenistic sources. The Roman material was much of it common property by now. He says he consulted 'ancient annals'; but there can be little doubt that his chief debt was to more recent scholarship. One source of material as well as inspiration must have been Livy's new history, as we can detect from verbal similarities in the versions of the stories of the Fabii and Lucretia.

Since the chief authorities he is likely to have consulted have survived at best only in fragments, there is little to be gained from trying to deduce his debt to each. More interesting, and more vivid, are the passages in which he claims to be drawing on his own experience. Already in the *Amores* he had shown his enthusiasm for old ceremonies by describing the festival of Juno which he chanced to witness at his wife's home-town of Falerii. In the *Fasti* he mentions that he himself has taken part in the rites of the Parilia on April 21, carrying the means of expiation, bean-straws and the ashes of a burnt calf, jumping over the three fires arranged in a row, and letting himself be aspersed with water from a laurel branch. He had drunk, too, of the spring in the awesome shrine of Diana beside Lake Nemi, and perhaps caught a glimpse of its priest, the prowling 'King of the Grove', who, having slain his predecessor in single combat, reigned till another appeared and slew him in turn. (Readers of the *Golden Bough* will remember that it is from this grove, whose Latin inmate Virbius was identified with the Greek Hippolytus, that Frazer began his world-wide pilgrimage.)

Ringed with dark woods under Aricia's lee
There lies a lake of age-old sanctity.
Here lurks Hippolytus by horses rent
(Hence to that grove no horse may e'er be sent).
Tablets on threads the long-drawn fences crowd,
Thank-offerings for the goddess' favour vowed;
And many a woman brings, for answered prayer,
Torches from Rome, with garlands on her hair.
The strong of arm and fleet of foot there reign,
And as he slew each slayer will be slain.
A pebbly brook flows fitfully murmuring nigh;
Oft have I drunk of it, but sparingly;
Egeria, Numa's wife and counsellor,
Loved of the Muses, doth that water pour.

Other stories that are vivid he claims to have picked up in talk. On April 19, it appears, foxes were let loose in the Circus Maximus with burning torches tied to their tails, as part of the shows in honour of Ceres, and Ovid tells a myth to account for this.*

At Carseoli the land is cold, unfit
For oliveyards, but corncrops thrive in it.
Passing that way to my Pelignian dale,
My little home whose waters never fail,
A friendly house I entered, oft a guest,
When now the Sun had loosed his steeds for rest.
My host was wont to furnish for my pen
Many a tale, and this he told me then:
'Once on the plain out here'—he waved his hand—
'A frugal wife and husband had some land.
He with the plough his little plot would work,
Now use a sickle, or again a fork;

* Frazer thought that a fox bound up in straw was burnt on April 19 simply as a warning to foxes to leave the fields alone.

While she would sweep their humble, wood-propped farm,
Anon put eggs under a hen to warm,
Or gather mallows green or mushrooms white
Or keep the hearthstone's cheerful blaze alight,
And tireless yet find time to ply her loom,
Weaving defences 'gainst the cold to come.
A son she had, mischievous as his age—
Twelve years he'd run of earthly pilgrimage—
Who caught a fox beyond the willow-den
That from the coop had stolen many a hen;
He wrapped the wretch in straw and hay, and gan
Set fire to him: he felt the fire and ran;
Where'er he ran he set the crops alight
And breezes fanned the flames' destructive might.
The event, forgot, has left memorial,
For here to name a fox is criminal;
And penance still is done at Ceres' feast,
When, as he burnt the crops, so burns that beast.'

This glimpse of the eager listener is followed shortly by one of the eager inquirer. Returning one evening from Nomentum to Rome—the date was April 25—Ovid fell in with a crowd clothed in white for ceremonial purity which was escorting a priest to the grove of a typically Roman deity—Mildew (*Robigo*). (The procession of the Robigalia was long continued on this day by the Church, still as a protection for the crops against mildew but now under the patronage of St Mark.) He immediately approached the officiating Flamen Quirinalis, to find out why he was going to burn the entrails of a dog and a sheep at the grove, and overheard his prayer, which was designed not only to protect crops but to divert the deity, in his cognate capacity as rust, from agricultural to warlike implements. Having put on the flames the entrails, which apparently caused a shudder to the sensitive poet, used though he must have been to such sights, the Flamen answered his question, at least as regards the dog: it was a substitute for the parching Dog-star.

The personal approach that we find everywhere in the *Fasti* is a happy legacy from the *Aetia* of Callimachus. One might be tempted to suppose that Ovid was merely enlivening his work with the fiction of autopsy, but the thought is banished by a passage such as this:

I have a daughter (may she me survive,
For while she lives 'tis joy to be alive).
When I would fix her wedding-day, I sought
To know which times were lucky, which were not.
After the sacred Ides of June, 'twas said,
Was most auspicious both for man and maid:
June's earlier half ill sped the marriage yoke.
For thus the holy Flaminica spoke:
'Till yellow Tiber to the sea consign
All that is purged from Ilian Vesta's shrine,
I may not cut, I may not groom my hair
With boxwood comb, my nails I may not pare,
Nor touch a man, though priest of Jove he be
And mine by law in perpetuity.
So haste not thou, nor make thy girl a bride
Till fiery Vesta's floor be purified.'

There is something quaint and very Roman about this incident of the sceptical poet consulting the grave lady with her elaborate taboos, whom on another festival he had seen begging ceremonially for the *februa* (means of purification) and being given, for some reason, a sprig of pine; but whatever he may have thought himself, he was not the one to disregard the feelings of his daughter, and anyway many hardened rationalists have their superstitions. The idea that the whole of May as well as the first half of June was unlucky for marriage was deep-rooted, though Ovid ascribes it only to the *vulgus*;* Frazer says that it persists in England, and Ripert claims to have seen a throng of wedding parties in their best besieging the *mairie* of Marseilles on April 30. On another occasion Ovid, returning down the *Via Nova* at the time of Vesta's festival, was astonished to see a lady descending barefoot, till an old woman who lived near by invited him to sit down beside her and explained that this custom was a survival of the distant days before the *Cloaca Maxima* and other sewers drained the Forum, when the *Lacus Curtius* was indeed a lake.

Now and then he gives us what purports at least to be a glimpse of his work in progress: 'For a long time I fondly imagined there were images of Vesta, but then I discovered there are none under her dome'; or again, 'Three or four times I went all through the calendar, but

* One of Plutarch's suggestions, 'Is it because in that month many of the Latins sacrifice to the dead?' is probably correct.

could find nowhere the Day of Sowing, till the Muse, observing me, interposed, "That day is appointed each year: why look for a movable feast in the calendar?"'* This co-operation of the Muses and other deities, a feature of the *Aetia* of Callimachus, is the commonest piece of 'stage business' with which Ovid seeks to enliven his poem. As the weird, impressive train of Cybele passes, the poet takes courage, in spite of the awe-inspiring din of flutes and cymbals, to ask the goddess of whom he may inquire their purpose, and is referred to her grand-daughters, the Muses. Indeed, various deities themselves are freely summoned for cross-examination. As he ponders, tablet in hand, on the identity of Janus, the house grows brighter and suddenly the god himself appears, with his two faces, his staff and key; the poet is duly terrified, his heart frozen and hair standing on end. But elsewhere, by way of variety, he turns to account his *not* having seen Vesta, whose temple no man might enter. Rapt in prayer he *felt* the presence of divinity, and a glory shone around; and with no apparent instructor he felt his ignorance enlightened and his errors banished.

In arranging his work Ovid seems to have sought to keep his books roughly equal in length; thus, Book IV having reached 950 lines, he postpones treatment of the rites of Flora, which began on April 28, until the book on May, since they conveniently extended into that month. In spite of the licence he took of expatiating on one topic and merely referring to another, he seems to have felt constrained to devote two hundred lines to so well known a story as that of Ceres and Proserpine, even though he was telling it elsewhere at still greater length, introducing it with a not very reassuring apology:

> The Virgin's rape must here perforce be told:
> Some may be new to you, though most be old.

How did it come about that the *Fasti* were never completed? Four lines in the *Tristia* tell us the beginning of the story. The first says that the *Fasti* comprised twelve books, and the second merely adds that each book covered one month; the third tells us that it was written recently, and inscribed and dedicated to Caesar (who must be Augustus), and the fourth that the poet's exile interrupted the work. We know in any case, even if we could not have guessed, that twelve books were

* That is, the *permanent* calendar.

planned, since he thrice postpones a topic with a promise to treat it in its proper place in one of the last six months, and presumably '*scripsi*' indicates that the last six books were indeed to some extent drafted.

Six books, then, were reasonably complete, but the remaining six only in a rough form. If Catullus found it hard to write poetry at Verona, separated from his library at Rome, how much harder would it be for Ovid to continue the *Fasti* on the confines of barbary. He says as much in the *Tristia*: 'I have here no supply of books, to stimulate and sustain me.' Even if he took a modicum of source-books with him, he would lack the help and stimulus of daily observation and discussion, and, indeed, the minute recollection of what went on in Rome might be painful to him. He put the *Fasti* aside, and turned his energies to poems designed to compass his recall. That was his prime objective, and while he nursed a spark of hope that he would succeed there was every reason why the torso of the *Fasti* should remain on the shelf.

The rest of the story is guess-work, but reasonably certain. In A.D. 14, six years later, Augustus died. Tiberius, his successor, presented little hope of a relaxation, but his nephew and adoptive son Germanicus might be sympathetic. He was a charming and popular prince with an interest in literature. He had at some time for Quaestor Ovid's stepson-in-law Suillius, whom the exiled poet begged to intercede with his adored master and act as intermediary. And when, after establishing peace by his operations in Germany, he was appointed in the autumn of 16 to go on a mission to the East next year, Ovid's hopes must have soared. He did eventually visit the Sea of Marmora and look on the Black Sea; and though by then the poet was dead, the rumour of his plans may have long preceded him.

This would amply account for the fact that the *Fasti* as we have them are dedicated, not to Augustus, as stated in *Tristia* II, 551, but to Germanicus. The death of Augustus had in any case made some changes in the *Fasti* necessary; and besides, the ageing poet, now close on sixty, could scarcely hope to conceive and complete against time a new poem of any weight: what he could perhaps do was re-dress the abandoned *Fasti*. But our text shows clearly that he only succeeded in treating Book I before death overtook him about the end of 17. An executor presumably gave to the world Books I–VI much as he found them, and if he came upon any draft of Books VII–XII, decided that it was too rough to publish.

Thomas Keightley, in the Preface to his edition of the *Fasti* (1848), commented on the variety of their appeal and exclaimed: 'There is not, perhaps, in the whole compass of classical literature a work better calculated to be put into the hands of students.' That begs many questions, and in assessing the poem we must distinguish at least three main aspects—its relation to the Roman public for which it was written, its contribution to our knowledge of religious history and cognate subjects, and its merits for us as literature. Let us deal with these in turn.

The close of the *Metamorphoses*, as we have seen, was a highly rhetorical eulogy of Julius Caesar, extolling his conquests and deploring his murder, and of Augustus, as his still greater successor. The contemporary *Fasti*, with more frequent opportunities, display the same spirit of unbridled adulation, which goes beyond anything in the other Augustans, and presages the excesses of the Silver Age poets. Julius Caesar deserved his place in the story for his reform of the calendar, but Ovid must needs inflate by suggesting that the interest of 'that god' in the stars was prompted by a desire to have foreknowledge of the heavenly mansions to which he was destined. If a compliment is paid in passing to Pompey, it is only to make the point that his conqueror had an even greater name; there is nothing of the republican sympathy of a Livy or a Lucan. The tyrannicides were sacrilegious murderers (but Venus foiled them, for it was only a wraith of Caesar they stabbed), and the revenge taken at Philippi had been the prime duty of his successor.

It was, however, in token not only of this but of his recovery of the standards lost over thirty years before by Crassus at Carrhae that Augustus erected in his own new forum the great temple of Mars the Avenger. The fact that such a signal and symbolic diplomatic victory could be won without bloodshed made a great impression at Rome and gave peace-loving poets their chance. The *Fasti* dwell singularly little on fighting. It is as peacemaker that Augustus is chiefly hailed by Ovid: 'let others sing of Caesar's arms: I Caesar's altars—' and greatest among these altars was the Altar of Peace, voted in 13 B.C. when he returned from pacifying Spain and Gaul, and dedicated four years later.* Ovid rises to the occasion:

> Thy braided tresses wreathed with Actian bay
> Come, gentle Peace, in all the world to stay.
> If but our foes be gone, let triumphs go:
> Thou on our chiefs more glory shalt bestow.
> Save to quell arms, no arms let any take,
> Nor trumpet sound save in religion's wake,
> Lands near and far Aenead valour prove,
> And who feared Rome too little, learn to love.
> Burn incense, priests, at Peace's festival;
> Anointed let the snow-white victim fall;
> And pray the gods, disposed such prayers to hear,
> The House that brought may have her all the year.

The surprise ending 'learn to love' (not learn to serve) is an indication of how the Augustan attitude to empire had progressed even beyond Virgil's 'spare the surrendered and subdue the proud'. Julius Caesar's experiments in clemency had become an ideal for imperialists. No praise could be too high for the man who had secured peace and was yet content to be *princeps*, not *dominus*, whose door by Senatorial decree was decorated not only with the laurels of victory but with the crown of civic oak for preserving his fellow-citizens; he is already *aeternus*, and the poet does not hesitate to compare him with Jupiter. Opportunities would occur for other gods of the *Fasti* also to be ranged on the side of peace, and not merely Ceres or Janus, but Mars himself.

Rome was now at the height of her power and prosperity, and her citizens realized, with wonder as well as pride, that what they were already calling 'The Eternal City' had become in a sense the whole world. The poet who composed four centuries later the much-quoted line 'thou has made the City what was once the world' was merely rewriting a line from the *Fasti*. Events were moving fast: Ovid remarks that by the time the Senate, Knights and People decreed for Augustus the title of Father of his Country (2 B.C.) history had already conferred it; and now also, though even that is too late, it is giving him the true title he has long in fact earned of Father of the World.

Their wonder was chiefly expressed by contrasting in imagination

* Impressive reliefs from this that survived have now been embodied in a reconstruction on the Tiber bank beside Augustus' Mausoleum—if indeed they are from this.

the rural simplicity of the site which Evander and then Romulus chose with its eventual destiny. This theme, familiar from *Aeneid* VIII and beloved of Augustan poets, occurs time and again in the *Fasti*; a single instance may be quoted, where Evander, guided from Arcadia by his prophetess mother Carmentis, comes upon the spot:

> And now, at sage Carmentis' word, he neared
> A river-mouth, and up the Tiber steered;
> Till she the bank Tarentum's pool beside,
> A lonely spot with scattered huts, espied;
> Then straight before the poop, with streaming hair,
> Wildly she stood and checked the steersman there,
> And, arm outstretched towards the right-hand shore,
> With frenzied foot thrice smote the pinewood floor.
> Scarce, in the nick of time, Evander's hand
> Saved her from leaping, fain to reach that land.
> 'All hail!' she cried, 'Gods of this long-sought place,
> Thou land that shalt increase the heavenly race,
> Rivers and springs this hospitable ground
> Enjoys, and groves where naiads dance their round!
> Greet with good omen me and this my son,
> And bless the foot that steps your bank upon.
> Shall not these slopes give place to walls immense
> And every nation justice seek from thence?
> These hills, 'tis promised, shall possess the earth.
> Wondrous such destiny should here have birth!'

In the same way the Augustans loved to contrast the simplicity of the first Roman buildings with the splendour of those they now saw, to think of the wattle huts of King Numa's day with roofs of thatch where now stood great buildings roofed with bronze, and of his palace on whose foundations the small round temple of Vesta was said to stand, or contemplate the rude shack on the edge of the Palatine still shown as the dwelling of Romulus. Jupiter in those days could scarcely stand upright in his little temple, and the thunderbolt he held was of clay; and men carried foliage to the Capitol where now they carry jewels. Such thoughts stir feelings that spring from deep in the human heart. Ovid was moved by the contrast of Romulus, son of Mars and destined for heaven, asleep on his humble pallet:

> How sound he slept, content on straw to lie,
> Yet from that couch ascended to the sky!

In that couplet lies half the appeal of what was to be the Christmas legend.

The *Aeneid* is the inspiration of the fine rhetorical passage with which Carmentis concluded her prophecy. Particularly moving is the apostrophe to Pallas, the young son of Evander whose death in Book x so roused Aeneas against Turnus: her first thought is to save him, but instantly she checks herself from seeking to frustrate in the interest of her own personal feelings the great purposes of destiny:

Soon shall Dardanian vessels touch these shores;
Once more a woman shall give rise to wars.*
Pallas, dear grandson, why gird on thy bane?—
Gird it! a hero shall avenge thee slain.
Thou, conquered Troy, shalt conquer, overthrown
Shalt rise: that ruin shall thy foes cast down.
Triumph, ye flames, o'er Neptune's Ilium hurled:
Yet shall its ashes overtop the world;
Aeneas shall his gods and sire convoy,
Both sacred: Vesta, welcome gods of Troy!
Some day shalt thou and earth one guardian share:
A god himself shall for thy service care;†
The Augustan line shall keep the fatherland,
The reins of empire destined to their hand.
The third, though fain the burden to decline,
God-born, shall handsel it with mind divine;
And, e'en as altars shall be raised to me,
Julia Augusta shall a goddess be.‡

The *Aeneid* and the history of Livy are the greatest monuments to the Augustan desire to reawaken in the Roman people a pride in their past, but the *Fasti* too could play its part. In a long passage Ovid traces the descent of Romulus through his mother Ilia back to the Trojan dynasty and to Jupiter himself, not omitting to mention Solymus, a companion of Aeneas, who was the mythical founder of Sulmo; in another he speaks of the proud titles, derived from the conquest of this land or that, or from some other achievement, which were engraved under the ancestral masks displayed round their halls by Roman

* Lavinia, daughter of Latinus, betrothed to Turnus, whom Aeneas married.

† Augustus transferred the sacred fire of Vesta to his own house on the Palatine.

‡ The last four lines belong, of course, to the second draft. For Tiberius' reluctance see Tacitus, *Annals* I, 11. Livia became Iulia Augusta after Augustus' death, by his will; she did not in fact become a goddess until Claudius' reign.

aristocrats. True, he only rehearses these in order to lead up to the glory of the Emperor, who would be entitled to a *cognomen* drawn from every race in the world, and whose surname of Augustus is distinguished from those above by its associations with the divine; yet nevertheless the very roll of names awakens echoes of the sixth *Aeneid*.

As for Augustus' 'charge of morals and laws', the author of the *Ars Amatoria* makes a couple of references in the *Fasti* to the Emperor's zeal for chastity, and one, more interesting, to his gesture against luxury in destroying the huge palace of the infamous Vedius Pollio, though he had himself inherited it. But the main emphasis is naturally on the religious revival, which he inaugurated as early as 28 B.C. with a great programme for the restoration of temples, amplified with the Secular Festival in 17, and furthered by becoming Chief Priest in 12.

In fact Ovid could hardly have put his pen more completely at the service of the regime. The trouble is that, while no doubt it did not go against the grain for him to do so (since in any case he does not seem to have been a man of strong principles), he cannot in his heart have cared genuinely about such propaganda. Nothing that we know about him from his previous works would suggest an enthusiasm for moral regeneration; while as for the religious revival, we may reasonably suppose that Augustus himself merely took the view that, irrespective of belief, it is the greatest security for a decent degree of social order; and are we to suppose that Ovid was more religious than the Emperor? Roman religion was a formalistic affair, deserving for the most part to be called rather superstition; deities like Cardea, goddess of hinges, Limentinus, god of thresholds, are the barest of abstractions, well deserving St Augustine's mockery. It would perhaps be better to call it *Latin* religion, for it goes back to the animism of the agricultural community that preceded the miraculous growth of the city. At first everything around a man seemed somehow alive and part of a universe where magic ruled. Next came a vague belief in spirits that had to be propitiated, leading in turn to the idea that certain places were particularly holy, which the Romans expressed by saying that there must be a divinity there—*numen inest*. Many *numina* acquired names and special functions. Out of such beginnings, overlaid with the highly developed structure of Greek religion and mythology, grew the complicated round of ceremonies that marked the Roman year. Among the educated that godfearing habit of mind, to which Polybius attributed this people's rise to world-power, faded with the influx of Greek philosophy and rationalism in the second century; but the other great national characteristic of conservatism ensured the survival of the rites themselves.

In general, Ovid treats this religion with an affectation of naïve faith: it would have been out of place to indulge either in theological speculation or in open irony. But once or twice the old Ovid peeps through the mask. Saturn, warned by an oracle that his son would overthrow him, devoured his offspring as soon as they were born; fretting at this, his wife Rhea swaddled a stone, and he swallowed it instead of the new-born Jupiter. In telling this grotesque Hesiodic tale the poet cannot help interjecting, surely not without irony, 'antiquity is believed in default of good evidence: do not shake established belief'. His Flora, about to recount how she contrived the virgin birth of Mars out of Juno, expresses a hope that Jupiter may never find out, which makes him comically anthropomorphic, and Mars in turn is grotesquely fooled by Anna Perenna. Ovid's Claudia Quinta, the Vestal falsely rumoured to be unchaste, is not, as others might have made her, 'of a holy, cold and still conversation', but a gay and high-spirited girl:

> Her style, her varied coiffure, and a tongue
> That answered back old carpers did her wrong.

The Augustan ideas were at least new when Virgil and Horace proclaimed them, but it is hard to believe that where they seem to us trite and mechanical in Ovid they did not seem trite and mechanical to his contemporaries also. No brilliance of expression could refresh them. A whole generation had had them dinned into its ears. However, a large part of the *Fasti* comprises legends or descriptions of old customs. It is true that, even when treating of these, Ovid remained a man of his generation: 'we praise the ancients, but act according to our own times'. He was not like Livy, who said that when he told of ancient times he became an ancient in soul: in the words of Gaston Boissier, 'il ramène à lui l'antiquité au lieu d'aller vers elle'. But in a literary or antiquarian way he does seem to have relished them, so that from time to time his verse-almanack does come to life.

This brings us to our second question—what profit can antiquarians, astronomers or students of comparative religion derive from the *Fasti*? Sir James Frazer thought it worth a monumental edition in five volumes, and Warde Fowler in his Preface to *The Roman Festivals* asserted that the only sound method of exhibiting the religious side of the Roman character was to follow the Roman Calendar, testimonies which sufficiently indicate that at lowest the work forms a convenient text or basis for discussion of the topics it deals with.

First of all, let us clear away the astronomical portions. Cicero remarked that Aratus, 'a man ignorant of astronomy', had written an excellent poem on that subject, and ignorance of astronomy would not deter Ovid or seem to his readers a *prima facie* disqualification. But he was indeed as ignorant as most of us are, and these portions are full of blunders, exposed in detail by Ideler more than a century ago. Admittedly some of his mistakes are traceable to the Julian calendar itself, for Caesar's astronomer Sosigenes came from Alexandria and sometimes followed works based on observations made in that latitude, while others, un-Julian but common to Ovid and Columella, were presumably derived from another source. But he had clearly no understanding of the principles of the subject, being a townsman writing a work of literature for townsmen who had long since regulated their lives by looking at calendars instead of stars. They had recently acquired a reliable one, and Ovid's astronomy could have no practical value except as an advertisement for it; nor can it have much practical value for us, since it gives a distorted version of contemporary knowledge, let alone of scientific truth.

As for the rest of his material, there is no good reason to doubt that he consulted many authorities, though he names none. His other works suggest that he was a voracious reader. He twice bids his reader inspect a number of calendars of Latin and Sabine towns, reporting what will be found in each with the implication at least that he himself has had access to them, though some of his statements about them conflict with other authorities, and of course he may be relying on some previous collator. What he professes himself to have witnessed we have no reason to suspect.

What we may suspect is that he did not think deeply about what he read. He will give us five possible derivations of the *Agonalia*, or four possible reasons for Romulus having divided the year into ten months, or seven possible origins of the custom of fumigation, and leave the matter there. His ideas about the derivation of words strike us aghast, though these are no more absurd than etymologies found in Varro and other more scholarly ancients. More reprehensible, he will support one version in one place, and another in another, from sheer literary opportunism. In I, 123–4 the gates of Janus are shut to keep War inside, whereas in I, 281 it is Peace who is to be confined there for safety. Where Romulus is to be glorified, the murder of Remus is ascribed to Celer, and his brother's grief is emphasized; but where Augustus is to be glorified by comparison with Romulus, then it is implied that Romulus was the murderer. Let us accept the fact: Ovid was interested primarily in literary effect, and only secondarily in truth. In an important passage Wissowa gave a warning against unwary use of Ovid as a source for scientific deductions. He characterizes him justly as 'a poet equipped with neither very extensive nor deep knowledge, and very little understanding for the peculiar characteristics of Roman religion, but compensated for this with a rich imagination and an outstanding gift for painting'. A most revealing passage is I, 89, where Ovid says, 'But what god am I to say you are, Janus of double shape? For Greece has no divinity like you.' Whenever he could, he equated a Latin with a Greek deity, and was at once supplied with material; for Latin mythology in itself was jejune.

There is a common idea that the *Fasti* are a source of unique importance for knowledge of Roman religion, but in fact most of the information it gives could be derived from other sources. No, it is as literature that the poem must stand or fall, as a popular introduction to Roman religion; and Warde Fowler, who undertook to expound the Roman festivals month by month, has as much right as any to sum up. After frankly acknowledging Ovid's shortcomings as an authority he concludes with his own experience, that 'When after the month of June we lose him as a companion, we may feel that the subject not only loses with him what little literary interest it can boast of, but becomes for the most part a mere investigation of fossil rites, from which all life and meaning have departed for ever.'

We come, then, to the final task of estimating the value of the *Fasti* as literature. The scheme of the *Metamorphoses* is an ingenious, imaginative *jeu d'esprit*; that of the *Fasti* is a convenient but prosaic rule of thumb. It is true that Roman mythology lacked the coherence which Greek had acquired, while Roman religion largely consisted in scrupulously doing the traditional thing on the traditional day, so that Ovid had less opportunity here to attempt an artistic whole; but we have had occasion before to note his passion for being exhaustive. 'The place requires...': having once chosen to follow the calendar, he can leave nothing out. Moreover, the superficial order of the *Fasti* makes things, in some ways, more chaotic. Thus the beginning of Hippolytus' story is told in Book VI *à propos* the rising of the constellation Anguitenens; its natural sequel has already occurred in Book III, in connexion with Egeria. The legends Ovid tells from early Roman history, when marshalled by Frazer in chronological order in his Preface (VII–IX), might lead one to expect a continuous pageant corresponding to the early books of Livy, whereas in fact, of course, the stories are told haphazard wherever opportunity offers. As for the risings and settings of the constellations, their bare intrusion is most inartistic when no story is told in connexion with them.

I have already spoken of an element of triteness, and perhaps also of underlying insincerity, in the sections which can specifically be classed as Augustan propaganda, and there is a certain rhetorical conventionality about other passages. The abandon of youth, outrageous but alive, has faded into the respectability of middle age, a development which, however gratifying to the moralist, has taken some of the edge off Ovid's writing. We have the conventional praise of old, rugged, military Rome uncorrupted by the arts of Greece. Contrast this Philistine utterance, 'not yet had the conquered arts been handed over to the conquerors by Greece, an eloquent but weakling race', with Horace's generous enthusiasm, 'captured Greece took captive her uncivilized conqueror, and introduced the arts into rustic Latium'. Who would ever have thought to hear the gruff voice of old Cato grumbling on through Ovid's mouth? Janus' condemnation of the modern scramble for wealth is eloquent and pointed enough, but it is a rhetorical school-piece, and how often we have heard it before! Even that mystic-sounding eulogy of astronomers as being above worldly thoughts strikes one in Ovid as having become by now a conventional purple-patch of Pythagorean-style 'sublimity'. And who can read with much enthusiasm the story of Aristaeus and the bees as told in a few neat couplets when Virgil has told it at length in one of the loveliest passages in all Latin poetry. One feels continually that Ovid has come into the field too late.

This much said, we can turn to the less invidious task of selecting from the five thousand lines of the poem some examples of what can give pleasure. To begin with there are passages which stand out as interesting for their subject-matter, though of course what seems interesting varies from age to age, and even from person to person. I have already quoted passages which are alive because Ovid is reporting scenes he actually saw, or local tales he heard. Even in bare prose the account of what happened at the festival of Venus on April 1st must intrigue us, if only for its curious details and its difference from anything thinkable today:

Duly do you worship the goddess, Latin mothers and brides, and you too who wear not the fillet and long dress [prostitutes]. Take from her marble neck the golden necklaces, take off her rich adornments: the goddess must be bathed entire. Now dry her neck and restore its golden necklaces; then give her other flowers and fresh roses. Yourselves too she bids to bathe wearing wreaths of green myrtle, and for a certain reason which I will reveal. Once naked on the shore she was drying her oozy locks, when a wanton crew of satyrs espied her. She screened her body with myrtle: thus she was protected, and she bids you to do likewise. And now learn why you should offer incense to Fortuna Virilis [Success with Men] in the place that reeks with warm water.* All of you strip when you enter there and every blemish in your body is exposed; Fortuna Virilis enables you to hide this and conceal it from men, if supplicated with a little incense. Nor disdain to take pounded poppy in white milk and liquid honey squeezed from the comb: Venus drank that when first she was escorted to her husband; from that time on she was a bride.

Ovid's eerie description of the private rite of appeasing ancestral ghosts at the *Lemuria* in May is our only full account of this primeval superstition.

When now full midnight lends silence to sleep and the dogs and birds of every sort are hushed, the man, mindful of the old rite and fearing the gods, rises (no knot on his feet†) and makes a sign with fingers joined about his thumb,‡ lest in his silence an unsubstantial shade may meet him. After washing

* In the men's baths. Only women of humbler rank did this.

† For knots as obstacles to magic see Frazer, *ad loc.*

‡ This is the only mention in ancient literature of a gesture against malignant influences still commonly used to avert the Evil Eye.

his hands clean in spring water he turns, and first takes black beans and throws them away with face averted, saying, 'Lo, these I cast; with these beans I redeem both me and mine'. This he says nine times without looking back; the ghost is believed to gather the beans, following unseen behind. Again he touches water and clashes Temesan bronze, and begs the ghost to depart from his house. When he has said nine times, 'Shades of my fathers, avaunt!' he looks back; for then he deems the rites duly performed.

Such passages take us far from our world, but there are not a few in which we recognize customs that have counterparts or survivors in modern times. The votive tablets for services rendered and the candles dedicated by grateful women in the shrine of Diana are now offered in many places to another Virgin. We have a passing reference to what would surely have been the climax of the poem if Ovid had completed it, the Saturnalian festivities of December 'welcome to mirthful spirits'. The Purification of the Virgin at Candlemas (February 2) may be a relic of the purificatory rites (*februationes*) from which, as Ovid tells us, the month took its name. The bonfires which peasants in east Europe light, or till recently lit, on St George's Day, and those which Italians lit two thousand years ago on the *Parilia* two days earlier, have probably a common Aryan ancestor. And our pagan rites of May Day are akin to those of the *Floralia*.

Again, how reminiscent of a Bank Holiday crowd on Hampstead Heath is Ovid's description of the carnival of Anna Perenna, which took place beside the Tiber on the Ides of March, a picture worthy of Frith, and incidentally a piquant background to the murder of Julius Caesar:

The populace arrives, and scattering in knots all over the grass drinks, with each boy lying beside his girl. Some rough it in the open air, a few pitch tents, some make themselves huts of leafy boughs. Others again put up canes for uprights and stretch their gowns over them. With sun and wine they warm up and pray for as many years as they can drain cups, drinking by numbers. There you will find a man who can drink himself as old as Nestor, a woman whose bumpers would make her as old as the Sibyl. There too they sing snatches picked up in the theatre, and keep time to their song with waving hands, and tread uncouth measures around the bowl, while sweethearts in their best dance with streaming hair. On the way home they reel and provide amusement for the crowd, and all who meet them bless them. I met such a procession lately and thought it would make a good story: there was a drunk old woman dragging a drunk old man.

The *Fasti*, considering their length, have less humour than we should expect from Ovid: he has become, in the words of Peeters, 'une sorte de *vates*, inspiré, grave, et respectueux', somewhat to our regret. There is some rather boisterous fun over the bald and fat Silenus standing greedily on his ass to eat honey from a hollow elm and suddenly mobbed by a swarm of hornets (how Bacchus and the Satyrs laughed!); and the dénouement of the merry tale of Faunus, who attempted to assault Omphale and found she had changed clothes with her bedfellow Hercules, smacks strongly of the *Reeve's Tale* in Chaucer. More typically Ovidian is the scene where the babies born of the Rape of the Sabines are being used by their mothers as peacemakers between their parents' families:

> Those who could speak 'Dear Grandfather!' did cry:
> Those who could hardly speak were made to try;

or the account of the shopkeeper's visit to the spring of that notorious thief Mercury:

> There is a fountain near the Capene Gate,
> Hallowed by Mercury, its clients state.
> The loose-clad vendor comes and, duly pure,
> Takes water thence in fumigated ewer.
> Some bay-leaves dipped in this will sprinkle dew
> On wares he destines for an owner new;
> He sprinkles too with dripping bay his hair
> And utters in his trickster's voice a prayer:
> 'Absolve me from my lies in times gone by;
> Absolve me from this day's duplicity;
> Whether I called thyself to witness or
> By Jove, too high to hear me, falsely swore,
> Or against any god with knowledge sinned
> Or goddess, may my words be as the wind;
> And may the coming day bring scope for lies,
> Nor any god regard my perjuries.
> Give me but gain and joys that gain confers,
> And make it pay to have tricked my customers.'

The graceful rococo charm of the *Metamorphoses* is seldom given play in the *Fasti*, but once or twice it appears when the poet is describing his fictitious relations with the various deities from whom he seeks information. The opening of Book IV on April, the month of Venus, gave an obvious chance, and Ovid handled it to perfection:

'Be gracious, Mother of twin Loves', I said.
The goddess to her poet turned her head:
'What would'st with me, pledged to a higher strain?
Doth that soft heart still feel some ancient pain?'
'Thou know'st about the pain', I answered: she
Laughed, and thereat half heaven of clouds was free.
'Wounded or whole, allegiance still I pay
To thee, my earliest theme, my theme for aye.'

Ovid pleads that more serious themes befit his present age, and Venus graciously gives him both absolution and inspiration.

On another occasion history is happily linked with astronomy. The calendar gave for April 6 the Battle of Thapsus, the setting of Libra, and the expectation of rain: Ovid combines the three:

'Twas on the games' third day: I well recall
My oldish neighbour at the festival,
Who said, 'This day it was, on Libya's coast,
That Caesar crushed proud Juba's treacherous host.
He was my captain, and it is my pride
As tribune to have served him at his side.
This seat of honour war on me confers,
But peace on you and all your Decemvirs.'
A sudden shower cut short this episode:
The Balance hung in heaven shed its load.

Nearly a third of the *Fasti* consists of narrative pieces of from twenty to two hundred lines each. In content many of these stories are only moderately entertaining for sophisticated readers, being in any case familiar, and much depends on the telling. The freely flowing metre of the *Metamorphoses* allows the expression to adapt itself to the subject, whereas the fetters of the couplet allow the *Fasti* to succeed fully in one kind of narrative only, the swift and exciting. Here indeed it does excel, with its rapid fire of direct speech, commands, apostrophes, questions, interjections, parentheses, and short dialogue. One is reminded of those stories in Livy where, as the tension increases, he breaks into a panting movement of short sentences. No story was better suited to this style than that of Lucretia, which may serve as a specimen of Ovid's narrative power in elegiacs at its best. It is too long to give in full, but I will summarize it and quote the most characteristic passages.

The last of the Tarquins is king, and the Romans are conducting a tedious siege against Ardea. While they are beguiling the time in talk, the king's son Sextus raises the question, 'Are we as dear to our wives as they are to us?', and a lively contest of wife-praising ensues over the wine, till Collatinus, the husband of Lucretia, proposes a simple solution:

> Up rose Collatia's namesake and its pride:
> 'Why bandy words? Believe your eyes!' he cried;
> 'Night lingers yet: to horse, and let's to Rome.'
> Agreed, they saddled horse and soon were home.
> There first they sought the royal residence.
> Without they found no guard in evidence;
> Within the princely matrons met their sight,
> Garlanded, wassailing the livelong night.
> Thence to Lucretia straight. Behold, she span,
> Baskets of wool in front of her divan.
> Her maids around by frugal lamplight plied
> Their stints allotted, while she softly cried:
> 'Come, hasten, girls: this cloak our hands have wrought
> Must to your master presently be brought.
> But what's the news? You can hear more than I.
> How much more fighting do they prophesy?
> Soon, Ardea, you to better men must bow:
> Wretched, why keep them absent from us now?
> Ah, safe return is all: for mine is rash
> And, sword in hand, through thick and thin will dash.
> I faint whene'er his image I behold
> Fighting, and in my heart my blood runs cold.'
> Tears drowned the rest; she dropped her stretchèd thread
> Of yarn and on her bosom sank her head.
> E'en this became her: tears lent virtue grace,
> And worthy of her heart appeared her face.
> 'Fear not; I've come!' her husband cried. She flung
> Her arms around his neck and cherished hung.

But Sextus meanwhile is fired with love for Lucretia, and not least by the challenge of her chastity. The young men return to the camp before Ardea, but he cannot get her out of his mind; ever fresh and pleasing images of her keep recurring; love continues to surge in his heart like a wave in the sea raised by a wind which has now dropped, and he begins to plot the rape. He mounts, and rides at sunset into Collatia.

> As friend this foe to Collatinus' hall
> Was welcomed: kinship made it natural.

Ah, human blindness! All unwitting she
Prepared a banquet for her enemy.
The feast was done, and sleep its hour claimed.
Night fell, and through the house no taper flamed.
He rose, and drew his gilded sword, and hied
Straight to the chamber of that innocent bride,
And kneeling on the bed, 'Lucretia', breathed,
''Tis I, Prince Tarquin, with my sword unsheathed!'
She nothing spake: she had no power to speak,
Nor any thought in all her heart to seek,
But trembled, as a lamb from sheepfold strayed,
Caught by a wolf, lies under him dismayed.
What could she do? Struggle? She could not win.
Cry out? His naked sword would intervene.
Escape? She felt his hands upon her breast,
Never before by hand unlawful pressed.
With prayers and bribes and threats he sought to assail:
No prayer or bribe or threat could aught avail.
'What use? I'll mingle death and calumny,
Rape, and accuse you of adultery;
A slave I'll kill, say you were caught in sin.'
Fear for her name prevailed, and she gave in.

Morning comes and she summons her father and husband from the camp. At first she cannot bear to tell them of her shame, but finally she forces herself. They forgive her, but she cannot forgive herself, and straightway stabs herself and dies. Brutus appears, and snatching the dagger from her body swears to avenge her. Her wound is shown to the people, and in fury they drive the Tarquins out of Rome.

This story was, of course, well known already: Livy had told it in his first book, and at times Ovid echoes his very words. But no prose could equal the swift economy of Ovid. How well he uses the figures of speech which were the rhetorician's stock-in-trade! In a scene so dramatic as this neither they nor even the occasional conceits seem forced. It is a masterpiece of writing, and no wonder the young Shakespeare was impressed.

CHAPTER IX

BANISHMENT: 'TRISTIA' I AND II

PURSUIT of the story of the *Fasti* down to the abortive revision has led me to anticipate. Before coming to the crisis of Ovid's life I must pick up the thread where I left it at the end of chapter I. By A.D. 8, when the *Metamorphoses* were virtually completed and the *Fasti* half completed, his brief marriage with his second wife had ended, whether through death or divorce, which was commoner at Rome than it is in Europe today and implied no stigma; and he had now been married for some time to a third, who proved as loyal to him, in success and in disaster, as he was devoted to her. She had a daughter, who married P. Suillius Rufus. He speaks also of his parents with warm affection, of whom his father had lately died a nonagenarian, followed by his mother. His daughter, twice married already, has had a child by each husband.

The nineteenth century, which to a large extent is still with us, dealt harshly with Ovid's character. It recognized no love that was not romantic, and it made 'morality' mean chiefly conventional sexual standards. For both these reasons the *Ars Amatoria* ('L'art d'aimer sans amour', as Ripert calls it) was naturally condemned, not to mention the *Amores*. Again, it was for the most part an age of piety, in which pagans who treated their religion with reverence earned more marks than those who did not, especially when, as in the case of Virgil, there were signs of a groping after monotheism and of a sympathy with speculations about human survival of death. Finally, it was an age of patriotism, and in Britain especially, of imperialism, so that enthusiasm for the beneficent power of Augustan Rome found a ready echo, and those who, like Ovid, were tardy in toeing the line did not obtain full credit. In fine, the Stoic type was at a premium, the Epicurean at a discount.

Let us admit immediately that Ovid could not be called a man of principle. He had a facility such as was encouraged at Rome by the prestige of the bar and by the declamation schools for maintaining whatever suited the purpose in hand; and no doubt he was irresponsible about the possible social effects of his earlier works. His generation, unlike that of Virgil and Horace, which came through the horrors of the Civil War, had grown up under the Pax Augusta, so that he took it and the endeavour that had gone to its making for granted. He had not the passion of a Lucretius for truth, nor any mission to redeem his fellow-men or to wrestle with the problems of metaphysics. But there are many people who, having all those virtues and offending no conventional code, are nevertheless immoral in the true sense of the word and unpleasant into the bargain. Let us scrutinize our values before we condemn Ovid's character. His salient characteristic was *humanitas*, humane good feeling akin to that charity without which, we are assured, all other qualities are as nothing.*

Again, though we have no evidence that he was a systematic thinker, he had a respect for the intellect. We have seen evidence of this in his deliberately making the clever Ulysses triumph over the stolid Ajax. He trusted in reason and spoke slightingly of augury and of superstitions such as belief in spells and witchcraft. Lucretius himself would have approved of his outburst against the idea of ritual purification from murder: 'Ah, men too lax, who think that the gloomy crime of murder can be washed away by river-water!' He must also have lived a life of intense and incessant intellectual activity, always reading and composing, a bee, not a butterfly. The Italian attitude of *dolce far niente* was not for him—'idleness is death to me'—nor did he care for gaming or even for the all-night drinking parties of Roman society, being, as he reminds a friend from exile, almost an abstainer.

As for beauty, we have had abundant evidence of his love of it as displayed in nature, especially where it is associated with peacefulness. In everything aesthetic he gives an impression of good taste. What he liked to see in women was *cultus*, which the French call *chic*, the opposite of *rusticitas*. This did not involve expensive adornment, as the vulgar

* It is a relief, after Victorian censoriousness, to turn back to Macaulay's summing up: 'He seems to have been a very good fellow; rather too fond of women; a flatterer and a coward; but kind and generous, and free from envy, though a man of letters sufficiently vain of his literary performances. The *Art of Love*, which ruined poor Ovid, is, in my opinion, decidedly his best work.'

imagined; the tasteful simplicity which made Horace's Pyrrha irresistible was his ideal. A touch of the hand can make or mar a coiffure; and what suits one woman may not suit another. As for men, they too should rely on *munditiess*—neatness and cleanliness both of person and dress. But what mattered most in both sexes was personality and character, the only sure basis of lasting affection. *Amabilis* was the word used by Seneca to describe Ovid's own showing in the oratorical schools: 'his style was elegant, neat and attractive'. His good taste extended into the sphere of conduct. How heartily one assents to the eloquent passage in which he adjures lovers not to boast of their experiences, or still worse, their fictitious experiences! More than once he asserts his belief in the civilizing power of love. Lovers are bound to each other only by the ties of love: 'in you love performs the office of law'. Unlike Propertius and Tibullus, he thinks constantly of the woman's point of view. He bids a man be chivalrous in forgetting, and helping her to forget, any blemishes she may have, especially if she is past her prime, and insists that in the act of love the woman should have equal pleasure with the man. Nor does he forget to put in a word for the lady's maid, so often ill-treated by her mistress in a fit of temper as she does her hair. And in a striking passage he pleads that, if love must end, it should fade decently with mutual goodwill, not explode in a quarrel or law-suit and leave rancour behind:

> To hate a girl once loved's a rank offence,
> An end more fit for beasts than men of sense.
> Indifference is enough: who ends in hate
> Loves still, or else will shed his misery late.
> Woman and man, now one, then foes straightway!
> 'Shame on *such* strife!' would even the Appian say.*
> The man who sues his girl may love her yet:
> Where there's no grudge, love fades and both forget.
> One for whom I was acting, while his wife
> Stayed in her litter, seethed with threats of strife;
> When his turn came to accuse her, 'Let her come
> Forth!' he exclaimed: she came, and he was dumb;
> Dropping his hands, dropping his tablets twin,
> He took her in his arms and cried 'You win!'

* Venus Appia, conceived as being accustomed to look down on the strife of the law-courts from her temple in the Forum Iulium.

> Surer and seemlier 'tis to part in peace
> Than sink from marriage-vows to court-decrees.
> Unchallenged let her all your gifts retain:
> A little loss is oft a greater gain.

So even the ostensibly cynical author of the *Amores*, *Ars* and *Remedia* sometimes betrays that he has really a heart; and when in the later poems he emerges in his own person, we find him a loved and loving husband and father. We are often warned, and as often forget, that Roman erotic poets did not expect their characters to be judged from their poetry.

Ovid's third wife was possibly by birth, and certainly by personality, a woman of some consequence, who had early won the approval and friendship of Augustus' aunt, the younger Atia, and paid court apparently in person to the Empress Livia. She was a member of the household of Paullus Fabius Maximus, in what capacity we cannot tell; she was at all events a beloved protégée of his wife, Marcia, the daughter of Atia. She had herself already a daughter by another husband when he married her, but was still quite young when he went into exile. His letters from exile contain many expressions of his love for her, and tributes to her devotion, loyalty and competence as guardian of their property.

Paullus Fabius was an influential noble, consul in 11 B.C. at the earliest age of eligibility. He provides an interesting link between Horace and Ovid. When Horace published the last book of his *Odes*, some time after 14 B.C., he placed first in it a wistful poem deprecating the renewal of Venus' assaults upon him now he is close on fifty. He bids her go revelling to the house of Paullus Maximus, who is ripe for love: for he is noble and good-looking and an eloquent pleader for anxious prisoners at the bar, and a young man of a hundred talents; he will carry far and wide the standards of her warfare. When she did finally triumph in the young man's marriage, it was his contemporary Ovid, already approved by him as a poet and perhaps already married to a member of his *entourage*, who composed the wedding hymn. Later Horace's phrase 'and not silent on behalf of wretched men in dock' was to wake a poignant echo, when the exile begged Paullus to plead with the Emperor for him: 'May your voice, I pray, soften for me the imperial ears, your voice so often an aid to trembling prisoners.'

But Ovid's first allegiance was to the house of his patron Messalla, on whose death he composed, only a few months before his banishment, the elegy to be recited in the Forum. Though a devoted adherent of Augustus, Messalla had resigned the new post of Prefect of the City after a few days and devoted himself thenceforward to the bar and the patronage of literature. His elder son, Messallinus, inherited his rhetorical talent; but though a few years younger than Ovid, he knew him only as one of his throng of clients, and the exile, when he seeks his support, is embarrassed by the recollection that he had not waited on him as often as he might profitably have done. But if Messallinus was to him remote 'as a Caesar', it was far otherwise with his brother, Cotta Maximus, who was some twenty years younger than the poet and was born after he had joined Messalla's circle. He was a gentle soul and a poet, whose generosity to poets was indeed proverbial to Juvenal nearly a century later. Ovid always addresses him with deep gratitude and affection, as here:

> Then were you moved by friendship's constancy,
> Which even before your birth began for me,
> Remembered you were born my friend, not made,
> And how I kissed you in your cradle laid,
> From youth devoted to your family—
> So old was your responsibility.
> Your noble father, Latin eloquence
> Incarnate, owning like pre-eminence
> In speech and birth, first bade me dare confide
> My verse to fame: he was my genius' guide.
> Your brother too will scarce remember now
> The distant day when first I made my bow.
> But you especially I did embrace:
> Whate'er befell, you were my only grace.

He had other patrons in high places whom he was to remember in time of need, including the wealthy Sextus Pompeius, consul in A.D. 14, last scion of the house of Pompey the Great; but, apart from Cotta and Fabius, his closest friends were naturally men of similar social status to himself, of whom we know nothing from elsewhere, particularly one Atticus, of whose companionship he gives a lively picture in recollection.

> Much of our time in serious talk we spent,
> Nor little, I recall, in merriment;

Often our converse made long hours fly;
Days were too short for my garrulity.
Often my latest song was read to you,
Your judgment sought upon some poem new;
What you had praised I deemed the world approved,
And this reward for guiding care you loved;
To make erasures your advice I took,
That a friend's file might polish up my book.
Together we appeared in squares and streets
And porticos and curving theatre's seats.

Of his less intimate friends some were naturally fellow-poets. From Macer, the companion of his youthful Grand Tour and indeed some connexion of his own wife, he had somehow drifted apart; but there remained others. Roman poets were by no means always free from jealousy, but from the very first Ovid shows generous enthusiasm for his colleagues. As a young man he looked up to his elders as gods. He speaks appreciatively of all the other elegists of that generation, and particularly of the dead and disgraced Gallus, to whom he insists on giving the benefit of the doubt—'if the charge of treachery to your friend is false'. From exile he asks the poets at home to drink his health, but only if he has deserved their favour by his kindness and done no harm to letters by any criticism, and if he has not fallen into the common fault of disparaging modern writers because of his reverence for the ancient. Of these moderns he gives a complimentary, and no doubt over-indulgent, list in his last Pontic Epistle. It would appear that there was a society of poets, and it has been suggested that *Tristia* IV, 3 reflects an annual custom of meeting at the Liberalia under the patronage of Bacchus, long recognized as an inspirer of poetry.

I have already indicated a certain analogy between the circle of Ovid and that of Oscar Wilde. The *Ars Amatoria* was not written in a vacuum; it was the reaction of a witty and high-spirited member of a sophisticated circle to a puritanical and sometimes hypocritical orthodoxy backed by power. Half the point would have been lost if there had been no respectable people to shock. But whereas Wilde was secure, so long as he did not break the law, because he risked only the disapproval of society, Ovid lived under a velvet-gloved despot who had personally initiated a not very successful campaign against sexual irregularity.

It is scarcely surprising that there is no evidence of a personal relationship between Ovid and the Emperor—if there had been one, he could hardly have failed to mention it in his appeals from exile. His early attachment had been to Messalla, and in any case Maecenas, who might have won him betimes for Augustanism, as he won the equally unpromising Propertius, and introduced him to Court, had fallen from grace in 23 and died in 8 B.C. The advances tardily made by the poet in the *Metamorphoses* and *Fasti* could not efface the strong impression of indifference or even contempt which the work of his first forty-five years had created, even though he was now without doubt the most famous and talented poet in the Empire. In face of the eulogies in Virgil and Horace of the hardy old Sabine way of life he had scoffed in the *Medicamina Faciei*:

> Old Sabine dames preferred at Tatius' date
> Their holdings, not themselves, to cultivate.

For himself, he rejoices that he has been born into a latter age of sophistication:

> Others may crave old times; thank God, I thrive
> In these: today 'tis bliss to be alive.

One wonders how the Emperor liked to read in the *Ars Amatoria* that his famous mock naval battle had been a splendid occasion for picking up foreign girls, or that the porticos dedicated by his sister in memory of Marcellus and by himself in honour of his wife were among the gallant's best hunting-grounds. Not that he would have minded about casual affairs with freedwomen; but despite the poet's repeated assurance that he was only concerned with this class, the greater part of the poem could apply equally well to wives of citizens, especially as the assumption is often made that the girl will have a *vir* who has first claim on her. Sometimes too Ovid seems to forget his disclaimers, as when he recommends the theatre as a place often fatal to chastity, refers to the intrigues he is facilitating as 'offence', 'fault', 'sinning', compares the married state adversely with free association, or assumes that even a bride can scarcely hope to enjoy her bridegroom for long without rivals, and that wives regularly deceive their husbands.

He was aware that the *Ars Amatoria* had provoked criticism in some quarters, but feeling secure in his profession that he was dealing only with freedwomen and in the applause of society, he castigated his critics with hybristic gusto in the *Remedia Amoris*:

> Let charming Elegy sing quivered Loves
> And lightly wanton as the spirit moves;
> Achilles in Callimachēan verse,
> Cydippe in Homeric—which is worse?
> Who could endure the offence, if in a play
> Andromache should Thaïs' part portray?
> My theme is Thaïs: here free love's supreme:
> No fillets here, for Thaïs is my theme;*
> If but my Muse this playful part sustain,
> I triumph, and my critics' charge is vain.
> Burst, Envy, burst: e'en now my name is great,
> Greater to be, so it maintain this rate.
> But stay! I hope to live to vex you more:
> My mind has many another song in store.
> For fame is sweet and honour spurs intent;
> My panting steed has scarce begun the ascent.
> Elegy owns a debt to me no less
> Than epic doth to Virgil's self confess.

That was written about A.D. 2, when Ovid was at the height of his popularity, and already Nemesis had her eye on Hybris. It was just about the time when the first book of the *Ars Amatoria* took Rome by storm that Augustus discovered that his daughter Julia was a notorious adulteress. It is hard to imagine a more devastating blow. He had made such a point of the sanctity of marriage, and himself sponsored the Julian Law on Adultery. And now his own daughter, the apple of his eye, had not only violated it, but done so in the most dignified of public places in Rome; and her paramours included Antonius Iullus, son of his old enemy Mark Antony and Fulvia, whom Octavia had induced him, with rare generosity, to bring up with the other children of the palace. He relegated Julia to the Isle of Pandataria, and banished her known adulterers, except for Iullus, who was driven to suicide. When he imagined the mocking *Schadenfreude* of fashionable society, he could hardly help thinking of it as crystallized and perpetuated in the *Ars Amatoria*, now on everyone's lips. For the moment he took no action against Ovid, whereas he might have deprived him of his

* The fillet was the badge of respectable women. Thaïs, the famous Athenian courtesan who went on Alexander's expedition to the East, here typifies her class.

knighthood at the periodical review of the knights; but for some years he brooded, and it is possible that the extravagant flatteries of the *Fasti* and *Metamorphoses* were motivated by palpable grounds for anxiety.

A second blow fell in A.D. 8. Augustus found that Julia's daughter, also called Julia, was in her turn committing adultery. Her paramour, Junius Silanus, went into voluntary exile on being declared no longer *persona grata*, and she herself was banished to the island of Trimerus off Apulia. But these penalties were light compared with the doom that fell upon Ovid at this time. For nearly two thousand years men have been speculating on the cause. No new evidence is likely to come to light, and the poet himself remains our sole authority, so all we can do is to steer clear of wild imaginings and support what seems the most plausible conjecture.

It is probable that the *Ars Amatoria* was the true as well as the official cause. Fourteen times Ovid speaks of his poetry as being responsible for his downfall, on four occasions specifying the *Ars*. Incensed at his continued failure to reform society, Augustus chose the most obvious representative ('I was found') of what he wished to crush, and made him a scapegoat in a most public and extreme way. The 'error' to which Ovid recurs even more often, and round which the curiosity of later ages has buzzed, was probably only the occasion. A long chain of circumstances had led to his being present and accidentally witnessing something culpable. His offence was shameful, but not heinous. He attributes it to *simplicitas*—naïveté,* aggravated afterwards by what he has to call timidity (which may simply have been a decent disinclination to tell tales). Yet although, if he could explain all, his guilt would be seen to have been trifling, for reasons he cannot explain he must forbear even long after to go into details. It was natural that the Emperor should resent his error, but he had meant no harm and broken no law.

Since all must be obscure because Ovid intended it to remain so, let us not waste many words where too many have been wasted down the ages. There are only two theories that deserve mention, though each

* He uses the obvious parallel of punishment for an unintentional offence: 'unwittingly Actaeon saw Diana unclothed'. This led to the crowning absurdity, the theory that he was banished for accidentally seeing the Empress in her bath.

has variations. One is that the poet became involved in the dynastic tension between the Julians and the Claudians. The former were represented by Agrippa Postumus, son of Agrippa and the elder Julia, whose ill-temper, which disqualified him for succession, had been aggravated by indiscretion resulting in his banishment in A.D. 7; the ageing Emperor is reputed to have continued to nurse an affection for him. The latter were represented by Tiberius, son of the Empress Livia, adopted in A.D. 4 by Augustus and made heir apparent. Ovid's offence might have been that he became involved with the cause of Agrippa, perhaps through Paullus Fabius Maximus, and so offended Livia. But it is hard to imagine in that case how his offence could have been, as he so often asserts, to have *seen* something wrong. In any case he had long since withdrawn, almost ostentatiously, from public interests.

The second theory is that Ovid became undesignedly an accessory to Julia's adultery. It has the advantage of establishing a connexion with the other charge, concerning the *Ars Amatoria*, and so accounting psychologically for the surprising savagery of the Emperor; for the poem had gone unpunished for some eight years, and it is clear that the other offence, however misconstrued, was not in itself sufficient to warrant so extreme a penalty, being one of complicity rather than action and not a legal crime. Ovid makes it clear that the *Gens Iulia* was involved: 'Such is your family feeling for all who bear the Julian name that you think yourself injured when any member of it is injured.' Either of the theories would square with that; my own inclination is towards the second.

When the storm burst Ovid was on Elba, with Cotta Maximus. Rumours soon reached the Island, and he was questioned by his young friend and patron. In a touching passage written long afterwards from exile he recalls the scene to him:

> Aethalian Elba last saw me with you,
> Whose soil my tears of misery did bedew.
> When you demanded whether the report
> Was true, that evil rumour of me brought,
> Half I denied yet half did I confess,
> And wavered, fear betraying my distress;
> And as when watery Auster melts the snow,
> Down my numb cheek a welling tear did flow.

Cotta was angry at first, but Ovid claims to have heard that the anger turned to sympathy when he learnt the full story of his 'error'; he was one of the first to send him a letter of consolation and raise his hopes that Augustus might relent; and he even (if, as seems probable, he is the addressee of *Tristia* IV, 5) undertook to finance him in the event of his property being confiscated.

There could be no question of a public hearing: one charge was too general and the other too embarrassing for such treatment. Ovid was summoned to appear before the Emperor who, after delivering a stern rebuke, issued an edict that, being guilty of *maiestas* (degradation of the national dignity or insult to the imperial family), he was to retire to Tomis. Technically his punishment was *relegatio*, not the severer *exilium*, though he sometimes loosely calls it exile; he thus retained his property and civic rights, but in other respects the penalty was crushing. Tomis, in Moesia, was a bleak outpost on the Black Sea, at the site of the modern Constanza, insecurely held against the barbarians of the steppes. We may gather that he was given no opportunity of publicly stating his case, and the result was unfortunate for him as for us, at least as regards the second charge, which he himself conceived to be the chief. Instead of getting it out of his system, he spent the rest of his life in chewing it over, unable to turn to fresh pabulum. The necessity of concealing the details of his 'error' drove him to the futile alleviation of dropping hint after hint.

His poems were removed from the public libraries, and though no steps were taken against privately owned copies, such censorship had been most unusual in Rome. With regard to these he had a case that could be openly stated, but it was based on general principles and required time and leisure for its organization. It reached Rome towards the first summer of his exile as Book II of the *Tristia*, a single poem 578 lines long addressed to Augustus. It is a 'backstairs' speech for the defence, all the more elaborate and effective for being matured after the event. Though written afterwards, perhaps on the voyage to Tomis, it bears on the time of the edict, when ideally it should have been delivered, so that we may properly anticipate and deal with it here.

It is duly arranged according to the principles of the rhetorical schools. The first part (1–210) is servile in tone. The poet reproaches himself with being, in Wilde's phrase, 'the spendthrift of my own genius', and his pleas are pathetic conceits: If I had not sinned, Caesar, what would you have had to pardon? My plight has given you an opportunity of showing mercy. And so on. For all its eloquence this *probatio* repels us by its abjectness, though it derives a certain interest from the incidental information it gives about the nature of the poet's previous life, his sentence and its cause. With the *refutatio* a remarkable change comes over the poem. We all know how hard it is, when we are indignant and wish to get a decision reversed, to imagine the reactions of the person to whom we are appealing and address him with tact and moderation that may have some chance of achieving the desired end, giving him an opportunity to save his face, refraining from putting him in the wrong or making him feel foolish. How irresistible is the temptation to let ourselves go, making the most of our case and scoring every conceivable point! To this temptation Ovid now yielded, vainly imagining that a seasoning of gross flattery would counteract the effect; and at this distance our anxiety at the harm he risks doing thereby to his own fortunes is overcome by our delight at seeing the old Ovid re-emerge from the wastes of the Dobruja to discomfort his not invulnerable oppressor. He may even have fondly believed at this time that his cause might be helped if he appealed over the Emperor's head to public opinion.

Leaving out most of the flattery, his gist is as follows. There are two offences, 'poem and error'. I must not reopen your wounds by dealing with the latter, but will defend myself against the charge of encouraging adultery by my *Ars Amatoria*. Even divine minds can sometimes be mistaken; they have so much else to think about, without reading what is only intended as fun. If you had ever had time to do so, you would have found my *Ars* innocuous, if frivolous. It counsels nothing illegal, being concerned only with lawful affairs with courtesans, as I made clear in four lines of Book I.

Ovid now proceeds to answer criticisms severally:

> 'But wives can emulate the not so pure
> And learn, though not addressed, the art to allure.'
> Then let a wife read nothing, for there is
> No poem but can tutor her amiss:

Whate'er she touch, if she be bent on sin,
She'll find encouragement to vice therein:
Opening the Annals (what could be more stern?),
The cause of Ilia's motherhood she'll learn;
Beginning 'Mother of Aeneas' race',
She'll ask how Venus came to have that place.*

Nothing benefits that cannot also do harm. My poem can harm no one, if it is read in the right frame of mind. But supposing it could: by the same token you must condemn all sorts of innocent places used for assignations, and also temples, where one is constantly reminded of the gods' adulteries, including your own Mars Ultor.

But grant it: are not our dramatic shows
Suggestive too? Then every theatre close.
Many must answer for liaisons planned
While gladiators battle on their sand.
The Circus is a snare—away with it!—
For there strange men beside a girl may sit.
Should colonnades be open, just the place
Where women keen to meet a lover pace?
Temples are holy ground, but let her fly
Even from these, who tends to lechery:
Standing in Jupiter's, she will recall
The women Jupiter made mothers all;
Near by in Juno's worshipping, reflect
How Juno grieved her rivals to detect;
At sight of virgin Pallas, ask why she
Reared Erichthonius, child of infamy;
In Mars the Avenger's, your own gift, behold
Venus with Mars, her husband in the cold.†

After all it is no crime, he continues, to read amorous verses; pure women may read of many things they must not do, just as severe matrons and Vestals often see prostitutes exposed naked, yet brothel-keepers are not prosecuted.

'But why is your book excessively wanton, and why does it en-

* The *Annals* of Ennius, a pattern of rugged ('hirsute') virtue, included the seduction by Mars of Ilia, the mother of Romulus and Remus. The *De Rerum Natura* of Lucretius begins, 'Forebear of the sons of Aeneas..., Venus', Aeneas being Venus' son by her liaison with Anchises.

† Venus, as ancestress of the Julian house, had a place of honour by Mars in Augustus' new temple, while her husband Vulcan's statue apparently stood outside the door. Ovid mischievously adduces the notorious intrigue of Mars and Venus.

courage *anyone* to love?' I admit the criticism, but not the implication that I should rather have written epic or panegyric, for which I am unsuited. I should have feared to treat of your own deeds, in case I could not do them justice. You think I instructed wives in adultery, but I never addressed them, and indeed I have no knowledge of the subject, having never been under suspicion of that crime. No one should judge my character or any poet's from what he writes.

Ovid then embarks on a list of all the famous poets of love whose work has gone unpunished, a list which acquires a touch of irony from its similarity to the eulogistic roll in *Amores* I, 15, and is, as usual with him, too long because he cannot resist bringing in everyone. 'These', he concludes, 'stand on the open shelves mingled with great works of literature, made available to the public by the generosity of our leading citizens.'* Moreover there have been many Roman writers equally wanton. Catullus' verse openly admitted his adultery; and, on the other hand, who could be such a warrant of immunity as the highly respected Hortensius or Servius? Sisenna had translated the lascivious tales of Aristides without penalty, and Gallus suffered, not for celebrating Lycoris, but for not holding his tongue when drunk. As for Tibullus, he devotes a great deal of attention to hoodwinking his mistress's husband, and Propertius is similar. (Ovid characteristically underlines his refusal to mention names of living poets—not that it would be beyond Augustus' wit to think of appropriate ones.) But all have been spared, both in life and libraries, save him alone.

He turns next to those who have written with impunity on games of hazard. It is true that technically these were forbidden, except at the Saturnalia or for old men, and Horace in one of his more censorious odes refers to 'illegal dicing'; but the law was already becoming a dead letter, as such laws are apt to do. Why does Ovid make so much of it? Partly, one may guess, because he enjoyed the mental gymnastic of bringing the various games into verse; but partly also because Augustus was known to be so keen a player.

Suppose he had written mimes, he continues. These are all about

* Asinius Pollio started the first public library at Rome in 39 B.C., and Augustus included a public library in the precincts of his shrine of Palatine Apollo; Ovid's bitterness at the removal of his books from them is natural, but his way of expressing it was hardly calculated to convert the Emperor.

adultery, very indecent and very popular. Praetors pay high prices to put on 'such scandals', and nor merely praetors:

> Augustus, scan your sums on games defrayed:
> High prices for such shows you've often paid,
> Watched them in person and produced them free
> (So genial ever is your majesty),
> And with those eyes that all the world engage
> Smiled at adulteries upon the stage.

Indeed his own poems have been performed as mimes, and sometimes before the Emperor. Even the fortunate, favoured Virgil in his youth wrote of Phyllis and Amaryllis, and the most popular part of the *Aeneid* is that in which (irreverent phrase!)

> Arms and the man were put to Dido's bed.

Why should he now be punished for juvenilia, especially as he has written major works since then which are full of tokens of his loyalty? Having attacked no one, he divines that no one at Rome is glad of his troubles and many are sorry. In conclusion, he pleads that his penalty be mitigated so as to be commensurate with his error.

This *refutatio* is rather patchy and cavalier as a defence, if the charge is taken seriously. To tell someone not to read a book is to ensure that she reads it, whomever it claims to be intended for, and there is little difference between the technique of 'legitimate love' and that of adultery. The fact that Penelope was a wedded wife did not prevent Ovid from citing her as an illustration in the *Ars*. As for the contention that even the most solemn and approved works might suggest adultery, one cannot seriously maintain that to salute Venus as 'forebear of Aeneas' sons' is in the same class as an incentive to, or sanction for, adultery as the *Ars Amatoria*. To the assertion that the latter has in fact corrupted certain matrons Ovid opposes a simple denial. Such accusations are seldom easy to substantiate. It cannot be denied that books have on occasion led to deeds:

> Galeotto fu il libro e chi lo scrisse;

but how often, and in what circumstances, and with what kinds of character? Ovid has an answer to the last question at least: 'perverse minds will be corruptible by anything'. But though 'to the pure all things are pure' sounds a conclusive motto, it does not square entirely with human nature. On the other hand, though a colonnade may be a convenient place for an assignation, there are other places nearly as good, and to allow is not the same as to encourage. As for the argument about the suggestivity of temples due to the legends told of the gods, it is on a par with that about the opening of the *De Rerum Natura*.

When he proceeds to deal with the question why his Muse has 'too much wantonness' and why it encourages anyone at all to love, it may well be that he is introducing a charge never strictly made, in order to broaden the basis of his defence. He cannot deny it, but he can rope in everyone else as equally guilty or more so, and thus make it seem that he is being unfairly singled out. There was hardly a great man in recent Roman history to whom indecent verses were not ascribed, let alone the famous Greek and Roman poets of the past. His excursus on Tibullus as an advocate of adultery is slightly disingenuous, since the word *coniunx* in his elegies need not mean a husband, *maritus*, but merely, as K. F. Smith says, 'the man who at the time happens to be furnishing the mistress of the elegiac lover with a house door'; and Ovid was surely aware of this. The games of hazard are a red herring. On the other hand, the final plea, that he is being punished for an offence committed too long ago, has force, to our way of thinking.

The whole rebuttal is more akin to satire in spirit than to anything else. The case against Ovid rested on degree; the *Ars Amatoria* was in a class by itself because of its exclusive and expressed intention, its scope and its shamelessness. His reply depends largely on mischievous and fantastic disregard of degree; it is a riotous *reductio ad absurdum*, and what is meant to seem absurd is the attitude of the Emperor. It must have been all the more discomfiting because of the personal record of that upholder of the sanctity of the marriage tie, on which the poet could hardly touch. In his youth, having fallen in love with Livia, he had forced her devoted husband to surrender her, though she was pregnant; and later he had, for dynastic ends, made first Agrippa and then Tiberius divorce a wife to marry his daughter Julia. Suetonius says that even his friends excuse rather than deny his adulteries, though we must be duly suspicious of the examples he quotes. Various writers mention him as author of indecent verses (Martial quotes an alleged specimen), and indeed he would have been exceptional if, at least in his younger days, he had not followed this fashion. Ovid may have gone further than others in the *Ars Amatoria*, but his surprise at the reaction is perfectly understandable. He was a real scapegoat, a vicarious expiator of the sins of others as well as a conspicuous warning. There may well be justice in Aurelius Victor's remark in this connexion, that Augustus was 'a most severe punisher of vice, in accordance with the way of men, which makes them be harsh in punishing those vices in which they themselves most freely indulge'.

A time limit was set for Ovid's remaining in Italy, and he stayed till the last moment, paralysed into inaction while others bustled around him. Many supposed friends avoided contagion with him, but a few were notably loyal, and if he ever seriously thought of suicide, a friend talked him out of it. Some of his slaves were to go with him (we hear nothing of their feelings about this, and should be surprised if we did). His wife begged and begged to accompany him, but it was essential that she should remain to keep the home together and work for his return. The famous poem recalling his last night in Rome sounds as sincere as anything he wrote. It has hardly a trace of the old artificialities. Instead of the piled-up parallels we have three isolated and passing references—one to the desolation of the last night of Troy, limned for ever by Virgil in everyone's imagination; and that is all, in over a hundred lines. More significant, there is hardly a trace of straining after epigram or point. It is a sincere and vivid record of a poignant personal experience, a thing rare in ancient poetry, except on the subject of love or death, though Cicero's Letters offer us counterparts in prose. It is too long to quote in full, but a short selection may convey its quality:

The day drew near when Caesar's firm decree
Compelled me leave the bounds of Italy.
Nor time nor spirit had I to prepare:
My mind was atrophied by long despair.
Of slaves, of company I took no heed,
Or clothes or comfort for an exile's need,
But stunned I was, like one by lightning hit
Who lives but yet is unaware of it.
When pain at length itself had cleared my brain
And all my senses were restored again,
I said my last farewells to one or two—
Of all those former friends alas how few!

My loving wife wept loud in our embrace,
Tears undeserved ran streaming down her face.
My daughter, somewhere far on Libya's shore,
Could not be told about my fate in store.
From every side laments and groans arose,
Filling the house as with funereal woes:
In every corner men and women all
And children wept at this my funeral.
If little things to great we may compare,
Troy's aspect on her fatal night was there.

Then follows one of those touches of vivid imagination that suddenly lift Ovid's verse on to an altogether higher plane:*

At last all noise of men and dogs was still.
The moon was driving high o'er heaven's hill.
I looked at her and, silhouetted plain,
The Capitol, our neighbour all in vain:
'Divinities whose fanes we dwell beside
And temples I shall never see', I cried,
'Gods of Quirinus' city reared of yore,
Hail and farewell for ever, ever more....'

It is true that the image serves a practical purpose, to enlist the all-seeing gods of the Capitol to intercede with the new god of the Palatine, who has been misled; but who can doubt, in this case at least, that the poet had really seen that vision of the Capitol with its temples outlined in the moonlight, towering above his home? The stars revolved, and night sped on relentlessly; did Ovid, like Marlowe's Faustus recall with poignant irony on that last night the prayer in his youthful *aubade* of love—'run slowly, horses of Night'? The whole house was in mourning, the symbolic fire before the Lares extinguished. He tried to tear himself away from so much that was dear to him, and snatched at any pretext for delay. His wife was distracted, and when she pleaded once more to accompany him, 'I will be but a small additional burden to the ship of exile', we hear again, and perhaps are meant to hear, an ironic echo of Briseïs in the *Heroides* begging to be taken too if Achilles sails away from Troy. His last thought is of her, how he saw her behaving then, and how he heard she had behaved after he left.

* Goethe, on his last night in Rome, paced the Colosseum in the moonlight declaiming this passage.

Ovid was forced to sail, probably from Brindisi, in November, at a time of year when sailing was by no means safe or comfortable. The events of the voyage are told in the first book of the *Tristia*, which seems to have been sent to Rome soon after his arrival at Tomis. He assures us in the Epilogue (XI) that he composed on shipboard, even in the midst of storms. Granted that he may have made phrases in his head, and even jotted them down, in such conditions, we should take this claim with a drop of salt water. The poems are ingeniously constructed; they average 67 lines apiece; and II, which is ostensibly written at the height of a storm, extends to 110. Here the threatening waves serve in fact not only to arouse pity for his state, but as a metaphor for it and a text for reflexions on it. Certainly these descriptions, even if inspired by emotion recollected in tranquillity, are none the less vivid for that. Ovid brings before our eyes the slow, huge, relentless alternation of billow and trough. Yet the reflexions are the *raison d'être* of the poem. He begins by begging the gods of the elements not to abet but to mitigate the wrath of the god who has punished him. The complaint that the wind and waves will not let his prayer be heard leads into a description of the storm designed to emphasize his sufferings, and pity is heightened by his thoughts of his wife, the half of his life, bitterly bewailing his banishment without realizing that he has any more trouble than that. The sky thunders, and increases his terror; it is not so much death he fears as the horror of drowning in that terrible sea. He then turns to thoughts of his deserts. If Caesar has spared his life, the gods of the elements should concur; he could himself have drowned him, had he wished. Yet if his life is spared now, what sort of a life remains for him? He contrasts the pleasure of his youthful voyage, to study at Athens and visit the cities of Asia, with the bleak prospect of Tomis, and does not know what to pray for. He resolves to submit, acknowledges his fault while protesting his innocence in intention, and outlines the plea he was later to develop as the *probatio* in *Tristia* II. Finally he sees, or thinks he sees, signs that the gods have heard and the storm is abating. With considerable finesse he has woven themes suggested by the storm into an appeal to Caesar.

No. IV describes more briefly a storm in the Ionian Sea which with pathetic irony drives the ship back into sight of Italy and threatens to cast the exile back on the forbidden shores of his native land. Once again, the appeal is to pity, the description only a means to it.

Nos. X and XI enable us to trace the wintry voyage. From Italy the ship crossed to Greece and went up the gulf to Corinth, putting in at its western port of Lechaeum. Thence Ovid traversed the isthmus to Cenchreae and embarked on another ship, which crossed the Aegean by the stepping-stones of the Cyclades, and so reached the Hellespont. From there it made a diversion to Samothrace, where he left it to pursue its voyage to the Black Sea without him. 'The sea', says Euripides' Iphigeneia, 'washes away all the troubles of men.' Ovid seems to have become attached to this ship, with its image of Pallas, the patroness of poets, and the valediction he wrote to it, suggested by Catullus' poem on his yacht, which had made the same voyage in a happier direction, is almost serene:

> A painted helmet gives my ship her name.
> Pallas, her guardian, guard her still the same!
> Sailing, she runs before the lightest breeze;
> Driven with oars, she makes her way with ease;
> And not content her comrades to outstrip,
> She overtakes the long-departed ship.
> Both waves and calm expanse of ocean well
> She cleaves, and ships no water in a swell.
> I met her first at Corinth's Cenchreae;
> Guide and companion of my exile she
> Through thick and thin, though windswept billows chafe,
> Under Minerva's aegis has been safe.
> Still safe may she the Black Sea gateway cleave,
> And on the Getic coast her goal achieve.

The landsman had apparently, however, had enough of the sea. He preferred the short passage from Samothrace to the mainland opposite and the land journey across Thrace. He later recalled with gratitude that the wealthy Sextus Pompeius had, to save his purse, thoughtfully provided him with means of protection for this journey through bandit-ridden territory. It is possible that he re-embarked on the other side; the Epilogue at least affects to be written in a storm, and there are indications that it may be on the Black Sea.

The rest of the book is composed of letters written to individuals, but it is intended for the ear of the general public, and of Augustus in particular, and each poem, directly or obliquely, enlists sympathy for the poet. Thus no. IX, congratulating a friend on some advancement, is a warning of how those whom prosperity attracts desert a man in adversity, and an appeal for continued fidelity, which Caesar himself would surely approve on principle. No. VII is to his publisher, who has told him that he wears his likeness, the head crowned with the Bacchic ivy of poetic inspiration, engraved on the stone of a ring. In thanking him Ovid commends to him a still better image of himself—his poems, particularly the *Metamorphoses*, happily preserved from his own despairing rage, which will keep his memory green at Rome. That was the most important thing; at all costs he must not simply be forgotten. But he was also anxious for his readers to know that the work is unrevised. In the central position, *honoris causa*, is no. VI, to his wife, who alone can enlist friends to protect the family fortunes against the designs of a sinister 'someone', a letter full of trust and affection. Even this has one eye on the Palatine, for he suggests that her uncommon virtue comes from association with the Empress. By way of contrast to VIII, a denunciation of a faithless friend, no. V is to one who had given him the first word of kindness in his downfall, and so the will to go on living; the calamity has at least had this good result—without it he would never have known the extent of that loyalty. The second half of this poem is an exhaustive comparison of his lot with that of Ulysses, showing how on every count he is worse off. This defeats its own end; we find ourselves congratulating him on each new point he wins in this odd contest of rivalry. But the opening lines are a simple expression of gratitude and affection, flowing on freely over the bounds of the couplets and so doubly reminiscent of the sincerity of Catullus:

> Friend whom no friend for me will e'er dethrone,
> Who most have felt my trouble as your own,
> Dearest, who first dared speak and comfort me,
> I well remember, in my agony,
> And gently wooed me life again to try
> When my poor spirit only yearned to die,
> Unnamed, you know by tokens whom I so
> Address, and what you did for me you know.
> Deep in my heart I'll keep remembrance due,
> And always I shall owe this life to you;

Yea, this my breath shall into air expire
Leaving my body on the smouldering pyre,
Ere time the memory of your kindness blot
And your devotion be at last forgot.
To you may kindly heaven such fortune send,
Unlike to mine, as needs no helping friend;
Yet if a favouring gale still wafted me,
Should I have ever known that loyalty?

'Where there is sorrow there is holy ground.' One is reminded of that man, who likewise had to be anonymous, mentioned in *De Profundis*, who raised his hat to Wilde as he passed handcuffed down a crowded corridor after his condemnation.

These five poems, nos. V–IX, are a cross-section of the verse Ovid was to write henceforward. It is something that he could write at all, that his Muse was maimed rather than murdered, and he tells us of the wonder and relief he felt when he found that, even amid the surge of the sea and of his troubles, his genius was still alive. His conclusion is charming:

The storm, indignant that I dare to write
For all its menaces, pursues the fight.
To storm I'll yield—on terms of armistice,
That this my song and it together cease.

So, with a touch of his old wit, he ended his Epilogue; and to round off the book he added a very skilful Prologue, giving instructions to the volume itself, which, albeit in the garb of mourning, plain and unadorned, can at least enter the city. By this engaging device he was able without offence to make an oblique appeal to the Emperor. This carefully arranged plea for pity he despatched, perhaps accompanied by Book II, as soon as he arrived at Tomis.

CHAPTER X

'TRISTIA' III–V, 'IBIS', 'EPISTULAE EX PONTO'

THE eighty-four elegiac epistles which Ovid sent home from exile after *Tristia* II range from 22 to 166 lines in length, and fill seven books (i.e. rolls—*libelli*) averaging about 750 lines each. In the *Tristia*, apart from his wife, the girl Perilla, and members of the imperial family, he does not name those he addresses for fear of doing them harm by advertising their association with him. Modern scholars have tried to identify them where there is any hint of a clue. It seems fairly sure, indeed, that IV, 4 and 5 are to Messallinus and Cotta respectively, and perhaps the association of the poet with Messalla's house was too well known to call for more than a perfunctory concealment. But it is significant, for instance, that in seventeen cases where Lorentz ventured to supply a name Némethy either did not venture or supplied a different one, and in the only case where they did agree they seem to be wrong.

The *Letters from the Black Sea* (*Epistulae ex Ponto*) follow hard on the heels of the *Tristia*, and differ from them, as the poet himself avows, only in that they no longer conceal the recipients' names. To a friend who is represented as having demurred to this publicity he protests that he had himself offended previously in crediting the Emperor with so little humanity as to suppose that he would persecute those who comforted an exile. (Perhaps he had received a hint.) There is a curious passage, probably addressed to Cotta, in which Ovid exclaims: 'In my enthusiasm I almost let out your name! But in any case you will recognize yourself, and fired with desire for honour would fain cry openly, "I am that man".' This is a strangely inappropriate conceit if we are to suppose that the poem was sent to the recipient personally. Yet it is natural to assume that each poem addressed to an individual would be so sent, not kept in cold storage till the poet had enough of them by him to fill a volume; and in the case of the *Pontic Epistles* he tells us that this was in fact so. But each was intended also for circulation, as the occasional intrusion of *vos* or *o lector* sufficiently testifies. And finally, each was intended for the imperial eye. Even in an invective against a detractor Ovid contrives to glance at Augustus' clemency and his certainty of apotheosis, and few of the poems have no reference to him.

About once a year between A.D. 8 and 13 he made up a book of these elegies. In the books of the *Tristia* he arranged them, not chronologically, as a modern poet might do, but on principles of variety and symmetry such as we find operating in other ancient collections of poems. The dates emerge as follows:

A.D.	*Tristia*
8–9	I
9	II
9–10	III
10–11	IV
11–12	V

The decision to mention his friends by name so stimulated Ovid's Muse that by the end of A.D. 13 he had enough *Pontic Epistles* (30) to fill three rolls. These he caused to be published together, arranging them in no special order and consigning them in a prologue and epilogue to his friend Brutus. The poems in Book IV that can be dated fall between 13 and 16. Since it contains some 200 lines more than the others and, unlike them, has no prologue, it is presumed that they were collected and published after the poet's death in 17–18.

If we may believe Ovid, he sometimes had fits of rage or despair in which he burnt what he had written, as he had done on the eve of his exile. But just as the *Metamorphoses* had survived that holocaust so, he claims, it is relics saved 'by chance or stealth' from the flames that are preserved in these books. He may, of course, only be trying to shock his readers by the thought of such losses to Latin literature, as one more stimulus for his recall; but there is nothing surprising psychologically if what he says is true. At all events, the surviving poems average one for every month. For all his facility, he did not now find writing easy. He had no books to nourish his Muse, no privacy, no one to consult when at a loss for a word or name of person or place, no friendly circle of poets to listen and criticize, no audience to spur him with applause: 'to write a poem you may not read to anyone is like dancing in the dark'. Nor had he now a succession of new experiences, such as had diversified the first book of the *Tristia*, and obsession with his wrong precluded his seeking any. As time went on he felt that his genius, living on capital, was drying up; and even so fastidious an artist found eventually that he had no longer the zest to face the labour of amending faults in his verse which he clearly recognized. Why cast pearls before the Getae?

Whatever gleams of reviving spirits flickered in Ovid as his voyage proceeded, they were rudely quenched by the realities that confronted him on his arrival at Tomis. The Emperor had doubtless chosen the place because it was as far as possible from Rome; but he could not have chosen better if his object was to break the spirit of one who had thrived on the comfort and the pleasures of a brilliant capital. Ovid's charity or discretion preferred to suppose that he simply did not realize what he was doing. Here was no frontier-fort built and garrisoned by the Romans, but an old Milesian colony which had no doubt seen better days, existing because it was the only port on a desolate coast, and sustained partly by fisheries, partly perhaps by the passage of goods from ships that would have entered the Danube but for delta-silt. It had no mineral wealth, and the only product the poet could find worth sending to Rome as a present was a quiverful of arrows. Brackish lagoons afforded distasteful and unhealthy water, carried in jars on women's heads, to one who had been used to the clear hill-streams that flowed through aqueducts into the fountains of Rome. Nor were there vines to produce so much as a *vin ordinaire*; indeed, marauders allowed little cultivation at all around the town; there was a certain amount of grazing, though the women had not learnt how to work or dye the coarse wool; for the rest, wormwood scrub and an occasional barren tree were all the vegetation on the vast no-man's-land of steppes that, with the leaden sea, extended to the horizon on all sides.*

* The coasta lagoons are formed by Danube silt moving southward. Before the Dobruja was taken over by the Rumanians in 1878 most of it was, as in Ovid's day, uncultivated steppe covered with brushwood, with frequent marshes that made it unhealthy (*Guide Bleu*, 1933, p. 6).

In lines familiar to schoolboys Ovid has depicted the scene:

> Snow lies, and ere it melt in sun or rain
> Comes Boreas and hardens it again;
> Ere one dissolves, another fall is here,
> In many a place to lie from year to year;
> And Aquilo such fury can display,
> 'Twill level towers and carry roofs away.
> Breeches and furs keep out the cruel cold:
> No feature but the face can one behold.
> Icicles tinkle when men shake their hair,
> And rough beards glister with the rime they wear.
> Stark stands the wine, the wine-jar's shape preserved,
> And from it chunks instead of draughts are served.
> What of the rivers bound in icy bonds,
> And brittle water quarried out of ponds?
> Danube himself, who mingles with the sea
> Wide as the Nile through many mouths as he,
> Feels his blue waters by the wind congealed
> And creeps to ocean with his flow concealed.
> Men cross on foot where ferries lately plied,
> And horse-hooves echo o'er the frozen tide,
> While on new bridges o'er the flood's domains
> Sarmatian oxen haul outlandish wains.

Even the Black Sea was liable to freeze near the coast, and everything from fish to ships became ice-bound. (Provoked by rumours that his readers at Rome are sceptical about this, Ovid launches into a discourse on the reasons: the prevailing wind is north-east, with no relief from the mild south-west; the great rivers pour into the almost land-locked sea fresh water which, being lighter than salt water, rises to the surface.) No wonder the poet's health suffered. During his first winter he fell ill, and there were no suitable quarters for him, no medical attention or proper diet, no pure water, no one to talk to. Next winter he is ill again, and doubtful of recovery; a year later he is suffering from pains in the side (? pleurisy) which he attributes to the cold. Later, fearing he may have caused undue alarm by his account of his health, he reassures his wife; he has become inured in body, though not in mind. Indeed, he is aware that his illness is largely due to psychological causes. He has no taste for his food, even when he is not actually ill, and meal times bring him no pleasure; at night he suffers from feverish insomnia, and from sheer fretting he has become emaciated and prematurely old. His own wife would scarcely recognize him now.

The freezing of the sea and of the Danube, thirty-five miles west-north-west at its nearest point, brought fear to aggravate the attendant cold. Dacian barbarians on horseback poured over these normal defences of the Empire to plunder:

So whether Boreas with bitter blast
Has gripped the sea or bound the river fast,
When dry North Winds have smoothed the Danube's back
Swiftly the mounted savages attack.
With horse and long-range archery supplied
The foe lays waste the country far and wide.
Some flee and leave their fields an open prey;
Their undefended wealth is driven away,
Poor country wealth such as a peasant has,
A creaking waggon and an ox or ass.
Some, caught and led away with pinioned arms,
Vainly look backward to their homestead farms;
Some, pierced by barbèd shafts, fall cruelly dead,
For poison clings to every arrowhead.
What cannot be removed is wrecked entire,
And harmless cottages are set on fire.

And it was not only Dacians taking such intermittent opportunities who were to be feared. The surrounding country was only half pacified. While Tomis and the other towns of Greek origin were self-governing outposts, under Roman law and subject to the distant jurisdiction of the Governor of the province of Macedonia, the hinterland was an outlying part of the half-controlled dominions of the Kingdom of Thrace, a satellite of the Empire. Ovid gives us a vivid picture of the constant state of emergency:

Unnumbered tribes around hold us at bay,
Who count it shameful not to live on prey.
Naught's safe without; even the fortress-height
Has puny walls to reinforce its site.
When least you think, like birds, a flock of foes
Swoops down and, scarcely sighted, robs and goes.
Often within the bolted gates' retreat
We pick up poisoned arrows in the street.

Few, then, dare till the soil, and they must farm
One hand on plough, the other on their arm;
Helmeted pipes the shepherd, and instead
Of wolves, his sheep marauding warriors dread.

And again: In youth I shunned all horrid martial fray,
Nor ever handled arms except in play:
Now, middle-aged, a shield and sword I bear,
And press a helmet on my grizzled hair.
For when the look-out raises the alarm,
We haste at once our trembling hands to arm;
Ere long on panting horse the savage foe
Circles the walls with poisoned shaft and bow.
And as a ravening wolf through wood, o'er wold,
Bears, drags a sheep surprised without the fold,
So any man caught ere he can regain
The gates' defence is by the invader ta'en;
Then either, neck in halter, as a prize
Is led, or by a poisoned weapon dies.

The savage horsemen battered at the gate, and their arrows stuck bristling on the thatched roofs of the houses inside. No wonder Ovid dared not venture much outside, though he would have liked to kill time by his old recreation of gardening. Even within the precarious fortifications he felt none too safe. The Tomitans were originally Milesian Greeks, but by now more than half the population consisted of Getic or Sarmatian barbarians. With rough voice, grim face, unkempt hair and beard they rode up and down the streets, long bow and quiver of poisoned arrows on their shoulder and dagger at their side. Their law was jungle law; often their disputes in the forum were settled with the sword. He hints vaguely at plots against his life. Moreover, 'even if you are not afraid of them', says the delicate Roman, 'you may well loathe the sight of their chests covered with hides or long hair'. More savage than wolves, they were scarcely worthy of the name of men. Even those credited with Greek descent had adopted (sensibly enough, in view of the climate) the native trousers which looked so outlandish to the toga'd race. They used the local languages among themselves, or spoke Greek with a Getic accent, and for some time Ovid could only make himself understood by signs. He, 'the master of the noble Latin tongue', was here a 'barbarian', a man who spoke a language unintelligible as *bar-bar*, which made the oafish inhabitants laugh. Indeed, whenever they laughed (one recognizes here the phobia common among the deaf), he imagined it was at him, perhaps even at his being an exile; and they in turn suspected his every gesture. Not a soul knew the commonest Latin words; he had to talk to himself for fear of forgetting how to speak his native tongue; perhaps even his poems—horrid thought, had it been sincere!—might contain barbarisms undetected by him. At length he could hold out no longer; he was compelled to learn to speak Getic and Sarmatian.

Since Ovid is practically our only source of information on Tomis, we must be cautious about taking him too literally. Though he claimed credence because he had no motive for lying, his perpetual object was to awake pity for his plight. He was naturally exasperated when he sensed that people sitting comfortably at Rome presumed he was exaggerating for effect as usual, and he appealed for confirmation to any visitor from civilization. Several times he speaks as though he were in the far north, 'near the Great Bear', though in fact he was no nearer to it than Florence is; and his Italian friends might well be sceptical about the rigours of a place which they may have vaguely known to be in much the same latitude as themselves. But there is in fact no reason to doubt the faithfulness of the general impression he gives. From modern experience the winters of the Dobruja might well paralyse an Italian. Icy north-east winds sweep down from the Russian steppes on to the unsheltered plateau, and the Danube does in fact freeze, sometimes for two or three months on end. The *Guide Bleu* describes the climate as 'très continental, assez proche du climat russe'. The winter is long, and the temperature can fall to $-30°$ or even $-35°$.

It is clear that Ovid kept up a continual prose correspondence with his friends at Rome. But he would have to rely on chance carriers, and letters might be held up or go astray. He reckoned it might take a full year for a letter to come and a reply to be composed and to reach Rome. Cotta sends him some speeches he has delivered in the Forum, and he reads them over and over again. He remains avid of any rumour from the civilized world. When spring breaks up the ice he looks forward to the arrival of ships again. Though they are unlikely to be more than coasters, or from the Sea of Marmora at the farthest, he will run down to greet their crew in the hope of finding someone who speaks Greek, or still better Latin, and can tell him some news.

'Oh for the wings of a dove!' In a wistful and beautiful passage he recalls those legendary figures who had made their escape by flying—Triptolemus who had come himself to the Scythian shores with his new gift of corn, Medea and Perseus and Daedalus who were exiles like himself:

> Oh in his heavenly chariot to stand,
> Who first put seeds into the virgin land!
> To harness now Medea's dragon-car
> Whereon she sped from Corinth's walls afar!
> Oh to be borne on wings impetuous,
> Soaring like Perseus or like Daedalus!
> That wafted through the yielding air above
> I soon might see the country that I love,
> My long-lost home, true friends about the place,
> And chief of all, my wife's belovèd face.

Meanwhile, for lack of anything else to do, cooped up as he was and without company or means of enjoyment, he continued to do what he had done for the past thirty to forty years—write elegiac verse. He sings as the shackled farm-slave, the heaving barge-puller or the galley-slave sings, to lighten his toil. He finds writing verse an anodyne, and it fills up leisure which would otherwise be intolerable. Besides, when he wrote he felt he was in some sense present with the friend he was writing for. 'You are here though you do not know it, and though absent you are most constantly present; from the midst of the City I can summon you to the Getae: do likewise for me, and since your country is the happier, keep me always there in your remembering heart.' We may well believe that he had all these subjective motives for writing; but he had objective aims as well.

In the first place he could not bear to think of being forgotten at Rome, of coming home, if ever he did, to find that his world had passed on. Here is one effect of his exile for which we should be grateful. It made him dwell in his poetry on himself, partly from motives of self-pity and self-justification, but partly also to keep himself alive in Roman minds and excite sympathy. So his later poems contain pieces of autobiography, such as his recollections of his youthful grand tour with Macer, and his detailed *curriculum vitae* in *Tristia* IV, 10 already cited, which are exceptional in ancient poetry and have special interest for our age, hungry for *personalia*; and they may also have encouraged other poets, ancient and modern, to tell their readers about themselves.

But his overriding object was to move the powers at Rome, either by arousing their pity and ingratiating himself through flattery or by provoking a public outcry for his recall. For tactical reasons he asks in the first instance only for transference to a safer and more civilized place of relegation, though return to Rome was avowedly his ultimate hope: 'What I seek is a punishment; for I do not balk at suffering, but only ask to be able to suffer in more safety.' Nearly all the poems come back to this. There is, indeed, something distasteful in his reply to a letter from Cotta breaking the news that their friend Celsus is dead; though genuinely moved, he is soon improving the occasion by recalling how Celsus had constantly assured him that Cotta, such is his loyalty, could be relied on to work for his recall; a dead man's wishes must be respected. But a sufferer must be pardoned his *idée fixe*.

His flattery of Augustus and members of the imperial family knows no bounds. They are of course deified, and he is careful to mention that he has a shrine dedicated to them in his house at Tomis, in which he offers daily incense and prayer. Nothing could be more fulsome than his poem acknowledging a gift from Cotta of a silver *objet d'art* with likenesses of the Caesars on it. Such adulation, largely derived from that of eastern monarchs, had for some time attached itself to the person of the Emperor, who was identified in this with the state; as Ovid says, 'Caesar belongs to all, and I, even I, have a share in the commonwealth'. His flatteries differ from those of previous Augustan poets only in assiduity. Thus his differentiation between the supreme deities of Caesar and Jupiter, 'of whom the one is seen, the other believed, to be a god', recalls the opening of Horace's Regulus ode; and he has nothing more fancifully extravagant than Virgil's invocation to the new god Caesar in the exordium of the *Georgics*. This phenomenon is distasteful to the modern mind, and was indeed to some of the ancients even under the Empire. It is painful to see a dog fawning on a master who is cruel to it. Ovid's adulation of Augustus is particularly nauseating because it is heaped on his oppressor; but we should be chary of blaming him, unless we have been through a similar experience.

What gave him hope was the fact that Augustus had deliberately prescribed for him what was considered to be the less severe of the two Roman forms of banishment. By not depriving him of his property or citizen's rights he seemed to envisage the possibility of his ultimate return. In the event this proved to be a cruel mitigation. Full exile instead of relegation would probably have involved not coming within a prescribed distance from Rome; but how gladly Ovid would have sacrificed all to be able to live, even in poverty, in some place of his own choice! Instead, Fortune cheated him at every turn. The disaster to Varus and his legions in Germany, A.D. 9, distracted the Emperor's attention for some time, besides making it unlikely that his mood would become more benign; then, when the situation had been restored and the Pannonian triumph of Tiberius, finally celebrated on 23 October A.D. 12, had generated an atmosphere which seemed more propitious, Ovid lost the most likely and influential of his advocates by the death of Paullus Fabius Maximus in the summer of 14. Even so, he had fancied that Augustus had begun to relent, when on August 19 of that year he too died.

From Tiberius personally he seems to have hoped for little, though he appeals briefly to him once amid prayers to his imperial stepfather, and indicates that he has composed an elegy on his triumph, though in no mood for such themes, as well as a poem, which has not survived, on the apotheosis of Augustus. His main hopes, however, were transferred to Germanicus, the nephew and adopted son of the new emperor. He does not seem to have known the prince personally, for he relies on the intercession of friends; but he knew his reputation as a humane and affable man who was interested in literature and himself something of a poet. Already during the lifetime of Augustus he had put at the head of the second book of *Pontic Epistles* a congratulatory poem addressed to him. He now promised him a gift whose worth he would appreciate, a name immortal in poetry, and took up the abandoned *Fasti* again in the hope of completing them in his honour.

We may now explore this extensive corpus of verse for what we can find to interest or move us. In the first place, nostalgia for the life he had left behind sometimes allowed Ovid to escape for a while in imagination, and once more to compose in a major key. His brief autobiography and his memories of happy days with Messalla and

Cotta, or with Atticus, have already been cited. On another occasion, overcoming any bitterness for supposed neglect, he recalls his youthful tour with Macer.

> The splendid Asian cities at your side
> I toured, and Sicily with you for guide;
> With Etna's flames we saw the heavens glow,
> Vomited by the giant pinned below;
> Saw Enna's lake, Palicus' pool that stinks,
> And where of Cyane Anapus drinks,
> And her who, Elis' river-god to flee,
> Ran 'neath the waves, and still runs under sea.
> There did I spend most of a gliding year
> (Alas, how different that land from here!).
> The merest fraction, this, of all we viewed,
> While you with gladness all my ways endued,
> Whether we clove the deep with painted keel
> Or bowled along on rattling carriage-wheel.
> Often our road seemed shortened by our talk:
> We had more words to say than steps to walk.
> Days proved too short, and we'd be talking yet
> After the lingering summer sun was set.
> 'Tis something to have shared in dread of seas
> And joined in prayer to ocean deities,
> Done things together and, when later met,
> Laughed over them with nothing to regret.

When at last spring comes to Tomis (but there promises little more than the melting of snow and ice), he thinks of the violets coming out in Italy, and the boys and girls going off to the meadows to pick flowers, the birds singing, the swallow building, the corn peeping above ground, the vines and trees budding; and then of the life of the city, the holidays when the business of the Forum gives way to a succession of festivals, contests on horseback or with arms, games with ball or hoop, young men after exercise bathing in the Aqua Virgo, and the intense dramatic activity and rivalries of the three theatres. If Cicero, sent to govern Cilicia for a year, yearned for the life of Rome—'stick to the City, the City, Rufus, and live in its limelight; all time spent abroad is dim and sordid to those by whose efforts Rome can be glorious'—how much more would Ovid, banished indefinitely to Moesia! When he is in the act of protesting to Severus, *à propos* the latest barbarian raid, that safety, not the pleasures of city life, is all he asks, honesty checks him in mid-couplet: 'And do not think that Naso is missing the amenities of city life—yet he does miss them'; and once again he reviews in imagination the piazzas, temples, theatres and porticos, the Campus with its green turf and the gardens, lakes, canals and fountains all about. He thinks too of his own gardens outside the city, of the plants he was not too grand to water himself, and of the trees he planted there, whose fruit another will be picking. In such surroundings, comforted by the love of his wife and the companionship of his friends, he had planned to spend his declining years; and he envies Severus, who can pass freely from Rome to his Umbrian home, or drive along the Appian way to his place in the Alban Hills: 'All men are drawn somehow by the sweet attraction of their native soil, which will not let them forget.'

There is something particularly touching in the obvious sincerity of the passages in which the professed cynic of the *Ars Amatoria* comes at last to express a deep and genuine love—for his wife. When he lies ill and sleepless, her face keeps recurring to his disordered mind:

> Memories throng, but you prevail o'er all:
> Half of my heart and more you hold in thrall.
> To you far off I speak, name you alone;
> No night, no day without you have I known.
> When my mind raved in feverish eclipse,
> They say your name was ever on my lips.
> If I should faint, and tongue to palate cleave
> Till drops of wine could scarce my drought relieve,
> Yet if one said, 'Your lady's come', I'd rise
> And hope of you my limbs would vitalize.

On her birthday, and on no other day of the year, he puts on the white clothing of good omen, builds an altar of turf, burns incense and pours wine upon it; pathetically he fancies that the smoke is wafted towards Italy. Time and again he likens her to Penelope, the faithful wife whom the wandering Odysseus preferred to an unageing goddess; she may indeed have aged when they next see each other, but he will kiss her whitened hair and embrace her wasted body with joy, as beyond all hope they talk face to face again.

She had wanted to come with him, and perhaps if he had been formally exiled, with no interests or property left at Rome, she would have done so; as it was, her presence there was imperative, and her courage and vigilance achieved the difficult task of keeping their home together. There were moments when, after several years of fruitless waiting, he doubted of her energy in pressing, through the Empress, for his return; but even when he urges her uncle, one Rufus, to spur her on, it is not without warm praise for her, and when he does once reply somewhat petulantly to her question, or supposed question, 'What can I do?', we discover that he is ill at the time. The cumulative impression is of a devoted husband sure that his love is returned. In a beautiful letter to her, in which once again emotion flows over the limitation of end-stopped couplets, he sets his own mind at rest:

> O Great and Lesser Bear that never dip,
> Guide to the Greek and to the Tyrian ship,
> Since set in highest heaven you witness all
> Nor e'er beneath the western ocean fall,
> And, circling with embrace the sky's whole girth,
> Your orbit never stoops to touch the earth,
> Look on those walls, I pray, which overbold
> Remus the son of Ilia leapt of old;
> Then on my lady shine, and bring me word
> If she remembers or forgets her lord.
>
> Ah, why be anxious when the answer's clear?
> Wherefore this wavering from hope to fear?
> Believe the pleasing truth, nor doubt what's sure:
> Have faith secure that her faith is secure.
> Expect no answer from the stars on high,
> But tell yourself in words that cannot lie:
> Your chiefest care is mindful still the same,
> And—this she can do—cherishes your name;
> Pores on your features, absent though you are,
> And, if she lives, still loves you from afar.

Thinking of her lying sleepless and miserable as himself, constantly reminded of him by his empty place in their bed, he is torn between wishing her happy for her sake and unhappy for his; but he knows in his heart that she cannot be happy. It makes him wretched to think that she who used to be so proud of him, indulgently so, may now blush to be called an exile's wife—yet she need not, for he has done nothing of which she need be ashamed.

The Perilla to whom the charming poem *Tristia* III, 7 is addressed, a girl whose promise as a poetess Ovid had fostered, is apparently not, as is still sometimes assumed, his own daughter (for then he would hardly have said 'and *as* a father to a daughter I was your leader and companion'). But she may possibly be his step-daughter. At all events, the supposition that she belonged to his own household, so that her connexion with him was patent, would account better than her youthful innocence for the fact that she is the only person apart from the imperial house whom he ventures to call by name (whether it be true name or sobriquet) in the *Tristia*:

> Go, greet Perilla, letter swiftly writ,
> True messenger my converse to transmit.
> You'll find her sitting with her mother sweet,
> Or mid her books and at her Muse's feet;
> Whate'er it be, she'll leave her work for you,
> Straight asking why you come, and how I do.
> Say that I live, though thus to live not lief,
> For all this time has not allayed my grief;
> Still seek the Muses, though they brought this curse,
> Marshalling words in alternating verse.
> 'And do you still our old pursuits maintain,
> Compose and yet avoid your father's bane?
> For nature did both purity of heart
> And rarest gifts of wit to you impart.
> 'Twas I that led to the Pierian Spring
> That fertile rill, to save its perishing,
> Which in your tender years I first descried,
> And like a father was your friend and guide.
> If in your breast that fire burns the same,
> Then none but Sappho shall outshine your fame.
> Yet do I fear my fate has set you back,
> My ruin caused your ardour to grow slack.
> Before, we read our poems, I to you
> And you to me, your critic, teacher too,
> Who lent my ear to each new verse you framed,
> Or, if you idled, made you blush ashamed.'

* * *

The bulk of the poems from exile is so abject that one finds relief in the occasional outbursts of indignation, whether real or feigned. In the first poem that Ovid wrote to his wife after leaving Italy, *Tristia* I, 6, he praises her in the following terms:

You are the pillar that sustains my tottering house: if I can count myself anything, I owe it all to you. It is your doing that I am not a prey, that I am not stripped by those who have tried to snatch timbers from my wreckage. And as a ravening wolf goaded by hunger and thirsty for blood tries to catch the sheepfold unguarded, or as a greedy vulture peers about to spy unburied carrion, so a mean creature, treacherous in my time of bitterness, would have come into my property, if you allowed it. But your courage, with the help of stout friends, repulsed him.

Tristia IV, 9, written a year or two later, is a less specific poem in the same vein. It is a spirited denunciation of an enemy, whose name and offences Ovid will at present forbear to reveal, with an incidental reminder that the Emperor has left him all his legal rights. The connexion between this poem and I, 6 is through that strange composition, the *Ibis*, written after Ovid had attained the age of fifty, and before he heard of the death of Augustus, hence some time in the early years of exile.

Invective had been a recognized form of literature from early times. Ovid got his idea from a riddling poem of Callimachus called *Ibis*, now lost, in which he had denounced an enemy under that pseudonym. Here was a form of literature canonized by the Master which Ovid had not yet essayed, though he had approached it in some of the *Heroides*. His poem, in elegiacs and 644 lines long, contains little that need have come from that of Callimachus, and more than one thing that cannot have done so; and, in fact, he invokes the curses of his predecessor as an *addition* to his own.

The first 66 lines state his purpose. Hitherto his writings have hurt no one but himself—a just claim and a rare one. However, he will not yet denounce the offender by name. He has only been sparring so far, but if the man continues in his ways, he will attack in earnest and draw blood. The alleged offence which purports to be the occasion of the poem is dealt with in the following terms, strongly reminiscent of *Tristia* I, 6, and it will be seen that even such a poem as this contrives to make its oblique appeal to the Emperor:

> He will not let me hide an exile's head
> To the North Wind's cold birthplace banishèd,
> Vexes my wounds that only crave repose
> And still my name about the Forum throws,
> Nor leaves my ever-constant wedded wife
> To mourn her wretched husband's death-in-life.
> Shipwrecked, the remnants of my barque I clasp:
> He tries to wrest the salvage from my grasp,

The man who should have quenched the sudden blaze
Himself to plunder from the fire essays.
Who strives to rob an exile of his store
For age, deserves that penalty far more.
The gods forbade, of whom I most revere
Him who willed not I should be needy here;
To him deservèd thanks, where'er I may,
For this his mercy I shall ever pay.
Pontus shall hear—nay, he may yet allow
A nearer land to witness what I vow.

The invective that occupies the rest of the poem, apart from a six-line epilogue, falls into two parts, lines 67–250 and 251–638, uneven in merit as they are in length. The poet is discovered standing before an altar and in priestly fashion preparing to utter his solemn commination. He adjures the bystanders to do everything of ill omen they can, and bids the shrinking victim don the sacrificial fillet and prepare his throat for the knife. The invocation rises to a solemnity worthy of Propertius:

Gods of the sea and land, and ye who share
With Jove the wide, superior realms of air,
Hither, I pray, and lend me all your mind,
That force to my petitions be assigned;
And thou thyself, O Earth, thyself, O Sea,
Thyself, O highest Heaven, give ear to me;
Ye Stars, and Sun's bright image crowned with rays,
And shining Moon with ever-changing phase,
Night, awful in thy shadows, and ye Three
That spin the appointed web of destiny,
River of waters unforsworn that flow
With fearful murmur through the vales below,
And ye with snake-entwinèd locks that sit
Before the portals of the gloomy pit;
Ye lowlier powers, each Satyr, Faun and Lar,
All rivers, nymphs and demigods that are,
Come, all divinities that have held sway
From ancient Chaos to this latter day,
Be present while a treacherous man is cursed
And grief and anger do to him their worst;
Assent to my petitions one and all,
Nor let one jot of them unheeded fall.

The curses then follow, line upon line, every rift loaded with venom. The poet is clearly interested in his own hyperbolic ingenuity, not in the efficacy of his curses or even in verisimilitude. It is clear enough from his other works that Ovid despised superstition; yet never had he written more compact lines than here.

> Thee even the all-devouring flames shall leave,
> The righteous earth thy loathèd corpse upheave,
> A lingering vulture rend thy guts apart,
> And hungry hounds worry thy treacherous heart;
> Thy body—so much glory I permit—
> Insatiable wolves shall fight for it;
> Then, banished furthest from Elysium,
> To dwell with damnèd spirits thou shalt come.

No one who has appreciated the *Metamorphoses* should imagine that there is anything serious in this 'flyting'; the *Ibis* has the qualities of the winning entry in a competition in invective set by a literary magazine. Who was Ibis? Let Housman answer. 'Nobody. He is much too good to be true. If one's enemies are of flesh and blood, they do not carry complaisance so far as to choose the *dies Alliensis** for their birthday and the most ineligible spot in Africa† for their birthplace. Such order and harmony exist only in worlds of our own creation, not in the jerry-built edifice of the demiurge. Nor does a man assail a real enemy, the object of his sincere and lively hatred, with an interminable and inconsistent series of execrations which can neither be read nor written seriously. To be starved to death and killed by lightning, to be brazed in a mortar as you plunge into a gulf on horseback, to be devoured by dogs, serpents, a lioness, and your own father in the brazen bull of Phalaris, are calamities too awful to be probable and too improbable to be awful. And when I say that Ibis was nobody, I am repeating Ovid's own words. In the last book that he wrote, several years after the *Ibis*, he said (*Ex Ponto* IV, 14, 44), "there is no man living that my tongue has so far wounded."'

We may grant the brilliance of the writing, but readers who are repelled by the *Ibis* may feel that Housman overpraised the first part because it was accordant with his own highly personal taste for invective. All will agree with him, however, in considering the second part of the poem (251–644) to be merely a display of erudition.

* July 18, the date of the defeat of the Romans by the Gauls at the Allia in 390 B.C., observed as a perpetual day of mourning and ill-omen: see l. 219.

† The African river Cinyps (22, 2), perhaps notorious for snakes; cf. *Metamorphoses* VII, 272.

At the close of his poem to Perilla (*Tristia* III, 7) Ovid exhorts her, not without a warning against love as a subject, to gather rosebuds while she may—from the garden of the Muses; they alone do not wither. As he writes, his old enthusiasm for poetry, which had inspired the envoy to his first book, *Amores* I, comes over him again, and for a moment, his heart getting the better of his head, he gives us a glimpse of his real feeling about the oppressor of his genius, 'Caesar could have no jurisdiction over this', and our sympathy for him, dulled by his flatteries, revives. Gone is the mood of III, 4, 'live your own life, and as far as you can avoid the limelight':

> In sum, no human blessing will abide
> Save those that mind and spirit do provide.
> Lo I, of country, home and you bereft,
> With nought that could be taken from me left,
> Have still my mind's own company to enjoy:
> No Caesar's interdict could that destroy.
> Aye, and though sword should take away my breath,
> Yet shall my fame outlive my body's death:
> While Rome shall from her hills survey outspread
> The conquered world, so long shall I be read.
> You too may happier themes than mine inspire
> To shun, for so you can, the approaching pyre.

In splendid lines at the close of his autobiographical poem he gives thanks to the Muse who can transport him from the Danube to Helicon:

> Thou, Muse, hast given me in life what Fame
> Gives rarely this side death—a glorious name.
> Envy, that crabs the living, yet hath bit
> With spiteful tooth no work that I have writ;
> Nor, though our age has mighty poets seen,
> Has Fame malignant to my genius been:
> While many I count greater, I am said
> To be as great, throughout the world am read.
> Therefore, if bards can truly prophesy,
> Earth, I shall not be thine, whene'er I die.
> But be this fame to worth or favour due,
> I owe, my gentle reader, thanks to you.

Passports to immortality these epistles from exile have indeed turned out to be. It was a consolation to Ovid that there was at least this one thing he could do for his wife. Paradoxically, many would envy her despite her husband's calamity, but for which indeed it would probably never have occurred to him that she deserved to be so honoured. And when at last it proved to be safe to reward his faithful friends also in this way, he was anxious that not one of them should be left out.

How do the poems from exile strike the modern reader? In giving our judgement we must be careful to make some distinctions. The first two books of the *Tristia* (as well as the *Ibis*) should be considered apart; for the changing scenes of the voyage give variety to the first book, and the second is a full-scale apologia. The remaining seven books of epistles may be treated as an entity, for they are all too homogeneous. The indulgence for which Ovid pleads is readily granted to him as a person by sympathetic critics; but too often, I feel, it has betrayed them into suggesting that these books as a whole are better reading than they are. They contain 5412 lines: a generous selection based on interest and literary merit would barely include a third of that total.

The chief trouble is that, although each poem is generally well constructed, ingenious and polished, they suffer as a collection, just as the *Heroides* do, from monotony of subject. It is generous but idle to deny this: Ovid recognized it himself, in his epilogue to *Ex Ponto* I–III:

> Though the words are always the same, I have not written to the same persons: in one voice I seek help through a number of people. Should I, lest the reader twice find the same matter, petition you alone, Brutus, of all my friends? That would not be worth the sacrifice—pardon the confession, men of letters: my salvation means more to me than the reputation of my work. In sum, when a poet thinks of his subject-matter for himself, he can introduce as much variety as he fancies; but my Muse is all too true an index of my troubles, and has all the weight of an incorruptible witness. My purpose and care was that each friend should receive his letter, not that a book should result. Do not imagine this work is a selection: I simply collected the letters afterwards and put them together unarranged. So be indulgent to my writings; for their object has been to secure, not personal glory, but advantage for myself and for others their due.

Nor is it only the subject, but the treatment also, that is monotonous. The old formulae and stock-in-trade of elegy, the hard-worked figures of thought and figures of speech, recur again and again. Must we wade through eight couplets full of examples of the healing power of time before being told that Ovid's pain is not healed by it, or eight couplets of examples of legendary heroes more fortunate in that their place of exile was somewhere intrinsically desirable? The wit that seasoned with its salt the poems of his happier days is still there, but it has lost its savour. When he remarks that Leander, had he lived among the Getae, could have walked over ice instead of swimming to his love, or that Acontius would have found there no apple to inscribe as a trap for Cydippe, we may admire his effort to smile even so wryly, but the pathos of his situation somehow precludes enjoyment; the contrast is too poignant. True there is some compensation in a new sincerity, especially in the earlier poems where the pain is fresh, but it is hard to agree that 'les élégies de l'exil restent toutefois les plus intéressantes que le poète ait écrites, parce qu'elles sont les plus sincères'. Let anyone compare the picture he conjures up of the scenes at Tiberius' triumph and its counterpart in the *Ars Amatoria* and he will see the difference. Ovid's genius was for composition in the major keys; forced by circumstances into the minor, he has a lowering effect after a time.

Gibbon observed that these poems have 'besides the merit of elegance, a double value. They exhibit a picture of the human mind under very singular circumstances; and they contain many curious observations, which no Roman, except Ovid, could have the opportunity of making.' That is true, but the picture is exhibited far too often, while the observations are tantalizingly few. Some Romans, such as the Elder Pliny, enjoyed information about strange people and lands and customs for its own sake; Ovid in the first years of his exile only mentioned them in so far as they could be pressed into the service of his pleas for transfer or recall. It is natural that we, whose appetite for knowledge of all kinds has steadily increased since the Renaissance, should regret this. What light an educated observer could have thrown on an obscure corner of history if he had had the zeal and patience of an ethnologist! But at first Ovid would not reconcile himself to thinking of his quarters at Tomis as home. Had he not still a home in the capital?

At last, however, after four or five years, there begin to be signs of resignation to his lot. In a notable poem (*Ex Ponto* III, 7) he apologizes to his friends for having so long pestered them with letters whose contents, now known almost by heart, they must divine even before breaking the seal. He resolves to face the facts:

> We hug our hopes when all are not deceived,
> While we can fancy every wish achieved;
> Next after this comes resolute despair
> That faces ruin once for all aware.

Not that he ceased to beg for the intercession of his friends—as he confesses, 'desire knows no moderation'; but he began at last to show signs of interest in what went on around him. He tells of the surprise of Aegisos, an old walled city of the Odrysians high on a hill near the Danube, by the Getae, who were in rebellion against the King of Thrace; and though his motive is still primarily to give his friend Severus an illustration of the constant dangers of Tomis, he adds a little picturesque detail and expresses his gratitude and admiration to the king for restoring the situation. Apparently he did not restore it without Roman help; for the interesting poem IV, 7 seems to recall the same occasion. There we are told that Vitellius brought troops down the Danube by boat to relieve the town. This elegy is quite exceptional in Ovid's work. It is addressed to Vestalis, a centurion sprung from Alpine chiefs who had risen from the ranks, and is a citation of his act of gallantry in leading the assault on the apparently impregnable site, regardless of the steepness and the hail of stones and poisoned arrows. Though wounded, he led his men to close quarters and did prodigies of valour in hand-to-hand fighting until the place was recaptured. It would appear from lines 1–2 that he had subsequently been given an administrative post in the area, which would account for Ovid's coming to know him personally.

Ex Ponto II, 9 is also addressed to a local character, Cotys, King of Thrace, who claimed descent from Eumolpus, the legendary founder of the Eleusinian Mysteries. If the fragment of 134 hexameters about sea-fish which is preserved as Ovid's by a ninth-century Viennese manuscript were really by him, as some believe, it would provide further evidence that he turned in his last years to local interests. It is not impossible that the author of the *Medicamina Faciei* whiled away his tedious hours by composing a didactic poem on this subject; but if he did, it is unlikely to have been the one we have.

More authentic as well as more interesting is the change that occurred in Ovid's attitude to the Tomitans themselves. In the earlier years of exile, when he had mentioned that he was learning to speak Getic and Sarmatian, it was only to shock his readers. And he had remarked sardonically that he believed he could even write a poem in Getic. But at length, by his own account, he not only learnt the language but actually wrote such a poem, on the apotheosis of Augustus. One may well wonder how he reduced the barbarian language to the kind of prosody with which he was familiar; and his synopsis of the subject-matter, so laudatory of the imperial house, and his account of the reaction of the approving circle of 'uncivilized Getae'—'Since you write thus about Caesar, you ought to be restored by Caesar's command'—are such as to arouse in those who know their Ovid enough suspicion to console philologists for the absence from his literary remains of any trace of so tantalizing a document. At all events, after some five years among the Tomitans he either became aware of them as human beings or decided that there was no longer any profit in proclaiming their savagery. They were not unnaturally offended when they got wind of what he had told the world about them in his poems; and his defence, that he had been misinterpreted to them, that he had criticized the place, not the people, will hardly bear scrutiny: 'let anyone', he protests, 'examine the record of my work: my letters have made no complaint about you'. (One wonders how he would have explained away *Tristia* v, 7 and 10.) Yet they do not hate him; and, indeed, his conduct has deserved no hatred, for he has retained his old sobriety and modesty, and even in this lawless country no man, woman or child has had cause to complain of him. And he in turn now refers to them as loyal folk whom he loves; their sympathy with him has shown that Greek blood still flows in their veins. For his sake they wish he may leave them, but for their own are eager he should stay. They have even recently, despite his disclaimers, crowned him publicly with a wreath; and not only they, but other neighbouring towns, have voted him the privilege, granted to no one else in that region *honoris causa*, of being exempt from taxation. Tomis is now as dear to him as Delos was to Latona, and he no longer refuses to call his house there *domus*, home. He can even realize that a barbarian might wish to escape from Rome to Moesia. We have no reason to doubt the truth of the information given here, for it is too specific to be false, nor the sincerity of the sentiments, for they are not such as would assist his pleas for recall. It looks as though the public honour accorded him by these simple people had surprised, touched, and perhaps shamed him.

When he first came to Tomis Ovid had dreaded the thought of dying far from home, where his wife could not comfort his final moments and perform the last rites for him, but at length he resigned himself bitterly to the idea. The end came not long after that, late in 17 or early in 18. He had lived for fifty-nine years, eight of them in exile. We may be sure that the Tomitans gave honourable burial to one who had nevertheless affected to fear that, if there were any after-life, his shade would flit in terror amid wild Getic and Sarmatian shades. He had confessed in the end that even his own Pelignian people could not have treated him more kindly; and today his statue stands in Constanza, as it does in Sulmona.

CHAPTER XI

THE MIDDLE AGES

WHEN Ovid claims in his autobiographical poem that, as he made a cult of the elder poets, so the younger made a cult of him, he is probably speaking no more than the truth. And neither his exile nor the banishment of his books from public libraries seems to have affected his popularity. Indeed, his vogue extended beyond the reading public. A friend wrote to tell him that he was having a success at Rome of a kind which he wearily disclaims having sought—passages of his works were being performed in the theatre to the applause of crowded houses, as had sometimes happened before the eyes of the Emperor in happier days.* Further evidence of his popularity is provided by quotations and echoes of his poems in inscriptions at Pompeii and elsewhere. He comes second only to Virgil in the frequency with which he is echoed in these scraps of verse from all over the Empire.

Whether artists who depict stories which he treated actually had him in mind we cannot tell; but there is no doubt about the poets. Traces of his wording have been found in many of them throughout the early Empire. He emerges as, after Catullus, the favourite poet of Martial. In the post-Augustan age poets did not innovate in metre: they chose a model, and Ovid was the favourite. He was also early paid the pathetic compliment of the self-effacing forger, who forfeits his own chance of an immortal name in the hope of endowing his child with one, though the spate of forgeries did not begin until the Middle Ages. As for prose writers, it was natural that the younger Seneca, whose plays show his influence clearly enough, should have dwelt in his days of exile on the memory of the poet of Tomis. Ovid's vogue in the rhetorical schools is amply testified by the elder Seneca. There is no evidence however of his early use in secondary education, which is surprising, for while one can understand that the erotic poems might

* In such performances a chorus recited the words in unison, with musical accompaniment, while a dancer interpreted them with elaborate gesture.

seem unsuitable, one would expect the *Fasti* at least, if not also the *Metamorphoses*, to be seized on by schoolmasters. Quintilian indeed was rather stuffy: while allowing that the *Metamorphoses* were 'to be praised in parts', he took the poet to task for being exuberant even in what purported to be epic. But he was writing a treatise on rhetorical education, not a work of pure literary criticism.

The second century was an age in practical organization rather than literary activity; and in the third there were constant civil wars and barbarian incursions, a foreshadowing of the Dark Ages. When, thanks to the reconstructive efforts of Diocletian and Constantine, learning and letters were able to revive in the fourth century and its successor, we find Ovid freely cited in the text-books of the grammarians who were characteristic of the age.

But meanwhile a new force was shaping the future, Christianity. What was the attitude of the Fathers to a writer like Ovid? Generally speaking, while the Eastern Church remained fairly tolerant of the Greek classics, the Western was largely hostile to the Roman, but the average layman would probably have been loth to exterminate paganism, if he realized that the cost might be the undermining of the Roman civilization he knew. Throughout the fourth and fifth centuries Ovid continued to be cited by grammarians and to influence poets, not only pagans such as Claudian (*c.* 400), the last important classic, but also Christians like Claudian's contemporary Prudentius. But he could no longer compete with Virgil, amid whose praises in the seven books of Macrobius' *Saturnalia* he is not even mentioned. It is hardly surprising that he should fade out in a society becoming rapidly, and indeed forcibly, christianized. Here, however, we should not forget the possibilities inherent in a feature of the period which presaged medievalism: the revival of the Stoic fashion of allegorizing myth and legend. Its absurdities pullulate in the commentaries; and the Christian writer Fulgentius, about the end of the fifth century, uses not only Virgil, but among other sources the *Fasti* and *Metamorphoses*, as a basis for his allegories in the *Mythologiae*.

The fifth century saw the final break-up of the Western Empire. Many provinces had already been invaded by barbarians, and now Rome itself was sacked by Alaric the Goth and Genseric the Vandal. Cassiodorus himself was in his earlier years a minister of the Ostrogoths, who put to death his less compliant contemporary Boethius, and brutal Lombards ruled much of the Italy in which St Gregory was Pope. Nothing would have preserved the classics had not Benedictine monks, under the impulse given by Cassiodorus, occupied their long leisure in transcribing manuscripts. It was rarely Ovid's works, however, that were transcribed, no doubt through disapproval of the erotic poems.* Few early manuscripts of them have survived—for some of the poems none from earlier than the eleventh century; nor do their titles occur often in the library catalogues of the eighth to tenth centuries. Citations in this period are also very few; at the end of the seventh century Aldhelm of Malmesbury, Bishop of Sherborne, wrote a treatise on metre, but he never refers to the great master of elegiacs. Nor is Ovid mentioned in the poem in which Alcuin gives an account of the Library of the School of York, where Latin verse composition formed part of the curriculum.

At the court of Charlemagne, however, there were writers who anticipated the Renaissance Humanists in that their poems tended to be personal and epistolary, not variations on school themes (and here Alcuin is as human as the rest). The poets who influenced them most were Virgil, Ovid and the Christian Fortunatus. The best of them, Theodulf, read his 'Naso loquax', wrote mainly in Ovidian elegiacs and often echoed Ovidian phrasing. The civilized intercourse of these high ecclesiastics and their beloved patron, revealed to us against a background of centuries of violence, was surely influenced by the *anima cortese* of Virgil, the *candor* of Ovid, the *urbanitas* and *humanitas* of Horace. To what extent they knew the works of these ancients except from anthologies it is hard to determine. It is noteworthy that Ovid is never quoted by Einhard, the learned biographer of Charlemagne, nor by Servatus Lupus, a great borrower and lender of classical manuscripts. In any case, this brief springtime was nipped in the bud by Charlemagne's death in 814.

The barbaric invasions of Norsemen and Hungarians in the tenth century plunged the Carolingian empire into chaos again, but by the end of it the former at least had been assimilated, the Islamic danger had

* Nevertheless an Oxford MS. contains, besides three other works, *Ars Amatoria* I. It once belonged to St Dunstan, who, before he became one of the strictest disciplinarians, had been in love with a lady at the Court. He has drawn a portrait of himself on the opening page.

receded, and learning had somehow survived. The great Benedictine monasteries of St Gall, near Constance, and Monte Cassino were at their most active, copying classical as well as Christian manuscripts, practising Latin verse composition, and studying Virgil and Ovid carefully along with the Christian poets. In Italy teachers and pupils felt themselves to be the heirs of the great classics; but it was chiefly in the cathedral schools of France that the humanistic spirit was kept alive, to reassert itself at the end of the century, with the gradual improvement of economic and social conditions, under the influence of such dynamic figures as Gerbert of Rheims and Fulbert of Chartres. But Ovid is never mentioned by Gerbert, who quotes freely from classical authors; he was as yet a formal model for composers rather than a spiritual influence.

It is only with the late eleventh- and early twelfth-century renaissance that he comes into his own. The Carolingian age had been, in Traube's phrase, *aetas Vergiliana*; now begins the *aetas Ovidiana*. Economic improvement has encouraged the lust of the eye and the pride of life, and turned men's thoughts to the varied interests of this world. The wit and point of satire and rhetoric, appreciated in the new courts, have become fashionable. Whether in their courtly poems in praise of beautiful ladies, or in their poetic epistles to friends, or in their versified tales from the Bible, the young poets of the cathedral schools made Ovid their master. Some of Hildebert's poems have from time to time been mistaken for work of the classical period. Ovid was the favourite poet of Baudry (1046–1130), who composed exchanges of letters between him and Florus based on the *Tristia*, and between Paris and Helen based on the *Heroides*. He also composed elegiac epistles to a girl in a convent expressing Platonic love, whose piquancy was in the paradox of Christian chastity venturing in Ovidian garb. Baudry was not a great poet, but he was a classicistic versifier of talent, typical of the earlier part of this period.

The elegiac and hexameter metres were used for all sorts of themes by poets free to study the classical authors who were now becoming increasingly available. France and England, then one kingdom, were the chief sources of poetry in the twelfth century. Especially popular in England were the so-called 'comedies', tales with a happy end dealing mainly with amorous intrigue and cuckolded husbands, not without satire at the expense of women. The content might derive at first from ancient comedy, but as time went on matter as well as treatment owed more and more to the poet whose name appears in the title of two of the most erotic—*Ovidius Puellarum* and *Ovidius Trium Puellarum*. An anonymous versifier told the incestuous story of Tamar and Ammon in the guise of the *Metamorphoses*; and some of Ovid's stories, Myrrha and Leucothoë for instance, reappear in the *De Nugis Curialium*, a medley composed by Walter Map at the Court of Henry II.

The twelfth century was the age of the 'Wandering Scholars', begging their bread and wine from monastery to monastery and court to court, largely independent of Church discipline and often critical of Church ways. Many of them were minstrels with a repertoire of sacred and profane verse. Somehow or other, perhaps first in England, there developed among them, wholly unorganized though they were, the fantastic conception of 'Golias'. Goliath of Gath was the antithesis of the holy singer David; and the medieval Golias was a sort of Bishop of Misrule (Master of a mythical *Ordo Vagorum*, a travesty of the monastic orders), on whom the Goliards fathered the products of their own gay, youthful outrageousness. Wine, women and song were their themes, and nothing was sacred to them. They were condemned by a Council of 1227 for singing parodies of the Holy Office. They would begin a begging poem with '*Ecce homo* sine domo', and change the Hymn to the Virgin from '*Verbum*' to '*Vinum* bonum et suäve', or the Hymn for Prime to

> Now that the daylight fills the sky
> We lift our cups immediately.

Prominent among them was the 'Archpoet' of Cologne, who wrote, in their characteristic metre, his famous burlesque confession. Their favourite poet was Ovid, and we can recognize his *bravura* in the Archpoet's

> In a tavern I propose in the end to die,
> With a flask conveniently near me as I lie.

A few odd facts may serve to illustrate the vogue of Ovid at this period. There was a curious verse form styled *cum auctoritate* wherein each Goliardic stanza ended with a classical quotation. In a twenty-stanza poem by Walter de Châtillon seven of the tags are from various works of Ovid; and in an *amorosa visione* Cupid appears in a vision by night and laments that the high standard set by Ovid's precepts is no more maintained, each stanza ending with a line from the *Ars* or *Remedia*. In the famous poem depicting a (doubtless apocryphal) Council held at the convent of Remiremont, in which young nuns debate whether knights or clerks are the more adept in the art of love, a 'quasi-gospel' is read from the works of that *doctor egregius*, Ovid. Once he is even called 'the Pope' of love, whose decrees have authority. But the chief evidence comes from the library catalogues, the numerous anthologies (*Florilegia*), and the ubiquitous reminiscences in secular poems of all kinds, metrical and rhythmic, Latin and vernacular. Ovid is also cited more frequently than any other poet by Vincent of Beauvais (d. 1264) in his encyclopaedic *Speculum Mundi*; and he provided a store of stock quotations for the monks of Canterbury. Many spurious works, classical and contemporary, were fathered on him.

Here is the medieval paradox for us with our puritan tradition, that neither profanity nor obscenity was felt to be so inconsistent with religion as it generally is today. The noblest cathedrals of the period are liable to flaunt grotesque and even obscene carvings. Compared with many Goliardic poems by ecclesiastics Ovid was demure, and we need not be surprised that he maintained his place in the forefront of recommended school-books. There are twelfth-century introductions to, and glosses on, Ovid's works, not excluding the *Ars Amatoria*, which were intended for schools. The cathedral schools were becoming more and more secular, the 'minor orders' of the inmates merely disguising the fact, and indeed the prestige of the classics they taught depended partly on their utility for such lay careers as law and medicine. Even the 'comedies', for all their bawdiness, were studied in school; and in his *Registrum multorum auctorum* (1280) Hugo of Trimberg includes a notoriously lascivious work with a light-hearted comment: 'Next comes *The Girls' Ovid*, which I do not think will be a rarity in any school.'

But we must not press this point too far. There are instances enough of prelates who repented of their youthful tastes and indiscretions. Marbod, a famous poet and head of the classical school of Angers, apologized for his early love poems, and in old age published what amounts to a denunciation of Ovid and all his corrupting works that are beaten into schoolboys. Herbert de Losinga, the first Bishop of Norwich, had a dream that compelled him to renounce the reading and imitation of Virgil and Ovid. Even Abélard, whose love-songs for Héloïse had been sung in every street of Paris, came eventually to ask, 'Why do the bishops and doctors of the Christian religion not expel from the City of God those poets whom Plato forbade to enter into his city of the world?' Nor should we, through concentrating for our present purpose on poetry and pursuits which hark back to Ovid, forget that this was the great age of hymn-writing and cathedral-building, of Christian chivalry and the Crusades. Whatever the corruption of the Papacy, it was in general a theocratic age of faith and piety. Frequent Councils, especially in the thirteenth century, denounced loose clerics, *vagi* and Goliards. The old suspicion of pagan literature as a whole, and immoral literature in particular, was easily awakened in many a Christian breast.

Naturally those who loved literature were at pains to defend it by every shift. It was easy to pick out from Ovid's voluminous works many lines that were edifying, partly because he was in many ways a man of sound morality, and partly because he knew what morality was and could put appropriate sentiments, for instance, into the mouth of Helen rejecting the advances of Paris. The *Florilegia* used in schools were full of unexceptionable lines culled from him, often pure statements of observation, such as the ever-recurring 'we strive ever for the forbidden, and yearn for what is denied us', which a chastened Abélard wistfully quoted to Héloïse, and Luther inscribed in a copy of St Anselm. King James I of Aragon, at an assembly of barons and bishops, led off with a quotation from the *Ars Amatoria* under the impression that it was from the Bible.

More strange is the attribution of moral purpose to Ovid himself. Of the *Heroides* we hear that 'the author's intention is to condemn illicit loves, to brand the frivolous and commend those whose passions are of the right kind'. The *Remedia Amoris* was taken seriously as an aid to chastity; it is pleasant to think of Brother Bertrand Ginesse settling down to transcribe it at 5.0 a.m. on the Vigil of the Conception and finishing his task at eleven o'clock that night 'to the praise and glory of the Virgin Mary'. It was also taken seriously by medical writers, and cited for cures for 'the loveres maladye of *hereos*' or *heroys*, defined as 'an alienation of the mind accompanied by immense and unreasoning concupiscence'. If the moral was not obvious, recourse was had to allegorization. There were many such expositions of the *Metamorphoses* in the twelfth century, the most famous being the *Integumenta* of John of Garland; even the love-stories of the gods and goddesses were allegorized for the use of nuns, who were thus free to read the text of Ovid without necessarily accepting the interpretations offered. One can see how the account of the Creation, Fall and Flood and the story of Philemon and Baucis 'entertaining angels unawares' would impress uncritical readers of the *Metamorphoses* nurtured on the Bible. They assumed that the author had had access to the material of the Old Testament. Early in the fourteenth century an anonymous author produced the *Ovide Moralisé*, in which a French translation of the *Metamorphoses* was encumbered with intellectual and moralizing commentary to the extent of 70,000 octosyllabic lines. This monstrous work was destined to have a great influence. A simpler, fundamentalist approach had relieved the conscience of Amarcius, a German poet of the eleventh century: unlawful loves had given ancient poets material for their songs, but though it was on the Muses that they called, it was God who had inspired them, for us to profit thereby. This could, however, be a dangerous expedient, for among doctors of Paris burnt in the next century for heresy were some who held that 'God hath spoken in Ovid, even as in Augustine'.

As the thirteenth century proceeded the classics continued to be copied, read and quoted. In the *Biblionomia* of Richard de Fournival, a probably idealized library catalogue (*c.* 1250), all Ovid's genuine works are given a place, even the rarely mentioned *Medicamina Faciei*. The *Metamorphoses* ('Ovidius maior') remained the indispensable source of mythology, and it is as such that it played an important part in the composition of the *Divine Comedy*. No poet, save Virgil, is so often echoed by Dante as Ovid. He is one of the *quattro grand'ombre*, with Homer, Horace and Lucan, encountered by the poets in Limbo. It was he who gave Dante Ulysses' noble line

Considerate la vostra semenza,

with his

este, precor, memores qua sitis stirpe creati,

he indeed who suggested the Dantesque conception of that hero. And yet Dante's whole approach to the classics is medieval rather than humanistic. He allegorizes, using Ovid's Orpheus as a typical example.

And though he shows in the *Vita Nuova* a knowledge of the poet of love, his peculiar conception of love has come to him refined through the Troubadours and the singers of the *dolce stil nuovo*, to be sublimated by his own religious vision.

In fact, during the thirteenth century there has been a shift of emphasis. Aristotle was driving the humanities out of Paris; there was now no time left for the *auctores*, when the *artes* had become so exacting, and by 1215 they had disappeared from the arts course there. Next civil law, driven by papal decree in 1219 from Paris because it was strangling theology, was admitted by papal decree in 1235 to Orleans, where it proceeded to strangle literature. The significant figure of the thirteenth century is not some humanist such as John of Salisbury had been at Chartres, but St Thomas Aquinas.

Fewer people than before may thus have known Ovid at first hand just at a time when his *name* was becoming known far more widely; and inevitably he underwent the medieval metamorphosis of ancient worthies. It was not merely among the peasants of his own Sulmo (for whom Ovidius survived as 'Uiddie', son of their eponymous founder Solymus the Trojan) that he was magician, necromancer, merchant, philosopher, paladin, prophet or saint. A famous poetic romance of the thirteenth century, the *De Vetula* ('The Hag'), which purported (not perhaps very seriously) to have been found in the tomb of Ovid at Colchis, was almost certainly written by Richard de Fournival, who must have known the real Ovid quite well. The poet himself is the hero; the hag is the nurse of the girl he loves; she deceives him by a stratagem borrowed from the *Fasti* and he loses the girl. But twenty years later the girl is herself now a hag, and Ovid realizes that Learning is the only reliable love. This enables the book to close in medieval fashion with meditations on philosophy, astrology and religion. In another legend popular with preachers, having been banished to the island of Tomos, providentially situated near Patmos, he is converted by St John and ordained bishop of the Tomitan land, which he evangelizes.

Meanwhile local Latin dialects were developing at different places into the vernacular languages, which triumphed in the thirteenth century. Latin might still be spoken at school, but it was ceasing to be spoken at home. About 1160 Chrétien de Troyes translated the *Ars*

Amatoria. His version is now lost, but he had a host of successors among the poets of chivalry. The earliest extant version, by Maître Élie, expands the original here, abbreviates it there, and modernizes as well, church taking the place of the theatre, and clerical mystery plays that of the racecourse, as suitable milieus for finding a mistress. Translations might be prejudicial to classical studies, but they were influential in familiarizing a much wider public with classical stories and ideas. In *Flamenca*, a Provençal poem of 1234, there is a list of stories a minstrel would be expected to have in his repertoire. Most are classical myths, and of these the majority come from Ovid's *Heroides* or *Metamorphoses*.

From the old popular poetry combined with the Latin heritage had emerged the songs of the Provençal Troubadours and the German Minnesingers. From Ovid, often no doubt by way of Latinate intermediaries, the Troubadours derived the conceptions of love as a sickness, as a form of warfare, and as a science that can be taught, besides various more particular motives. But their knowledge of him was superficial, consisting of stories from the *Metamorphoses* and sentiments from the amatory works; and they differed from him in that they sang in *praise* of women, generally of higher birth, and that their love was a christianized love involving service and sacrifice. One type of song was the *alba* (*aube*) or *Tageliet*, which apparently arose from the medieval watchman's song of greeting to the dawn. It is not until the end of the eleventh century that the theme appears in it of lovers parted by the dawn and chiding

Busie old foole, unruly Sunne.

Quite possibly this was introduced by some clerk who had read his Ovid. In any case it may be refreshing to pause here for a moment and go back to the fountainhead (*Amores* I, 13):

Lo, from her ancient spouse she comes away
Whose rimy car o'er Ocean brings the day.
'Stay, Dawn!—why hasten?—so may Memnon's shade
With yearly due of slaughtered birds be paid.*
Now most within my lady's arms to hide
I love, most now to feel her at my side;

* Memnon, king of Ethiopia and hence black, was son of Aurora and Tithonus. When Achilles killed him at Troy, his ashes became birds which yearly returned to Troy on the anniversary of his funeral, and fought to the death over his grave, on which they fell as offerings.

Now also sleep is downy, air is cool,
And birds' clear-fluting throats with song are full.
Why hasten, both to men and maids a bane?
Check with thy rosy hand that dewy rein.
Before thy rising sailors better may
Their stars observe nor in mid-ocean stray;
Thy coming wakes the weariest traveller, and
Puts weapons in the soldier's hardened hand;
Thou first the mattock-laden peasant seest,
And summon'st to its yoke the tardy beast;
Thou sendest boys to school but half-awake,
On tender hands the cruel lash to take,
And halest many a sponsor into court
Where one small word huge forfeit may extort.
Thee every sort of lawyer vilifies,
For each to tackle some new case must rise,
And women's arms that might awhile have rest
Back to their stint of wool thou summonest.
All else I'd bear: but who that's not forlorn
Of love could bear that maids should rise at morn?
How oft I've prayed Night should not yield thee place,
Nor stars in rout scatter before thy face;
How oft I've prayed the wind should break thy wheel,
Or cloud-drifts cause thy stumbling steed to reel.
Jealous, why hasten? Sure, thy Memnon swart
Was proof of blackness in his mother's heart.
Would that Tithonus might tell tales of thee!*
No woman's fame in heaven would fouler be.
'Tis to escape thy all o'er-aged mate
Thou mount'st betimes the chariot he doth hate;
But if thy Cephalus thou didst embrace,
Then would'st thou cry, "Night's horses, check your pace".
Why should I suffer for thy spouse's age?
Did I, forsooth, your misalliance stage?
See now, what hours of sleep doth Moon allow
Her youth adored,† though not less fair than thou!
And Jove the Father, fain to see thee less,
Made two nights one to prosper his success.'‡
So did I chide, and you could swear she heard:
She blushed—but daybreak was no whit deferred.

* Aurora had prayed Jupiter that her husband Tithonus should be immortal, but forgot to ask that he should also be ageless. Cephalus was one of her many other loves.

† Endymion, the beautiful sleeper of the Latmian cave.

‡ In his affair with Alcmena.

The thirteenth century saw the appearance of a great poem in the French language—the *Roman de la Rose*. The Rose, guarded in a tower, is the girl whom the lover must pluck—and does, after more than 20,000 lines. The first 4266 lines were written by Guillaume de Lorris about 1225–30. 'Courtly' or chivalrous love was different from classical, involving courteous and submissive deference to the weak and the idealization of virgin purity. Yet Guillaume, a young and idealistic dreamer (the quest is presented as a dream), heralds his poem as one 'où l'art d'amors est toute enclose', and draws much on Ovid. In 1270 it was taken up by Jean de Meun and completed in a total of 22,700 (octosyllabic) lines. Jean was a scholar, philosopher, wit and satirist, and it is not surprising that he used Ovid still more; for his part of the poem is a vast intellectual treatise on subjects more or less connected with the quest, and he puts, for instance, much advice from the *Ars* into the mouth of an old woman. In all, Ovid contributed about 2000 lines to the poem, which had a resounding success.

The true spirit of Ovid, and much of his mythological subject-matter, lived on in the vernacular, helped by translations, to reach England late through Chaucer and Gower. Chaucer, captured by the French in 1359 when less than twenty years old, chivalrously treated and then ransomed, began his literary career by translating the *Roman de la Rose*. In an age when publication still consisted, as in Ovid's day, in recitation or multiplication of manuscripts or both, there was no idea of copyright. Chaucer never thinks to mention Boccaccio, from whom he derived so much; but from across the Channel he was saluted with honour by Deschamps as 'Grand Translateur'. However, either a romantic and venial snobbery or reverence for the 'authoritee' of 'olde bokes' made an exception of the classics; and so it happens that he refers more often to Ovid by name, and to his works, than to any other author. In *The Hous of Fame* (1486–9) he gave him a statue with Virgil, Lucan and Claudian:

> And next him on a piler was
> Of coper, Venus clerk, Ovyde,
> That hath y-sowen wonder wyde
> The grete god of loves name.

In the same poem (712) he refers to his 'owne book', the copy of the *Metamorphoses* he possessed in an age when private libraries were small, and which he had had within reach at his bedside that night when he sought to beguile his sleeplessness by reading the tale of Ceÿx and Alcyone. 'Ovydes Art' was one of the books owned by the fifth husband of the Wife of Bath. In his earlier period he shows knowledge of Ovid's *Metamorphoses*, *Heroides* and *Fasti*, and of other classical works. But his reading seems to have been the skimming of a poet, not the study of a scholar, and he naturally had no true perspective of the classical world such as Shakespeare shows in his plays based on North's Plutarch. He seems, like Ovid, to have had a remarkable memory for what he read, for it is most unlikely that he composed at a table covered with the various books which he uses on occasion within a few lines; and, as with Ovid, his very slips are an indication that he is relying on memory.

The more obvious cases of his borrowings from Ovid of ideas, descriptions or stories have often been catalogued. The Man of Law in the *Canterbury Tales* maintains that Chaucer has told more tales even than Ovid, and then gives a list which reveals with charming irony that Ovid was in fact his chief source for them. There is still room for some debate as to how much came at second-hand, but no one can deny that the mature Chaucer relied mainly on the Latin originals. Like Ovid himself, he did not hesitate to select, alter, conflate, elaborate and invent. In *The Hous of Fame* the walls of the temple of Venus are painted with scenes from the *Aeneid*, which are briefly enumerated. But when we come to Aeneas' desertion of Dido, we are launched into a full-scale disquisition on the betrayal of a pathetic heroine in which the 'traitor' himself is hardly heard, while the plight of his victim is emphasized (239–432). 'The Epistle of Ovyde' has drowned the voice of 'Virgile in Eneidos'; and eight other of the *Heroides* are incidentally adduced as parallels.

Chaucer's *Book of the Duchesse* (1369–70) had been in the French medieval tradition, and the story of Ceÿx and Alcyone from the *Metamorphoses* plays only a casual part in it. But in 1372 and again in 1378 Chaucer had visited the Italy of Petrarch and Boccaccio; and *The Hous of Fame*, though still in the old tradition, is a transitional poem. It teems with Renaissance ferment and undigested classical lore. It was followed by a masterpiece, *Troilus and Criseyde*, full, as a love story was sure to be, of reminiscences of Ovid. Though based on

Boccaccio's *Il Filostrato*, it breaks free through the entirely new characterization of Troilus, Pandarus and Criseyde, which in turn necessitated the invention of new episodes. It is clear that the *Heroides* had already stimulated Chaucer's interest in feminine psychology, and the yielding of Criseyde, more subtle and lifelike than any treatment in medieval poetry of such a theme, was undoubtedly influenced by the yielding of Helen to Paris in Epistle XVII.

Troilus seems to have shocked conventional society, or at least the feminine half of it, for it represents a challenge to the whole conception of courtly love. *The Legend of Good Women* (1386), his palinode enjoined by the Queen, consists largely of stories from the *Heroides* or elsewhere in Ovid which deal with the constancy of 'Cupid's Saints', including those of Lucretia and the ever-popular Pyramus and Thisbe. How closely he sometimes followed his original may be seen from a specimen based on a passage already quoted (p. 41), about Ariadne:

> Right in the dawening awaketh she,
> And gropeth in the bedde, and fond right noght.
> 'Allas!' quod she, 'that ever I was wroght!
> I am betrayèd!' and her heer to-rente,
> And to the stronde bar-fot faste she wente,
> And cryèd, 'Theseus! myn herte swete!
> Wher be ye, that I may nat with yow mete,
> And mighte thus with bestes been y-slain?'
> The holwe rockes answerde her again;
> No man she saw, and yet shinèd the mone,
> And hye upon a rocke she wente sone,
> And saw his barge sailing in the see.
> Cold wex her herte, and right thus seide she.
> 'Meker than ye fynde I the bestes wilde!'
> Hadde he nat sinne, that her thus begylde?
> She cryed, 'O turne again, for routhe and sinne!
> Thy barge hath nat al his meiny inne!'

This is his last work to show much Ovidian inspiration, for although the *Knight's Tale*, adapted from Boccaccio, has a number of details traceable to the *Metamorphoses*, the liberating influence of the renaissance spirit, itself fostered by study of the classics, had already broadened his horizon and encouraged him to stand on his own feet. The lively episode of Deïphobus' dinner-party and the thunderstorm in *Troilus*, his own invention, presages the *Canterbury Tales*.

The Legend of Good Women is significant in another way for our subject: in it the Heroic Couplet, destined to be inseparable from our idea of Ovidian elegiacs, makes its first appearance in English literature. But as yet it is curiously un-Ovidian, considering that here the *Heroides* were being closely studied for their subject-matter; it is *enjambé*, and devoid in general of balance, antithesis, parallelism and the rhetorical figures of speech. There are of course couplets in Chaucer that sound Ovidian, such as one quoted by Dryden:

> Winsinge she was, as is a joly colt,
> Long as a mast, and upright as a bolt;

but they amount to little in the great bulk of his work in this metre.

It was Dryden who first drew attention to a similarity between these two:

> Both of them were well-bred, well-natured, amorous and libertine, at least in their writings, it may be also in their lives.... Both writ with wonderful facility and clearness; neither were great inventors; for Ovid only copied the Grecian fables, and most of Chaucer's stories were taken from his Italian contemporaries, or their predecessors.... Both of them understand the manners; under which name I comprehend the passions, and, in a larger sense, the descriptions of persons, and their very habits.

He was conscious, in his age, of defending a paradox when he went on to say that 'the figures of Chaucer are much more lively, and set in a better light', and for preferring Chaucer's thought, as distinct from his words, and deploring Ovid's 'boyisms' of untimely wit. But while we may now readily agree with him, we should not forget that in those touches which give life to a description Ovid surpassed his known predecessors as Chaucer surpasses him. In several respects we may extend the comparison between the two. The kaleidoscopic variety of mood which we noted as characteristic of the *Metamorphoses* is to be found in the (alternative) Prologues to *The Legend of Good Women*, and the Ovidian sense of fun and mischief in that work as a whole (and in both poets these traits have too often gone unrecognized). Both were sophisticated men given to an ironical affectation of naïveté. The element of burlesque so common in Ovid appears in Chaucer's own Canterbury Tale of *Sir Thopas*, while the ribaldry of Faunus' discomfiture in the *Fasti* bursts out in the kindred dénouement of the Reeve's Tale and in those other *fabliaux*, the Miller's and the Cook's

Tale. Both also discovered in mid-career that their *métier* was storytelling; and both were intensely interested in psychology, especially that of women.

I doubt whether we should attribute those similarities to direct influence of Ovid on Chaucer so much as to innate sympathy of temperament (Chaucer shows other marked affinities to Horace, with whose works he was not familiar). Nor should we stress them without also stressing the differences. Chaucer deliberately avoids the divine machinery and miraculous happenings that he found in his originals, thereby making his characters more serious and responsible human beings. Thus his practice of omitting metamorphosis begins in his earliest work; it would have marred his tale of Ceÿx and Alcyone in *The Booke of the Duchesse* because that is introduced as a prototype of the conjugal love of John of Gaunt and his first duchess Blanche, who had died in 1368 at the age of twenty-nine. Chaucer has better taste than Ovid, and far more concern for morality. The high seriousness which prompted him to translate Boethius is evident in Troilus' musings on predestination, in the Dantesque close of that poem, and in the Prioress', Second Nun's, and other Canterbury Tales. He has a sincere, if fitful, strain of religion.

The classical world he sees largely through medieval spectacles. His Dido and Procne go on pilgrimages; his Janus resembles a contemporary yeoman, his Aeneas a contemporary knight. And yet he is a bridge to the Renaissance. His Troy may be largely medieval, but significantly he added touches of true classical colour not found in *Il Filostrato*, so as to maintain the playful fiction that he is following an ancient authority. This is a first step towards getting the classical world into perspective. On the other hand, he actually relies less in his later work on classical authorities, for the renaissance spirit opened his eyes to the world around him, awakening him from medieval dreams of allegorical gardens to the observation of contemporary life and character, and into his Troy bursts the Shakespearian figure of Pandarus, forerunner of such realistic creations as the Wife of Bath.

CHAPTER XII

THE RENAISSANCE

THE phenomena we think of as being respectively medieval and renaissance spring from deep in the human heart, and co-exist perpetually in the same century, the same country, even the same individual; we can only say that in most centuries, countries and individuals the one or the other spirit is dominant. In the humanistic Florence of the Medici Savonarola struck a discordant note: 'You will say, "yet the Ovid of the *Metamorphoses* is good". I answer you, "Ovid the story-teller, Ovid the madman!";' and in the France of Louis XIV the austere Fénelon stood out against the prevailing Ovidian craze. In the sixteenth century alchemists were yet busy with the *Metamorphoses*; while far into the seventeenth and even beyond, we come across such typically medieval titles as *Les Fastes de l'Église*, *L'Arte d'Amar Dio*, *De Arte Amandi S. Mariam*.

Petrarch (1304–74) and Boccaccio (1313–75) are the significant figures of what may nevertheless be called the transitional period, each retaining a fair admixture of the medieval with what we recognize as forward-looking. Petrarch was steeped in Ovid. He took many of his mythological ideas from the *Metamorphoses*, the story of Daphne haunting him particularly because of the association of *laurus* with Laura. But most of his borrowings in his early, amatory period were from the erotic poems. His *Trionfo d'Amore*, for instance, was suggested by *Amores* I, 2. Later he became more critical of 'Naso most wanton of Poets', denouncing the *Ars Amatoria* roundly. Yet although he now cited him less frequently than Virgil, or even Horace, his echoes of Ovid betray the extent of his familiarity. Boccaccio in his youth was much more pagan. Steeped likewise in Ovid, he drew upon him freely in the early part of *Fiammetta*, where Venus is persuading the heroine to yield; nor can we dissociate the spirit of the author of the *Decamerone* from that of the author of the *Amores*. But in 1361 he was reconciled to Christianity, and turned his back on such frivolities.

For a hundred years after the death of these two no considerable poet appeared in Italy, nor for that matter in France, apart from Villon. But this was the springtime of Italian painting, and we may pause here to consider the role of Ovid in the visual arts. Even in the Middle Ages there were artists familiar with his stories. Pyramus and Thisbe were carved, about 1200, among the figures on the cathedral of Basel, and on the Royal and West Portals of the cathedral of Chartres, built in the episcopate of the widely-read John of Salisbury, appear incidents from the *Metamorphoses* involving centaurs. The first illustrated edition of Ovid's *Metamorphoses* was produced at Bruges in 1484 by the city's pioneer in printing, Colard Mansion. The illustrations were medieval in spirit, with costumes belonging to the period and district. This was followed in 1497 by another, with Italian translation, published at Venice by Zoane Rosso, one of the finest of all renaissance books, which was to exercise great influence on Italian artists for half a century, particularly on Giorgione and Mantegna. Many others appeared; indeed, no ancient author so often received this tribute.

It was the same with the large-scale arts. There were numerous tapestry workshops operating in the north from the mid-fifteenth to mid-sixteenth centuries, at Arras, for instance, as the name reminds us. The subject and spirit of their work were suddenly transformed by a wave of influence from Ferrara that swept through Brussels over the Low Countries and France. From being medieval they became mythological, the whole inspiration coming from Ovid's *Metamorphoses*.

Meanwhile in 1445 Filarete, carving the bronze doors of St Peter's, introduced sixteen stories from Ovid among those of the Christian tradition. The bridal chests of the period were mostly decorated, Vasari tells us, with scenes from Ovid and other poets or tales from Greek and Roman history. Painters in general began to turn their attention to secular subjects, among which the stories of pagan mythology were especially popular. It may be no coincidence that this fashion became widespread in the years immediately following the publication of the first printed Ovid in 1471. Early in the sixteenth century it reached a climax at Rome in Peruzzi's *Villa Farnesina*, where Raphael painted his *Galatea* and Sebastiano del Piombo decorated the lunettes with scenes from the *Metamorphoses*. The passion for mythology affected all the great masters of the High Renaissance, especially those of Venice, among whom Titian stands out as an admirer of Ovid and an inheritor of his spirit. The French kings in the middle of the century commissioned Rosso and Primaticcio to decorate the Palace of Fontainebleau with Ovidian pictures. Bernini's famous statue of Apollo and Daphne, and Rubens with his great series from the *Metamorphoses*, commissioned by Philip IV of Spain,* carry us on into the next century, when the passion gradually spent itself. From the lusty exuberance of Rubens' treatment we pass to the nostalgic, detached calm of Poussin and Claude.

In the arts it is especially difficult to determine in any particular case whether Ovid or any other writer is the direct source, for the myths became widely familiar through the handbooks; but we may justifiably assume considerable direct influence. In the seventeenth century two great technical works, one Dutch and one German, containing all that an artist should know, both conclude with a complete prose translation of the *Metamorphoses*.

Let us now return to literature. It was in Italy that bourgeois life had most chance to develop, and her cities had a tradition of culture more favourable to the revival of the classics than that of the courts of chivalry. In 1444 Aeneas Silvius Piccolomini, the future Pope Pius II, produced a Latin romance much influenced by Ovid, the *Historia de duobus amantibus*. This was translated into Italian some years later, and took its place with Boccaccio's *Fiammetta* in popular esteem. But it was the invention of printing that did most to spread classical influence in general. The *editio princeps* of Ovid appeared at Bologna in 1471, followed in the same year by an edition published at Rome, and in 1478 by a prose *Heroides* in Florentine dialect published at Naples. The earliest annotated edition of the *Metamorphoses*, by Raphael Regius, was published at Venice in 1492, and immediately became a standard work. Sixteenth-century Italy developed a flourishing literature in which pastoral and mythological elements were blended with major poets in Ariosto, Boiardo and Tasso. Many versions were made of tales from the *Metamorphoses*, while the *Amores* and *Heroides* contributed erotic colour.

* For the Torre de la Parada, 1636–8. Most of the 112 subjects were from the *Metamorphoses*; the sketches were made by Rubens, but he himself painted only some of the large works, leaving the rest to collaborators. This is the most grandiose artistic enterprise of all those based on Ovid.

In France meanwhile Ovid became a favourite of the Pléiade, with Joachim du Bellay aspiring to the title of 'l'Ovide français' and drawing on the *Tristia* for his *Regrets*. Ronsard, the greatest of the group, was much influenced by the Roman elegists, admiring Ovid most of the three, and taking from him hints for his love poems to Cassandra Salviati; but he owed still more to the *Metamorphoses*, especially in his *Odes*. In the first half of the sixteenth century boys in Paris schools read Ovid in the eighth class, and in 1551 we find the *Tristia* and *Ex Ponto* prescribed for the seventh class in Jesuit colleges. St Ignatius himself was interested in the production of expurgated classics for schools.

Spain had already felt the Ovidian influence in the Middle Ages, more from the erotic poems at first than from the *Metamorphoses*. A notable example is the *Pamphilus de Amore*, a Latin novel in dramatic form based on the *Ars Amatoria* and attributed to the poet himself. Another work of the late Middle Ages, the highly humanistic *Libro de Buen Amor* of Juan Ruiz (*c.* 1330), notoriously owes much to him, as well as the lyric *Cancioneros* of the fifteenth century. The stock comic figure of the Bawd, derived from *Amores* I, 8, became through Ruiz a popular feature of Spanish poetry, notably in the famous dramatic dialogue *Celestina* of F. de Rojas (1499). Piccolomini's romance was translated into Spanish in 1496, and had great influence in Spain, and numerous stories of the sixteenth century drew upon Ovid himself, though the aristocratic, chivalrous tradition at first remained dominant, and the Inquisition forbade the translation of the *Amores* and *Ars Amatoria*.

There are many other great European writers of the Renaissance who have been found to show Ovidian influence to a notable degree, such as Cervantes, Lope de Vega, Calderón and Camoëns. Montaigne, brought up by his father to speak Latin before French, first discovered the joy of reading when he came across the *Metamorphoses* at the age of seven or eight, though other writers were to please him more when he came to maturity. Apart from the French, Ovid's last and most distinguished devotee on the Continent was Goethe, who echoes him often in his *Roman Elegies* and whose journals constantly record that he has been rereading the *Metamorphoses*. In the vision of life at the end of *Faust* appear Philemon and Baucis.

An interesting side-line of the Ovidian tradition was operatic libretti. The first experiment in opera, made at Florence in 1594, was a dramatization by Ottavio Rinuccini of the story of Apollo and Daphne, with music by Peri and Caccini. *Daphne* was followed in 1600 by *Eurydice*. The novelty was that these works consisted of 'a magic circle of unbroken musical sound from the beginning of the story to its end'. Monteverdi, Gluck and others later exploited the same inexhaustible source of plots.

Yet while few would deny the pervasive influence of Ovid in the Renaissance, it is often difficult in literature to determine whether it is direct, though less so than in the visual arts because of the clues provided by verbal echoes. (Boccaccio's *De Genealogia Deorum*, the great link between medieval and renaissance mythology, for which he used and collated various ancient sources, was followed by many another handbook.) A late instance of this dilemma is provided by Keats; we know that he was indebted to Sandys' translation, with allegorical verses and commentary, of the *Metamorphoses* (1632), but we also know that he pored over Lemprière's *Classical Dictionary*.

In each country the Renaissance achieved for a time a harmony between Christianity and paganism, but this depended on a certain naïveté, and could not maintain itself for long against sapping of various kinds. The allegorical interpretation of the classics, or at least its feasibility, was accepted with varying degrees of sincerity. At least a perfunctory claim to be edifying was advisable until quite late in the period. But those who had religion most at heart, from Luther to the compilers of the Index of Trent, denounced even the well-meaning *Ovide moralisé*. Meanwhile the rationalistic spirit began to see through the allegorical fog, Rabelais deriding in the prologue to *Gargantua* the obscurantist interpreter of Homer and Ovid. It was a small step from this to travesty of mythology itself, which became fashionable in the seventeenth century following the publication in 1644 of Scarron's *Typhon*, with such works as Richer's *Ovide bouffon* and d'Assoucy's *Ovide en belle humeur*. Finally, the authority of the classics in general was weakened by the spirit that led to the famous quarrel of the Ancients and Moderns in the France of Louis XIV.

But to explore the fortunes of Ovid in renaissance Europe as a whole would be the work of more than a lifetime. In a book intended primarily for English readers I may be pardoned if I limit myself henceforward to some aspects of his influence on English literature and to his reputation in England, especially since, apart from the geniuses of Shakespeare and Milton, the insular development roughly paralleled the continental, with a certain time-lag.

After Chaucer and Gower, whose *Confessio Amantis* is full of stories borrowed from Ovid, there followed a medieval twilight of a century and a half, during which, although some knowledge of Ovid was part of the school and university curriculum, the classical stories were known mainly through medieval redactions, or through paraphrases of these by Lydgate and Caxton. In 1480 Caxton made an English prose version of the *Metamorphoses* from the French, which, however, was probably never printed.

We may make a fresh start with the establishment of a national system of education in the sixteenth century. When in 1512 Colet founded St Paul's School, destined to serve as a model for many, of the six Latin authors prescribed for reading in selection Ovid was not one, though Erasmus had recommended the *Heroides* as an aid in the exercise of letter-writing (it was being so used at Eton about 1528) and Ovid in general as chief master for the final exercise of rhetoric. But soon after, in Wolsey's instructions for Ipswich School (1529), the *Metamorphoses* and *Fasti* were added to the schedule. Even Sir Thomas Elyot, in his programme for the education of a Utopian prince entitled *The Governour* (1531), grudgingly admitted these two works, if suitably moralized. The *Tristia* makes its first appearance at Bury St Edmunds School in 1550; it soon became a staple, and Eton boys in 1560 were studying it along with the rules of versification. In 1530 we find Winchester boys learning twelve lines of the *Metamorphoses* by heart every week.

Such was the grammar-school grounding in Ovid that we may expect an Elizabethan poet to have had. To many his characters and stories would also be familiar from pageants, often a curious mixture of pagan with Christian elements, and from tapestries, though pictures were still rare in England. His immense vogue in the poetry of the age begins with the anonymous publication, in 1560, of a fairly close translation in seven-line stanzas of his story of Narcissus (some 200 lines of narrative being supplemented, in the manner of the day, by some 900 lines of moral). In 1565–7 appeared Golding's complete translation of the *Metamorphoses* into fourteeners, and also Turberville's *Heroycall Epistles*, followed in 1569 by Underdowne's *Ibis* and in 1572 by Churchyard's *Tristia* I–III.*

From now onwards his influence is paramount throughout the Elizabethan age.† We may consider it under three headings: literary form and subject-matter, spirit and treatment, and technique. Discussions of influence usually concentrate on borrowings, perhaps because these are the most tangible and demonstrable form of evidence; but spirit is surely more important and interesting, in spite of the danger of subjectivity.

Of literary forms little need here be said. Michael Drayton's most popular work was *England's Heroical Epistles* (1597). Instinctively the poets who imitated the *Heroides* turned for inspiration to the double letters, with their live situations and contest of wits. Beginning with the Fair Rosamond and Henry II, Drayton matched couples from history almost down to living memory. More important was the vogue of retelling Ovidian stories, spinning them out with rhetoric and Italianate embroidery.‡ From 1560 to 1575 this was commonly done in ballad form, but later we have poems in stanzas or couplets which are akin to the Greco-Roman epyllia.

The finest example of these last was actually based on a Greek epyllion of the fourth or fifth century A.D., Musaeus' *Hero and Leander*, well known and of great prestige because the author was naïvely identified with Orpheus' legendary pupil of that name. Marlowe's poem in couplets, of which he completed only two books, was entered in 1593. He blended the unadorned story of Musaeus with Ovidian elements taken from the Hero–Leander letters in the *Heroides* and elsewhere. Thus the temple of Venus, on which Musaeus spent one epithet,

* Marlowe's *Amores* was probably not published until *c.* 1595–6, under the title *Elegies*. '*F.L.*' produced a version of the *Remedia* in 1600 (incomplete); Watson may have made one much earlier. Thomas Heywood translated the *Ars*, Beaumont the *Remedia*. The *Fasti* had to wait for John Gower's version of 1640. I am indebted to Mr John Carey for information on these matters.

† At Elizabethan dinners select transformations from Ovid's *Metamorphoses* were exhibited in confectionery.

‡ Among the most popular were Pyramus and Thisbe, Cephalus and Procris, Narcissus and Echo, Apollo and Daphne, and Philomela.

provides the occasion for a brilliant description imitated from Ovid's palace of the Sun and web of Arachne:

> So fair a church as this had Venus none.
> The walls were of discoloured jasper stone,
> Wherein was Proteus carvèd, and o'erhead
> A lively vine of green sea-agate spread,
> Where by one hand light-headed Bacchus hung
> And with the other wine from grapes out-wrung.
> Of crystal shining fair the pavement was;
> The town of Sestos called it Venus' glass.
> There might you see the gods in various shapes
> Committing heady riots, incests, rapes:
> For know that underneath this radiant floor
> Was Danaë's statue in a brazen tower,
> Jove slyly stealing from his sister's bed
> To dally with Idalian Ganymed,
> And for his love, Europa, bellowing loud,
> And tumbling with the Rainbow in a cloud;
> Blood-quaffing Mars heaving the iron net,
> Which limping Vulcan and his Cyclops set;
> Love kindling fire to burn such towers as Troy;
> Silvanus weeping for the lovely boy
> That now is turned into a Cypress tree,
> Under whose shade the Wood-gods love to be.

By 1590 most poets were borrowing freely from Ovid, whether directly or indirectly. The greatest of them, Spenser, took allegorical and other descriptions from him. Marlowe's *Hero and Leander* was followed immediately by Shakespeare's *Venus and Adonis* (1593) and *The Rape of Lucrece* (1594). The former is based on the story in *Metamorphoses* x, with the description of the boar from Book VIII and the reluctance of Adonis imported perhaps from that of Narcissus (III) or Hermaphroditus (IV), though the debt to Ovid in detail is not great. The latter follows Livy I, but borrows also from the story in *Fasti* II. In 1595 the craze for Ovid was at its height, stories being especially popular in which the female, for a change, pursued the male, as in *Venus and Adonis*.*

And so we come to Shakespeare's plays. It has been estimated that he echoes Ovid in these four times as often as Virgil. He draws on

* E.g. Heywood's *Oenone*, Drayton's *Endymion and Phoebe*, Edwards' *Narcissus* and *Cephalus and Procris*.

every book of the *Metamorphoses*, and there is scarcely a play which shows no trace of its influence, which is found particularly in the lighter scenes. At first he used mythology like any other renaissance poet as a new and delightful toy; later a hint of burlesque and mockery creeps in, and still later, a sense of deeper significance in it. Let us marshal a few well-known instances in such a way as to display his attitude.

At *Much Ado About Nothing*, II, i, 99 occurs the following exchange:

Don Pedro. My visor is Philemon's roof; within the house is Jove.
Hero. Why, then, your visor should be thatched.
Don Pedro. Speak low, if you speak love.

No one can doubt the source of that. But Golding had used the salient word in his translation,

The roofe thereof was *thatchèd* all with straw and fennish reede;

and what is more, in a scene written in prose, these lines break into Golding's metre. Did Shakespeare then read Ovid in the original at all?

Quotations in Latin are rare in the plays. Nevertheless, it is made clear in T. H. Baldwin's masterly survey of this much-discussed topic that he did use the original *Metamorphoses* habitually along with Golding; and further that, although there is no direct evidence that he had or completed a grammar school education, his 'small Latine and lesse Greek' amounts to just so much as could be gleaned from the grammar-school curriculum of the Elizabethan age, which included the regular learning of passages by heart.* This opens up some interesting speculations. Suppose he began his classical reading, as so many did, with Mirandula's *Flores Poetarum*. The first excerpt he would come upon was from *Amores* I, 15, and it ended precisely with the couplet he prefixed to his *Venus and Adonis*. He would come across the name Titania, which Golding does not use, and also Autolycus, 'adept at all kinds of thieving'. Again, the heading of two excerpts from Ovid in the *Flores* reads 'Lachrymas puellarum arma esse'—'Women's weapons, waterdrops' (*Lear*, II, iv, 280). If he reached the highest forms, he would probably learn rhetoric from the standard Tudor textbook, Erasmus' *Copia* in Veltkirchius' annotated edition of 1536, a work full of Ovid.

* A lesson from Lily's Latin Grammar is burlesqued in *The Merry Wives of Windsor*, IV, i.

On the other hand, critics from Richard Farmer in 1767 onwards have pointed out apparent echoes of Golding's translation:

> Gallop apace, you fiery-footed steeds,
> Towards Phoebus' lodging; such a waggoner
> As Phaëthon would whip you to the west,
> And bring in cloudy night immediately.

'Waggoner' is Golding's word for *auriga* though coincidence cannot be ruled out here.

> In such a night
> Medea gathered the enchanted herbs
> That did renew old Aeson.

'Enchanted herbs' is Golding's phrase for *cantatas herbas*, though again it might be a coincidence. There are more certain echoes in *Venus and Adonis* and elsewhere, as we shall see. The use of a translation was no evidence of incompetence in Latin (Elizabethan schoolmasters had no prejudice against them, either for the boys or themselves); but if Marlowe at Cambridge could make the mistakes he did in rendering the *Amores*, we must not imagine that Shakespeare would read Latin with ease. However, he probably used Golding partly to cull *words*, and the phrases or ideas that the words even of a mediocre writer can generate in the mind of a fertile poet. Like Chaucer, in fact, he skimmed.

The *Metamorphoses* was not the only work of Ovid that Shakespeare knew. We have seen already from *Lucrece* that he knew the *Fasti*. It has been suggested that he wrote of Cleopatra and Antony with Dido and Aeneas in mind; and it was apparently Ovid's Dido rather than Virgil's, for Cleopatra uses words adapted from *Heroides* VII, 139, in taunting Antony with subservience to Fulvia when he leaves her for Rome:

> What says the married woman? You may go?
> Would she had never given you leave to come;

and like Ovid's Dido she hints that she is pregnant.

We must not imagine Shakespeare, any more than Chaucer, as borrowing allusions from source-books open before him. Sometimes his very slips of memory indicate the contrary:

> In such a night
> Stood Dido with a willow in her hand
> Upon the wild sea banks and waft her love
> To come again to Carthage.

When was this? Never, so far as we know. It seems to be a transferred recollection of Ariadne in the *Heroides*: 'And I fixed a white veil to a long branch, to signal to those who had, it seemed, forgotten me.' Sometimes he might make a careful preliminary study of some source, such as a Life in North's Plutarch; but the casual allusions, accurate or inaccurate, probably leapt up at the touch of association from a deep, retentive memory.

So much for gleanings of subject-matter: but what of the absorption of spirit? For thirty years after the Ovidian revival of 1560 the medieval attitude predominated. Imaginative literature could only be justified by allegorical and moralistic interpretation. The hounds that rent Actaeon were his own passions; Narcissus was a parable of the fate of vanity. Golding in a dedicatory Epistle and a Preface to his translation expounds the inner meaning of the *Metamorphoses*. And the tradition died hard, for 'the greatest repository of allegorised myth in English was the commentary which Sandys added to the 1632 edition of his translation of the *Metamorphoses*', and despite the rationalistic criticisms of Hobbes and others there were some even in the eighteenth century who still paid at least lip-service to that form of interpretation, including Pope in the Preface to his *Iliad*.

Spenser's tapestry is so vast that whole tracts are apt to be enjoyed without reference to their context. Thus in *The Faerie Queene*, III, xi, we are conducted with Britomart along a 'goodly arras of great majesty', displayed through sixteen stanzas, in which are depicted the victories of Cupid, many of them over fellow-gods, as known from the *Metamorphoses* or works derived from it. We begin with Jove himself and his seduction in ram's form of Helle and in bull's form of Europa, and then proceed in stanzas of radiant beauty:

> Soon after that, into a golden shower
> Himself he changed, fair Danaë to view,
> And through the roof of her strong brazen tower
> Did rain into her lap an honey dew;
> The whiles her foolish guard, that little knew
> Of such deceit, kept the iron door fast barred,
> And watched that none should enter nor issue.
> Vain was the watch, and bootless all the ward
> Whenas the god to golden hue himself transferred.

Then was he turned into a snowy swan,
To win fair Leda to his lovely trade.
O wondrous skill and sweet wit of the man
That her in daffodillies sleeping made
From scorching heat her dainty limbs to shade!
Whiles the proud bird, ruffling his feathers wide
And brushing his fair breast, did her invade,
She slept: yet twixt her eyelids closely spied
How towards her he rushed, and smilèd at his pride.

These last two lines, with their sly humour, might have come from Ovid's *Amores*, and the whole description is far from censorious. It is only later that we are reminded that this is the castle of the 'vile enchanter' Busirane, and that the worship paid to Cupid's golden statue by its inmates is 'foul idolatry'.

A still more surprising manifestation (though Boccaccio's *Ameto* might prepare us) is Chapman's curious poem, published in 1595, called *Ovid's Banquet of Sence*. Ovid is in love with Julia, the Emperor's daughter (Corinna to him). He hides in a garden, sees her bathing, and has the opportunity of gratifying in turn the five senses of hearing, smelling, seeing, tasting and—but he is interrupted before he can proceed to feeling. And to what is all this leading? To the neo-Platonic conclusion, as opposed to the Stoic, that it is through the exercise of the senses that man must initiate his soul if he is to become capable of aspiring to the higher love and the vision of divine beauty!

There is no reason to suppose that these poets were hypocrites, however conscious they may have been that pagans could not be allowed to show their true faces in a Christian world. Nor should we impute cynicism to virtuous men such as Spenser who, steeped in Italian literature, lavished their gifts on sensuous and appetizing descriptions of what they were proposing to condemn: if their subconscious ran away with them, they were only, like Milton, 'of the Devil's party unawares'. Nevertheless, it is easy to see how descriptions of the sort they sometimes inserted would come to be relished without their context in a thoroughly pagan spirit, especially now that the pastoral tradition had become merged with the mythological. Thomas Lodge, in 1589, was the first to come out into the open with an epyllion pretending to no hidden meaning. His *Scillaes Metamorphoses* is a longish poem in sixain stanzas, with luscious anatomical and other descriptions in the

Italianate manner. It is based on Ovid's tale of Scylla and Glaucus, though the scene is quaintly set on the banks of the Isis. Itself a poem of little merit, it heralds four years in advance the lovely *Hero and Leander* of Marlowe.

It was not so long since Marlowe had been closely rendering the *Amores*, and indeed two dozen apparent reminiscences of that work have been detected in this poem. But more important is the spirit of the Ovidian erotic poems in general, which he has infused into the simple narrative of Musaeus. No sooner has Hero seen Leander kneeling in the temple

> (who ever loved that loved not at first sight?)

than she reacts like a sophisticated Corinna with a pert aside:

> Were I the saint he worships, I would hear him.

After he had declaimed at length against virginity in general, and hers in particular,

> Thereat she smiled, and did deny him so,
> As put thereby, yet might he hope for mo.

Her whole frame of mind recalls that of the already slipping Helen of *Heroides* XVII:

> These arguments he used, and many more,
> Wherewith she yielded, that was won before.
> Hero's looks yielded, but her words made war;
> Women are won when they begin to jar.
> Thus having swallowed Cupid's golden hook,
> The more she strived, the deeper was she strook;
> Yet evilly feigning anger strove she still,
> And would be thought to grant against her will.
> So having paused a while, at last she said:
> 'Who taught thee rhetoric to deceive a maid?
> Aye me, such words as these I should abhor,
> And yet I like them for the orator.'

Repelling his embraces, she volunteers the information where she lives, blushes to have let slip unawares a 'come thither', then later lingers on the way home, and even drops her fan, in case he may not succeed in following her. In Book II Leander, who knew enough about 'Venus' sweet rites' in Book I, is suddenly discovered to be an ignoramus in love, who

Long dallying with Hero, nothing saw
That might delight him more, yet he suspected
Some amorous rites or other were neglected.*

The sole reason for this seems to be that it enabled the tantalizing climax to be still further delayed, though in all conscience Hero did her part in this:

Treason was in her thought,
And cunningly to yield herself she sought.
Seeming not won, yet won she was at length,
In such wars women use but half their strength.

And so at last to the point where Hero, like Corinna in *Amores* I, 5, was 'all naked to his sight displayed'. And there Marlowe, for whatever reason, broke off, leaving it to Chapman to add four other books. He had written a poem of voluptuous beauty whose whole intention was as erotic as anything in Ovid.

Venus and Adonis, which appeared in the same year, is less Ovidian, though still based on Ovid; it signally lacks his chief characteristic as a story-teller, swiftness and simplicity; instead it is spun out with conceit upon conceit, and the sugar that threatened to cloy in Marlowe's poem has become saccharine. *The Rape of Lucrece*, which followed in 1594, dealt more seriously with chastity, a virtue which the condition of the reigning sovereign and the third book of *The Faerie Queen* may well have rendered topical at this period. For its time it is archaic—indeed, it harks back to Chaucer. It is thirteen times as long as the episode in Ovid, being still more rhetorical, though less sensuous, than *Venus and Adonis*. Those who condemn Ovid as rhetorical might well read this poem before turning to him again.

Francis Meres, writing in 1598, made a well-known remark which no doubt represents the feeling of that decade: 'the sweet witty soul of Ovid lives in mellifluous and honey-tongued Shakespeare; witness his *Venus and Adonis*, his *Lucrece*, his sugared sonnets among his private friends'. We may feel rather that it is not so much in these poems as in certain of the plays that the true spirit of Ovid lives on, notably in *A Midsummer Night's Dream* and *The Tempest*, for both of which there is concrete evidence to support the impression.

The *Dream* is based on North's translation of Plutarch's Life of Theseus; but Professor Baldwin, discussing the phrase 'triple Hecate'

* How like the end of some stanza in Byron's *Don Juan*!

in Puck's song at the end, has expressed his conviction that before Shakespeare wrote the play he had read Ovid's story of Jason and Medea in the *Metamorphoses* with some care, using along with Golding's translation an edition containing the notes of Regius. And, indeed, it is natural that he should have turned to Ovid for ideas, since the scene is set in that prehistoric Greek world which was the background for so much of his masterpiece. In the hunting scene (IV, i) the hounds, as described by him, recall Actaeon's in Golding's version of *Metamorphoses* III, 206–25. Hippolyta has previously remarked,

> I was with Hercules and Cadmus once
> When in a wood of Crete they bay'd the boar
> With hounds of Sparta.

Why Cadmus, not at all a well-known hero? Because he was the grandfather of Actaeon, and the first 136 lines of this same third book are about him. But why Crete, with which he had no special connexion? Partly perhaps because of the provenance of Actaeon's hounds—

> This latter was a hounde of Crete, the other was of Spart—

and again

> The shaggy Rugge with other twain had had a syre of Crete
> And dam of Sparta;

but perhaps also from the chance association of the two names in the opening lines of the same book:

> The God now having layde aside his borrowed shape of Bull
> Had in his likenesse shewde himself, and with his pretty trull
> Tane landing in the Ile of *Crete*. When in that while her Sire
> Not knowing where shee was become, sent after to enquire
> Hir brother *Cadmus*.

Here then is another longish passage in the *Metamorphoses* that Shakespeare had been reading. And the whole performance of *Pyramus and Thisbe* in the last act follows *Metamorphoses* IV, 45–166 closely.

So much for the activities of the mortals. But what of the uncanny agencies that play tricks on them? Here we can put our finger on nothing tangible that is Ovidian save for the name Titania; and yet the whole atmosphere is extraordinarily reminiscent of the *Metamorphoses* —the magic and the freedom, the Puckish element, the blend of charm and moral irresponsibility, the sense that nothing that happens is really serious because it is all a dream, the interplay of pathos and humour, cruelty and love, the natural and the supernatural, the grotesque and the beautiful, Bottom with his Midas-ears fondled by the demi-goddess Titania.

It is just such a shifting world of fantasy and magic in *The Tempest* that reminds one again of the *Metamorphoses*—the mercurial spirit of Ariel changing from one shape to another, the beauty of the island, the boisterous humour of Stephano and Trinculo, the conjuring up of Iris, Ceres, Juno and the nymphs, the grotesque Caliban and the innocent love of Ferdinand and Miranda. This fairyland at least can produce evidence of direct descent; for it was recognized long ago by Farmer that Prospero's incantation is prompted by Medea's in Golding's Ovid:

> Ye elves of hills, brooks, standing lakes and groves;
> And ye that on the sands with printless foot
> Do chase the ebbing Neptune and do fly him
> When he comes back; you demi-puppets, that
> By moonshine do the green sour ringlets make
> Whereof the ewe not bites; and you, whose pastime
> Is to make midnight mushrooms; that rejoice
> To hear the solemn curfew; by whose aid—
> Weak masters though ye be—I have bedimmed
> The noontide sun, called forth the mutinous winds,
> And 'twixt the green sea and the azured vault
> Set roaring war: to the dread-rattling thunder
> Have I given fire, and rifted Jove's stout oak
> With his own bolt; the strong-based promontory
> Have I made shake; and by the spurs plucked up
> The pine and cedar; graves at my command
> Have waked their sleepers, oped, and let them forth
> By my so potent art....

And now Golding's translation of Ovid:

> Ye Ayres and Windes; ye Elves of Hills, of Brookes, of Woods alone,
> Of standing Lakes, and of the Night, approche ye everychone.
> Through help of whom (the crooked bankes much wondring at the thing)
> I have compellèd streames to run cleane backward to their spring.
> By charmes I make the calme Seas rough, and make the rough Sees plaine
> And cover all the Skie with Cloudes, and chase them thence againe.
> By charms I rayse and lay the windes, and burst the Vipers jaw,
> And from the bowels of the Earth both stones and trees do drawe.

Whole Woods and Forests I remove: I make the Mountains shake,
And even the Earth itselfe to grone and fearfully to quake.
I call up dead men from their graves; and thee, O Lightsome Moone
I darken oft, though beaten brasse abate thy perill soone.
Our Sorcerie dimmes the Morning faire, and darkes the Sun at Noone.

Clearly Shakespeare had Golding in mind, but it can be shown that he derived even more from the original.*

All the Elizabethan poets borrowed from Ovid, but it was Shakespeare who knew best how to value him. In *Love's Labour's Lost* Holofernes comments severely on Berowne's verses:

Here are only numbers ratified; but, for the elegancy, facility, and golden cadence of poesy, caret. Ovidius Naso was the man: and why, indeed, Naso, but for the smelling out of odoriferous flowers of fancy, the jerks of invention? Imitari is nothing: so doth the hound his master, the ape his keeper, the tired horse his rider....I will prove these verses to be very unlearned, neither savouring of poetry, wit, nor invention.

He is judging according to the principles of Quintilian, who was studied in the higher forms of the grammar schools. He may be a burlesque character, but the qualities he ascribed by implication to Ovid, 'elegancy, facility and golden cadence', are so aptly chosen that we may assume that he speaks here for Shakespeare. As Professor Baldwin says:

Shakspere agreed also with Quintilian that while the fundamental things in a writer are not mechanically imitable, yet an admired writer should be so mastered as to absorb his inimitable spirit. It was in this fashion that Shakspere had mastered Ovid, whom Quintilian would never have advised (Virgil was his favourite). But Holofernes—and Shakspere—thought that Ovid excelled in poetic invention and the other inimitable virtues.

In the sphere of technique we may trace the influence of Ovid on the development of the heroic couplet. We have already noted the general absence in Chaucer's myriad couplets of closure, balance, antithesis, parallelism and rhetorical figures of speech, which are the distinguishing marks of the couplets of Ovid, as of Pope. No regular decasyllabic couplets showing clear evidence of classical influence are

* Some of the ingredients in the witches' cauldron in *Macbeth* come from Medea's recipe (*Macbeth* IV, i, 4 ff., *Metamorphoses* VII, 262 ff.), and Hecate there is Ovidian. Prospero's other famous speech (IV, i, 148–58), 'These our actors, / As I foretold you, were all spirits...' also derives ultimately from Ovid, through Palingenius.

to be found before the period of Tottel's *Miscellany* (1557). But this collection included sixteen poems by Nicholas Grimald in couplets which are mostly closed and which have plenty of balance of a kind, together with classical allusions, rhetorical questions, and other figures such as apostrophe. We are still far from the real thing; but Grimald is groping for it. The first really significant step towards the Popian medium was taken in circumstances which make it certain that the decisive influence was Ovid. Marlowe, probably as an undergraduate at Cambridge before 1584, made his line-for-line translation of the *Amores* in heroic couplets which, published a dozen years later, achieved popularity as well as notoriety. In this every couplet was naturally closed, and the main technical features of the original were reproduced as far as possible—antithetical balance, apostrophe, rhetorical questions and so forth.

> Fool, if to keep thy wife thou hast no need,
> Keep her for me, my more desire to feed.
> We scorn things lawful, stolen sweets we affect;
> Cruel is he that loves whom none protect.

Or again:

> Jove, being admonished gold had sovereign power,
> To win the maid, came in a golden shower.
> Till then, rough was her father, she severe,
> The posts of brass, the walls of iron were,
> But when in gifts the wise adulterer came,
> She held her lap ope to receive the same.

What is more important, Marlowe proceeded to display these features, to a considerably greater extent than his predecessors had done, in a poem in heroic couplets for which Ovid is only a secondary source, *Hero and Leander*. They had become associated with this particular metre.

The development of antithesis is most striking in *Venus and Adonis*, of which Bush remarks, 'It is hardly too much to say that the whole fabric of the poem is woven of antitheses, as if Shakespeare had fallen in love with one of Ovid's tricks and worked it to death'. Lines such as

> Hunting he lov'd, but love he laugh'd to scorn,
> Ten kisses short as one, one long as twenty,
> He red for shame, but frosty in desire,

recall immediately the poet from whom the subject-matter also was derived. And this poem had great influence, running into at least ten editions in Shakespeare's lifetime.

In Drayton's *England's Heroical Epistles* (1597), which ran into fourteen editions by 1637, careful study of the Ovidian model is manifest from the vigorous, rhetorical style, the turns and antitheses and the closure of the couplets. Who can hear the lines,

> Punish my fault, or pity mine estate,
> *Read them for love, if not for love, for hate*,

without thinking at once of Ovid's,

> If hate I cannot, grudging will I love?

All that is lacking from the original recipe is the literary allusions.

Finally, in 1609, came Heywood's monstrous *Troia Britannica*, of which Cantos IX and X consist in a diffuse translation of Ovid's exchange of letters between Paris and Helen. (He had earlier translated the *Ars* and *Remedia*.) Here once more we see the influence of Ovid in shaping the English heroic couplet. I will quote some lines of Helen's, for comparison with those already given on p. 46; four couplets have become seven, but the style has left its imprint:

> Yet had I rather stainless keep my fame
> Than to a stranger hazard my good name:
> Make me your instance, and forbear the fare,
> Of that which most doth please you, make most spare;
> The greatest virtue of which wise men boast
> Is to abstain from that which pleaseth most.
> How many gallant youths (think you) desire
> That which you covet, scorcht wi' the self-same fire?
> Are all the world fools, only Paris wise?
> Or is there none save you have judging eyes?
> No, no, you view no more than others see,
> But you are plainer and more bold with me;
> You are more earnest to pursue your game;
> I yield you, not more knowledge, but less shame.

Shakespeare had already put into the mouth of Iago those sudden couplets pregnant with the future, beginning

> She that was ever fair and never proud,
> Had tongue at will and yet was never loud....

Heywood's 'numbers' may not be conspicuously smooth or harmonious, but it was now no great step to the art of Waller, Dryden and Pope; and it was Ovid who had prepared the way.

The fashion of elaborating Ovidian tales continued into the seventeenth century, with a bias towards the *risqué*. Iphis and Ianthe were the theme of *The Maid's Metamorphosis* (*c.* 1600); Beaumont may be the author of the *Salmacis and Hermaphroditus* (1602), and Barksted dealt with *Mirrha* (1607). Cowley, at the age of ten, retold the story of Pyramus and Thisbe, and published it five years later (1633). One of the last poems in the series was Shirley's *Narcissus*, which, though entered in 1618, did not appear until 1646. But by the turn of the century there were puffs of contrary wind; satire came into fashion, and with it a taste for burlesquing mythology and deflating rhetoric. Thus Nashe wrote a debunking prose version of the story of Hero and Leander entitled *Prayse of the Red Herring*, and an anonymous Jacobean composed a *Metamorphosis of Tobacco* in heroic couplets. The publication of the Frenchman Scarron's *Tryphon* in 1644 gave an impulse to the production of travesties, particularly of Ovid, which continued in England throughout the Restoration period.

One product of the early seventeenth century is worth more than a passing mention, not for its intrinsic merits, but because it portends the future—Ben Jonson's *The Poetaster* (1602). This 'comicall satyre' is in dramatic form, and the scene is Augustan Rome. The earlier part is largely taken up with a sub-plot about Ovid. He is discovered by his disapproving father composing *Amores* I, 15 (here represented in English couplets). Next Tibullus brings him an invitation to a party from his mistress Corinna, *alias* the Princess Julia. There they stage a masquerade of the gods, with Ovid as Jupiter and Julia as Juno. They are surprised by Augustus, Maecenas and Horace and banished, parting in a balcony scene reminiscent of Romeo and Juliet. In the latter part of the play Virgil figures as the great poet, and together with Horace (who represents Jonson himself) arraigns and discomforts two detractors of Horace's poetry, Demetrius (= Dekker) and Crispinus (= Marston). One scene is adapted from Horace's Satire about his encounter with a bore (I, 9). Now all this is light-hearted enough; but it represents, first, a classicizing attempt to see the ancient poets and worthies in their true historical setting (though Jonson's Rome is as cardboard compared with the Rome that Shakespeare conjured up out of North's Plutarch), and secondly, a step towards the replacement of a banished Ovid by Jonson's favourite Horace in the place of honour next to Virgil. The classical attitude to antiquity is beginning to oust the romantic. When Shirley came to write his short chamber drama *The Contention of Ajax and Ulysses*, printed in 1659, the plot came from Ovid indeed, but the dirge at the end, which is all we now remember, is one of the most *Horatian* poems in the language,

The glories of our blood and state....

About the end of the sixteenth century the young Donne in some of his Elegies was deliberately emulating the Ovidian *nequitia*, with 'apparently serious defences of outrageous propositions', as Mr Leishman calls them. But it must not be supposed that the growth of voluptuous pagan poetry in Elizabethan times took place without protest from the staider sort. John Stockwood preached at Paul's Cross against the reading of the erotic poets, including 'a great part of Ovid', and in 1582 the Privy Council prescribed patriotic literature for grammar schools instead of 'Ovide de arte amandi, de tristibus or suche lyke' (without much effect, it would seem). Marlowe's translation of the *Amores* was among books ordered in 1599, by the Archbishop of Canterbury and the Bishop of London, to be publicly burnt. In Jacobean times puritanism gained momentum. Prynne's portentous *Histriomastix* (1632) denounced everything that was pagan, let alone immoral, and Cowley in 1656, grown middle-aged, turned on his fellow-poets of previous generations, for both literary and religious reasons, as handling 'confused antiquated Dreams of senseless Fables and Metamorphoses'. And so we come to the complicated and quite exceptional position of Milton.

Milton must have been introduced to Ovid at St Paul's. He learnt, in the venerable European tradition, to compose in Latin verse, and faultlessly he did it. Along with the metre, he adopted, in the classical way, the turns of speech and thought appropriated to it. And so, in the first of his elegies, written to Diodati in 1626 while he was in rustication from Cambridge, after remarking in a rhetorical spirit that if only Ovid's exile had been as mild as his, he would have equalled Homer and Virgil, the future author of *Paradise Regained* proceeds to recount the pleasures of the London stage, and the attractions of the girls he sees in the suburban parks. The boy who could write of the theatre

There oft a maid the unwonted ardour proves,
Knows not what love is, yet unknowing loves,

was clearly on the most familiar terms with the *Ars Amatoria*; but it would not have occurred to him that Diodati or anyone else would take him too seriously. He was simply, in the classical tradition, composing a poem in which his personal situation was made a peg for elegiac commonplaces.* In the sixth Elegy, after putting it to the same Diodati that the revelry he reports should have stimulated his friend's lighter muse, he goes on to say that frugality and purity befit a poet with higher themes, and reveals that he himself is composing an ode *On the Morning of Christ's Nativity*. Steeped in the Latin of Ovid's works, he was a scholar of the new type, exemplified by Ben Jonson, who saw antiquity in perspective, understood its conventions, and knew exactly what he was about.

'Nothing places Milton more clearly in the Renaissance tradition', says Bush, 'than his attachment to Ovid.' His early passion for the amatory elegies could not be expected to last long in so serious a puritan, but his enthusiasm for 'Ovidius maior' was to remain unabated. We are told that the works he most delighted to hear read to him in his blindness were, after Homer, which he knew almost by heart, the plays of Euripides and the *Metamorphoses* of Ovid. Such was the power of this great pictorial poem to 'shine inward, there plant eyes'.

The Circean passages of *Comus*, though based on Homer, owe some details to Ovid; but the whole conception of this masque is in the medieval allegorizing tradition of the *Ovide moralisé*, which came down to Milton through his admired forerunner, Spenser, and perhaps through Sandys' elaborate *Ovid's Metamorphosis* of 1632. We have seen how Spenser's poetic conscience impelled him to present in alluring colours the things he meant to condemn. Milton was in the same dilemma. The first utterance he gives to Comus

The Star that bids the Shepherd fold....

is so beautiful in diction and imagery that it has us prejudiced in the villain's favour at once, forgetful of the previous warning given by the Attendant Spirit. But in maturity he was too rational, too sophisticated, to follow Spenser in carefree blending or juxtaposition of pagan and Christian elements, yet too much impregnated with the classics

* On the other hand he carefully changes any phrase he borrows that might otherwise seem lascivious. Who shall say whether the fair maid seen, loved and lost in Elegy VII, 61–102, ever existed?

to abjure their aid, even if he could. And so in *Paradise Lost* we find him adopting various shifts, though significantly allegory is no longer one of them. He could identify the pagan gods with the Satanic powers, a patristic and medieval notion already used in the Nativity ode. He could introduce a myth with a 'fabled how', or dismiss one with a 'thus they relate, erring', refer to pagan divinities as 'feigned' or to the Muse herself that Orpheus bore as 'an empty dream', though the convincing and supererogatory beauty of his treatment is apt to betray the conflict in him of poet with puritan. Similes from mythology could be justified by the assertion that some storied person, place or event was here surpassed (as in the '*Taccia*—' formula of Dante: 'over-go' was the old English verb):

> Not that fair field
> Of Enna, where Proserpin gathering flowers,
> Herself a fairer flower, by gloomy Dis
> Was gathered, which cost Ceres all that pain
> To seek her through the world, nor that sweet grove
> Of Daphne by Orontes, and the inspired
> Castalian spring might with this Paradise
> Of Eden strive.

Casual allusions to mythology could cause no offence. Nor could the borrowing of details in descriptive passages, where Ovid could be especially helpful. The most elaborate of Milton's evocations of dawn, at the beginning of Book VI, owes something to him:

> Morn
> Waked by the circling Hours, with rosy hand
> Unbarred the gates of Light.

He was invaluable, through his inventiveness which so many poets have applauded, in the long stretches of the narrative which the Bible did not cover; but particularly for the cosmic phenomena described in Book I of the *Metamorphoses*, Chaos, Creation, Paradise, Fall and Flood.

It is instructive to observe how the two poets deal with the Flood. Ovid begins thus at line 262 (Jupiter is the subject):

> Forthwith in Aeolus' cave he prisoned fast
> The North Wind and each cloud-dispelling blast,
> Then let the South Wind free. His wings all wet
> And awful face o'ercast with veil of jet,

Out flies the dark South Wind. His beard is hung
With heavy mist, and waters stream among
His hoary hairs. Vapour his brow enshrouds;
His breast and pinions drip. The hovering clouds
He presses with broad hand, and therewithal
A roar is heard; then down in floods they fall.
Juno's swift Iris, clad in varied hue,
Draws moisture up to feed the clouds anew.
Crops are laid low, and farmers mourn to see
Their hopes, a year's toil, ruined utterly.

Ovid is not here at his best. He lets himself be diverted from the scene by the temptation to play with the personification in a baroque way, and his metre, 'on the hand-gallop' as ever, conflicts with the subject-matter. Milton liked the beginning, but had no use for the rest:

Meanwhile the Southwind rose, and with black wings
Wide hovering, all the clouds together drove
From under Heaven; the hills to their supply
Vapour and exhalation dusk and moist
Sent up amain; and now the thickened sky
Like a dark ceiling stood: down rushed the rain
Impetuous, and continued till the earth
No more was seen.

The inspiration for that sombre sequence of gathering gloom, deathly hush, and sudden cloudburst came rather from the master of expressiveness, Virgil (*Georgics* I, 322–6). Note especially the effect of the colon-pause at 'stood', after the long syllables have brought the gathering to a head. Ovid next has an interlude equally little to Milton's purpose, in which Jupiter summons the rivers to receive their orders, but when he returns to description he can help again with suggestions of detail:

If any house resisted and could be
Unshattered by so great calamity,
Yet o'er its roof the burying waters reared,
And towers beneath the deluge disappeared.
Now sea and land had no distinction more:
Ocean was all, an ocean without shore.

After telling of the Ark ('secure with *beakèd* prow' a few lines later echoes Ovid) Milton continues with obvious indebtedness to the above passage:

All dwellings else
Flood overwhelmed, and them with all their pomp
Deep under water rolled; Sea covered Sea,
Sea without shore, and in their palaces
Where Luxury late reigned, sea-monsters whelped
And stabled.

Even these sea-monsters come from Ovid:

Where slender goats but lately cropped the grass,
Now wallowing seals extend their shapeless mass.

Another instructive comparison is provided by the scene in which Eve describes how she discovered her own beauty through reflexion from a pool, one clearly suggested by Narcissus' similar experience in the *Metamorphoses*.* Tempted by the paradoxes inherent in the situation, Ovid, as so often, pursues his idea too far; and again Milton borrows some details, but refines by transforming or omitting others:

Here, tired with heat and with the eager chase
The boy lay down, attracted by the place
And by its pool; and as he sought to slake
His thirst, he felt another thirst awake,
And as he drank, smitten by what did seem
A face, he loved an unsubstantial dream,
And what was shadow mere, did substance deem.
With fixed expression, motionless, amazed,
As if in Parian marble carved, he gazed;
Prostrate, he sees twin stars, that are his eyes,
Hair that with Bacchus' and Apollo's vies,
Smooth cheeks, an ivory neck, mouth full of grace,
And whiteness tinged with roses in that face,
What's admirable in himself admires,
Approves himself, fondly himself desires,
Seeking is sought, and burns with self-made fires.
How oft in vain he kissed the elusive pool,
Into the water plunged his arms, poor fool,
To clasp that neck, only to find it flee!
He knows not what he sees, yet burns to see;
What lures yet mocks him is the self-same thing.
Fond boy, why chase a phantom vanishing?

* III, 413–36. The pool has already been described, p. 81. Cf. *Paradise Lost*, IV, 457–69.

> You seek what is not: turn away, and lo
> Your love, a mere reflected shape, will go;
> Naught in itself, with you it came, it stays,
> With you 'twill leave—could you but go your ways!

And now Milton's Eve:

> I thither went
> With unexperienced thought, and laid me down
> On the green bank, to look into the clear,
> Smooth lake, that to me seemed another sky.
> As I bent down to look, just opposite,
> A shape within the watery gleam appeared
> Bending to look on me. I started back,
> It started back, but pleased I soon returned,
> Pleased it returned as soon with answering looks
> Of sympathy and love. There had I fixed
> Mine eyes till now, and pined with vain desire,
> Had not a voice thus warned me: 'What thou seest,
> What there thou seest, fair creature, is thyself:
> With thee it came and goes.'

Milton would feel nothing incongruous in the association of 'our general mother' with Narcissus. Giles Fletcher, in his *Christ's Victorie and Triumph* (1610), had gravely compared the ascending Christ with Ganymede. This mingling of pagan and Christian elements was characteristic of the poetic tradition from Spenser to Milton. Indeed, our modern sense of incongruity may be exceptional. Milton in his third elegy, on the late lamented Bishop of Winchester, feigns to have seen him in a dream of Paradise, and ends with a line, 'Often may I have the happiness of such dreams', which is unmistakably reminiscent of that with which Ovid concludes a very different poem.

By the time he wrote *Paradise Regained* the worldly fopperies of the Restoration had sharpened his sense of the cleavage between pagan and Christian, which had already caused him scruples in *Paradise Lost*. In the earlier poem his chief sources of ideas, apart from the Bible, were Homer, Hesiod, Virgil and Ovid; every book of the *Metamorphoses* except the twelfth has been found to have contributed something. But in the later the old mythological richness has almost disappeared. Significantly, its last flicker, in the description of Christ's temptations, is one of the few passages of the work that remain in the memory:

And at a stately side-board, by the wine
That fragrant smell diffused, in order stood
Tall stripling youths rich clad, of fairer hue
Than Ganymed or Hylas; distant more
Under the trees now tripped, now solemn stood,
Nymphs of Diana's train, and Naiades
With fruits and flowers from Amalthea's horn,
And ladies of the Hesperides, that seemed
Fairer than feigned of old....

Before the end of the poem he has, through the mouth of his Master, renounced his classical heritage. In the year of Milton's death, 1674, Thomas Rymer remarked of the Renaissance that 'it was the vice of those Times to affect superstitiously the Allegory'; and four years later Saint Evremond expressed clearly the spirit of the dawning Age of Reason: 'The genius of our age is quite the opposite to this spirit of fables and false mysteries. We love plain truth; good sense has gained ground upon the illusions of fancy, and nothing satisfies us nowadays but solid reason.' The strange, romantic marriage of Christianity and paganism has finally been dissolved.

EPILOGUE

Molière, like Milton, still loved the *Metamorphoses* in his old age, and had a copy always at hand in his bedroom at Auteuil. But with these two the Renaissance may be said to have come to an end, and in their lifetime the reputation of Ovid began to fade. In Italy, and still more in Spain, he was eclipsed. The scholars of the Low Countries, and some of their German successors, continued to admire him; but only in France did his vogue continue, reaching its height in the age of Louis XIV. His wit, his elegance and his analytical interest in the feminine heart have made him as congenial to the French as Horace has proved to the English. Racine, in 1661, read and marked the whole of his works, intending to write a play based on his life, which suggests that many passages of his own which are parallel to passages in the Roman may be ascribed to direct influence. In particular, the *Heroides* may have given him hints for the characterization of his women.*

In art Ovid had provided ideas for the garden-sculpture of the Luxembourg Palace, made for Marie de' Medici, and he continued to do so for Le Nôtre's work at the Tuileries and Versailles.† Frederick the Great summoned painters from France to decorate Sans Souci with scenes from the *Metamorphoses*. But after Poussin and Claude he ceased everywhere to be the painter's bible. Not that the *Metamorphoses* have failed to provide subject-matter for some far from classical artists since then, such as the Northumbrian John Martin, who painted scenes from them in the early decades of the nineteenth century, and Pablo Picasso, who in 1931 illustrated a *de luxe* translation with thirty etchings.

In England Ovid was congenial to the Restoration spirit, as we find it, for instance, in Congreve's *Way of the World*. Sir Aston Cockain wrote a play about him, *The Tragedy of Ovid*, as Racine had planned to do. Swift as a young man (1708) composed a charming adaptation of the Philemon and Baucis story, in which a village parson of Chilthorne in Somerset and his wife figure as the originals of two old

* As a young man Racine wrote Latin poems in elegiacs.

† It is unlikely, for example, that the subject of the Lycians turned into frogs, figured at Versailles and therefrom in the great fountain of the Spanish royal gardens at San Ildefonso, would have occurred to anyone who had not found it in Ovid.

yew-trees, and their cottage, of the church. Dryden's *Fables*, published in 1700, are largely taken from Ovid. But the translation of the *Metamorphoses* by Dryden, Congreve, Addison and others, issued in 1717, is the last great English monument of his former glory. He was now on the defensive. Gilbert Wakefield in 1799 still ventured to think him the first poet of antiquity, but his correspondent Charles James Fox was aware of temerity in putting him even next after Homer and Virgil.

Of course there have been odd individuals who have shown a kindred spirit to his—Byron in *Don Juan* and *Beppo*, for instance, or Peacock; there have been odd enthusiasts even later than Wakefield, such as Landor; odd poets who have used this or that Ovidian story, as Shelley did in his *Arethusa*, Swinburne in *Atalanta in Calydon*, Morris in the Pygmalion episode of *The Earthly Paradise*, though their spirit and intention have rarely been Ovid's; and schoolboys have read him as model for the Latin Verse Composition which until recently occupied rather too much of their time. But these instances are as nothing compared with the general neglect.

It is worth considering what causes may have contributed to the decline, at first gradual and then rapid, of Ovid's reputation. I would suggest that the following were among them, at least in England:

(*a*) He ceased to perform certain services which had been in fact largely a fortuitous by-product of his work. He was no longer the only obvious source, for writers and artists, of mythological lore, after the diffusion of handbooks such as Boccaccio's. Nor was he a leading purveyor of erotic stories, after the publication of works in the vernacular such as the *Decameron* and the Spanish romances, still less after the development of novels in which these topics were treated at length, such as *Moll Flanders* or *Tom Jones*. The novels also surpassed him, at a popular level, in the portrayal of character, whereas in the Middle Ages and the Renaissance he had been considered a master of psychological subtlety, particularly in the *Heroides*, but also in the *Amores*, *Ars* and *Remedia*. He had come to seem even less remarkable in this respect, owing to the general increase of awareness in the analysis and delineation of character, even before the deepening of our whole understanding of motives, and the revealing of unimagined complexities, by the discoveries of Freud and modern investigators.

(*b*) Ovid suffered a relative decline among classical authors in the seventeenth century, partly through the great advance in the study of Greek, and partly through the discovery of the more serious merits of Horace, particularly in the *Odes*. Later, the classical students of the nineteenth century, romantically preferring poetry with original rather than derivative subject-matter, intensified the study of Greek at the expense of Latin.

(*c*) The prestige of the classics as a whole began to decline in the seventeenth century. It became clear that they were of no direct help to the gentleman in fighting or managing his estate, nor yet to the middle classes for trade now that Latin was ceasing to be an international language. There was an increasing demand for an educational curriculum based on mathematics and modern languages. The latter received powerful support in the nineteenth century from the Prince Consort, when 'Modern Sides' were established in public schools. Some classical authors could be defended to utilitarians on their own ground, but Ovid was not one of these.

(*d*) In England puritan and Anglican sentiment gradually gained the upper hand. Hostility to paganism was shown by writers such as Blackmore, Addison, Watts, Spence, Johnson and Cowper; and laxity in sexual matters was no longer condoned because the author was a classic. This new strictness, already operative in the age of Addison and Johnson, became a passion in the nineteenth century, which somehow managed to hush up the abusive obscenities and adultery of its favourite Catullus, 'tenderest of Roman poets', to fall with Augustan severity on the polite flippancies of Ovid.

(*e*) The contrast between the fortunes of these two in that century is a pointer to the most powerful factor of all in Ovid's dethronement, the upheaval characterized by the *Sturm und Drang* in Germany, the Revolution in France, and the Romantic Movement in England. Ovid was typical of the *ancien régime*, of everything against which the spirit of the age was in revolt. The last considerable poet to make constant use of him, André Chénier, was significantly among the victims of the guillotine. In particular, his whole attitude to love was highly unromantic, a fault for which his incidental descriptions of romantic scenery could not atone.

(*f*) The nineteenth century also saw a broadening of men's interest in the subject-matter of the classics, as a result of which classical authors came more and more to be valued, especially at Oxford, for their contribution to our knowledge of history, philosophy or archaeology, and less for their purely literary merit. This tendency, at first salutary, has now gone far too far. For such purposes Ovid, apart from the *Fasti*, has little to offer; he is not 'important'. Nor, on the other hand, had he special interest for the fashionable occupation of textual criticism; as Housman was to remark *à propos* the *Heroides*, there were easier tasks to hand than 'gleaning after Bentley over a stubble where Heinsius has reaped'.

(*g*) Finally, there has been a fundamental objection to his mentality as revealed in his works, and to his works because of his mentality, which goes beyond the age-long puritan deprecation of his attitude to sexual morality. I believe it can be traced to the Romantic critics, with their insistence on the sharp distinction between what is poetry and what is merely verse and their biographical approach to literature. Sometimes it is expressed by saying that he has no heart. 'The quality of heartlessness', says Mackail, 'affects the whole book [*Decameron*], and the whole of Boccaccio's work. He shares it with or inherits it from Ovid. It is consistent with the highest gifts of the story-teller, but not with the highest gifts of the poet.' It is true that the *Ars Amatoria* is heartless—one shudders to think of its being written in any other spirit; and the *Amores* are heartless—but no one should mistake them for love-poetry *manqué*. Yet when we come to the poems from exile, the only ones that bear on the real life of the poet, we surely find that he had a heart after all.

More often it is a soul he is said to lack. Ever since 'Longinus' defined sublimity as 'the echo of a great soul', a criterion has been intermittently present in men's minds which Ovid cannot satisfy. His purpose was to entertain, as Homer's was in the *Odyssey*. He is not 'sublime'; nor is he 'profound'. 'Their poetry is conceived and composed in their wits', said Matthew Arnold of Dryden and Pope; 'genuine poetry is conceived in the soul.' Palgrave voiced the general verdict of Victorian men of letters on Ovid: 'Among world-famous poets perhaps the least true to the soul of poetry.' It was left for Professor Gilbert Murray to put up a belated defence of him: 'He was a poet utterly in love with poetry; not perhaps with the soul of poetry—to be in love with souls is a feeble and somewhat morbid condition—but with the real face and voice and body and clothes and accessories of poetry.'

That was published in 1921, and it was in the nineteen-twenties that the time was ripe for a revaluation of Ovid. T. S. Eliot, in his *Homage to John Dryden*, had staked out a claim for wit as an instrument of poetry. There was a reawakening of enthusiasm for Dryden, and also for Pope. The narrow Victorian idea of what was 'poetical' was breaking down, and long-excluded verse-writers were being re-explored. It was also a period of emancipation. Old values were being questioned. People were beginning to realize that to be shocked was not an adult response to literature; that one could appreciate it without necessarily endorsing its content; and that a man no more sublime in character than Baudelaire could be recognized as a great poet. The only sign in English classical circles of such a revaluation of Ovid was a humane essay by Mr T. F. Higham in the *Classical Review* for 1934. But classical circles are seldom in the forefront of movements in literary sensibility, and perhaps even now it is not too late.

INDEX OF OVIDIAN PASSAGES TRANSLATED

INDEX OF PASSAGES

INDEX OF PROPER NAMES
(SELECTED)